TERRY GILLIAM

INTERVIEWS

CONVERSATIONS WITH FILMMAKERS SERIES
PETER BRUNETTE, GENERAL EDITOR

Photo credit: Photofest

TERRY
GILLIAM

INTERVIEWS

EDITED BY DAVID STERRITT
AND LUCILLE RHODES

UNIVERSITY PRESS OF MISSISSIPPI / JACKSON

www.upress.state.ms.us

The University Press of Mississippi is a member of the
Association of American University Presses.

11 10 09 08 07 06 05 04 03   4 3 2 1
⊗
Library of Congress Cataloging-in-Publication Data

Gilliam, Terry.
Terry Gilliam : interviews / edited by David Sterritt and Lucille Rhodes.
p. cm.—(Conversations with filmmakers series)
Includes index.
ISBN 1-57806-623-9 (alk. paper)—ISBN 1-57806-624-7 (paper. : alk. paper)
1. Gilliam, Terry—Interviews.   2. Motion picture producers and directors—
Great Britain—Interviews.   3. Entertainers—Great Britain—Interviews.   I.
Sterritt, David.   II. Rhodes, Lucille.   III. Title.   IV. Series.
PN1998.3.G55A3   2004
791.43'0233'092—dc22   2003060036

British Library Cataloging-in-Publication Data available

CONTENTS

INTRODUCTION

M ANY FILMMAKERS have been misunderstood, but Terry Gilliam has been misunderstood by experts.

For years he was labeled a cartoonist and animator, yet he always aspired to direct live-action features. As the animation specialist for *Monty Python's Flying Circus* he worked in relative isolation from the troupe's other members, yet he relishes collaboration and has more than enough social skills to helm movie projects on an extravagant scale. Studio power brokers have deemed him a budget-buster and all-around loose cannon, yet movies as different as *Time Bandits* and *The Fisher King* have fared splendidly at the box office. He's been pigeonholed as a humorist, yet personal projects from the early *Jabberwocky* to the late *Fear and Loathing in Las Vegas* have revealed conspicuously dark streaks at the core of his creative personality—just as films like *Fear and Loathing* and *Twelve Monkeys* show a concern with up-to-the-minute social commentary that contradicts his image as a fantasist obsessed with the long-gone past and the still-unknown future.

So will the real Terry Gilliam please stand up? Not if he can help it. Like the legendary Orson Welles—another maverick considered too profligate and unpredictable for the system to put up with—he insists on navigating the movie world by his own idiosyncratic compass, never forgetting that unfettered imagination is the heart and soul of any art form worth practicing. Gilliam started life as an amateur magician (also like Welles), and he has never stopped being a trickster to his bones. Given the choice between pleasing the establishment and baffling it, he will choose the latter every time. "I like the idea of amazing and astounding people," he told Anne Thompson in her 1981 *Film Comment* interview. He has done that to many a studio boss, with many an uncomfortable result. He has also done it for countless movie-goers who admire him to the skies.

The paradoxes embodied by Gilliam's work may be rooted deeply in his mind and heart, but the vicissitudes of his professional and personal life have certainly helped bring them to the surface. Born in 1940, he spent his early years in a Midwest town and his adolescence in Los Angeles, where his family moved when he was eleven. His love of drawing, sense of humor, and incli-nation toward satire helped him land a job at *Help!* magazine a few years after college; there he worked with Harvey Kurtzman, a longtime idol who now became his valued mentor. The next major turning point came when he left the United States for England in 1967 over disgust at the Vietnam War and what he strongly perceived as American proclivities for political authori-tarianism, moral vulgarity, and cultural tunnel vision. Work as a comic-book artist led to employment as an animator on British television, and he was ready for action in 1969 when the opportunity came to join *Monty Python's Flying Circus,* the British Broadcasting Corporation's innovative new humor series.

Gilliam's years of successful work for the small TV screen encouraged his desire to stretch his talents—and his vision—in the field of theatrical fea-tures. He made the leap by codirecting *Monty Python and the Holy Grail* with Python partner Terry Jones in 1975, then went solo with the dark medieval comedy *Jabberwocky* two years later. His directorial career took an energetic upward turn with the 1981 fantasy *Time Bandits,* a hit on both sides of the Atlantic with audiences and critics alike. A downward turn—which immedi-ately became another upward turn—arrived in 1985 when Universal Pictures deemed his science fiction epic *Brazil* unreleasable, then grudgingly placed it in theaters after the Los Angeles Film Critics Association gave it multiple awards on the basis of private screenings the reviewers had attended. Things went down again in 1988 when *The Adventures of Baron Munchausen* ran badly over budget, reached the screen in a slightly truncated form, and fared poorly at the box office; and up again in 1991 when *The Fisher King* made a strong showing at ticket windows and in the Academy Awards race. *Twelve Monkeys* scored a solid success in 1995, but the horror-farce *Fear and Loathing in Las Vegas* did the opposite in 1998. Gilliam declined a seat on the official jury of the renowned Cannes International Film Festival in 2000 so he could begin filming his long-delayed pet project *The Man Who Killed Don Quixote,* and got to the jury after all in 2001 when the *Quixote* production collapsed. He then became the on-screen star of *Lost in La Mancha,* a documentary directed by young filmmakers Keith Fulton and Louis Pepe about the rise and fall of his *Quixote* dream, hoping it would help convince the movie world that the disaster was a result of bad luck and straitened circumstances, not profligate habits or irresponsible actions. *Quixote* would rise again, he insisted as forcefully as he could, sounding to some like a crusty cinematic survivor, to others like a self-propelled dreamer as incorrigible as Quixote and Munchausen themselves.

This saga unfolds in the interviews collected here, which cover the entire range of Gilliam's activities, from his early work as a TV animator through the opening of *Fear and Loathing in Las Vegas* and the subsequent ordeals he endured in his *Quixote* adventure. As with any such collection, a certain amount of repetition is inevitable from one article to another, but anyone reading the pieces in order—as they are arranged, according to the dates when the interviews were conducted—will find a steady stream of new material as well as a set of continually changing, mutually illuminating perspectives on the life and work of a truly protean artist.

Anne Thompson's interview for *Film Comment,* conducted when *Time Bandits* was having its American premiere in 1981, catches Gilliam at a key moment of his transition from TV to the wide screen. He acknowledges the influence of his Monty Python collaborators in loosening up his imagination and helping him master the virtues of economy, speed, and improvisation. He admits the difficulty of this transition as well, noting that it took him a couple of live-action films to realize that actors are "real people" who can find it "really painful" when he tries to situate them in a visual frame designed by the animation-oriented part of his sensibility. He also speaks about his interest in making a children's movie that owns up to the existence of "evil" and "dangerous things" in the world. Working on a fantastical scale is a way to avoid "growing into middle age or adulthood," he concludes, "because . . . growing up is about limiting."

He takes a closer look at his formative years with Monty Python in Tony DeSena's 1982 interview for the *Aquarian,* recalling battles with BBC censors—who allowed "only one 'shit' per program, and once objected to a 'huge penis' that was really a leg John Cleese was thrusting through a door"—and discusses the genesis of the Python movies *Life of Brian* and *Live at the Hollywood Bowl.* David Sterritt's 1982 interview from the *Christian Sci-*

ence Monitor returns to the clear-headed nature of children and elicits the interest in religion that Gilliam and *Time Bandits* cowriter Michael Palin shared. "The normal approach in a kids' film is to make the final character a wizard," he says. "But why not bring God into it? Why not stop fiddling around and get right down to things?" These words have extra resonance in the climate created by such later blockbusters as the Harry Potter and *Lord of the Rings* series.

Rick Lyman's 1986 interview for the *Philadelphia Inquirer* brings up *Brazil*, considered by many to be Gilliam's greatest film, and his ultimately success-ful struggle—unexpectedly abetted by the Los Angeles film critics—to make Universal Pictures take it off the shelf and put it into theaters where it belonged. "The businessmen who run studios think they are filmmakers," Gilliam says with mingled mischievousness and frankness. "But you know what? They're not."

Gilliam delves more deeply into the substance of *Brazil* in Owen Gleiber-man's 1986 interview for the *Boston Phoenix*, introducing his frequently voiced idea that Sigmund Freud's insights have made human experience saner but also less exciting. "I like the idea of actual demons sucking your brains out," he says, expressing his enthusiasm for the "more tangible" con-ceptualizations of the premodern world. "Whether 'libido' describes some-thing better than this great thing with horny hooves and all that—that seems to me as good a description, if not a better one." It is no wonder that Bruegel and Bosch are recurring points of reference in his interviews, as in his films.

David Morgan is a leading authority on Gilliam and his work, and Mor-gan's 1988 interview for the British film magazine *Sight and Sound* visits the writer-director on the set of *The Adventures of Baron Munchausen*, which had perhaps the most troubled production history of any film he has completed, despite the presence of towering talents like cinematographer Giuseppe Rotunno and art director Dante Ferretti in the crew. Morgan watches Gilliam lose his temper on the set, notes the disjunction between his rapid-fire imagi-nation and the mammoth technical scale of this project, and talks with the filmmaker about his constant recurrence to the "same old theme" of "Fan-tasy/Reality" and its implications for ideas about lies, truth, age, youth, and the beginning and end of life. Gilliam is also eloquent about the relation-ships among humor, artifice, and beauty in this flawed but hugely ambitious film. Steven Rea sounds him out further on the production's "helter-skelter" nature in his 1989 *Philadelphia Inquirer* interview.

Cities and urban life have fascinated Gilliam throughout his career, and Morgan zeroes in on this facet of Gilliam's imagination in "Gilliam, Gotham, God," an aptly titled 1991 interview for *Metropolis* magazine. Here the filmmaker discusses the differences he perceives in European and American cities, humanity's hubristic desire to compete with God by building massive things—"I'm as big as you, buster!"—and his exploration of architectural design in movies as different as *Baron Munchausen* and *The Fisher King.*

Focusing on another facet of Gilliam's personality, Paul Wardle's 1995 piece for the *Comics Journal* traces his kinship with comic books from the humor magazine *Fang* in his college days to his apprenticeship at the fabled *Help!* and the comix aesthetic that underlies much of his Monty Python and feature-film work. Gilliam also gives a particularly detailed account of his vexing experiences with studios and puts his basic political views on the table. "No matter what the system is," he says, "it always goes corrupt."

Gilliam maintains strong connections with the world of art, and Nigel Fountain's 1996 interview for the *Guardian* links the visionary look of *Twelve Monkeys* with the surrealistic "monument to categories and chaos" that Gilliam created for a London gallery during the same period in the form of an immense filing cabinet overflowing with objects and images. Gilliam dislikes categories, we unsurprisingly learn. "The minute that Adam started naming animals," he says, "that was the end of it."

Twelve Monkeys was one of Gilliam's most satisfying experiences in terms of personal expression via a studio production, and in a 1996 interview *Sight and Sound* editor Nick James talks with him about working with iconic Hollywood stars—Bruce Willis, Brad Pitt—and the challenge of combining his "found art" sensibility with the exigencies of big-budget filmmaking. Phil Stubbs, who stands with Morgan as a world-class Gilliam specialist, gets the director talking about his forthcoming *Fear and Loathing in Las Vegas,* which Gilliam sees as a "compendium" of his previous ideas as well as a bold foray in new directions.

Scholarly interest in Gilliam's artistry has grown alongside the evolution of his career. Paul Wells's 1997 piece for *Art and Design Profile,* evocatively titled "On Being an Impish God," examines the filmmaker's ideas on fundamental issues related to modernism, postmodernism, and especially the intricate interplay of so-called low and high art in contemporary aesthetics.

A high point is Gilliam's account of how cinematically rich he found his early *Jabberwocky* when screening it for Dutch distributors without the sound track! Gilliam's longtime romance with vintage movie cartoons (Tex Avery, Chuck Jones) arises again in the retrospective interview conducted by Jordi Costa and Sergi Sánchez for their book on his life and work. Here he looks back on his early years from the perspective of maturity, and discusses his tastes in painting in unusual detail.

Gilliam has found that with many of his projects the making of the film echoes the content of the film—for example, the moment-to-moment survival of *Baron Munchausen* seemed as iffy as the Baron's own often-precarious existence within the story, as Gilliam told Rea in 1989. This was again the case with *Fear and Loathing,* according to Bob McCabe's 1998 interview for *Sight and Sound.* As with the experiences of Hunter S. Thompson in the book that inspired the movie, the mood was "just go for it, leap off the precipice and see what happens." He also discusses his ever-evolving views on the United States with characteristic frankness.

Rounding out this collection are three comprehensive interviews that probe the past, present, and future of Gilliam's career in depth and detail. In a previously unpublished onstage interview with *Nation* film critic Stuart Klawans, the filmmaker discusses everything from the ambience of his childhood home town to the battle of *Brazil* to the challenge of whipping Brad Pitt into proper acting shape for his *Twelve Monkeys* role. Gregory Solman's interview, also done in the *Fear and Loathing* year of 1998, digs out Gilliam's ideas on video technology, his view of himself as a highly disciplined filmmaker, the political rage that drove him out of America in the 1960s, and his all-time favorite movies. He also gives a meticulous account of the dispute over writing credits that complicated the release of *Fear and Loathing.* The last interview, with David Sterritt and Mikita Brottman at the Toronto International Film Festival in 2002, finds him in a mingled state of trepidation over the *Quixote* catastrophe, candidly acknowledged vulnerability vis-à-vis the money-driven movie establishment that holds the reins over ambitious projects like his, and undimmed enthusiasm for what he hopes will be an exciting and productive future.

Along with his other commendable qualities, Terry Gilliam has been a good friend. One of us (Lucille) has known him since the 1960s, has visited him at home and on the set, and has collected memorabilia of his work with steady pleasure and growing admiration. She and Terry coproduced a CD-ROM based on his 1978 book *Animations of Mortality* some years ago, providing players with his complete library of animation elements to mess with—an exciting project that unfortunately bit the dust when the internet overwhelmed the computer-communications market. The other of us (David) first met him during the 1982 interview included in this volume and has particularly fond memories of a trek Terry made to his lower Manhattan apartment several years later on a snow-blitzed winter night, treating our subsequent adventures—including an arduous slog through knee-high drifts to a restaurant that turned out to have prudently shut down for the duration—with nothing but high spirits and good humor. He is, as you may guess from his movies, quite a guy.

In addition to Terry's cooperation, we have benefited from the efforts of many other people in preparing this collection. Seetha Srinivasan has been a superbly helpful editor, graciously putting up with delays and confusions arising from the events of September 11 and other causes. Charlotte Garson has been an extraordinary research assistant, tracking down the most elusive materials with unfailing ingenuity and patience, and continuing her indispensable assistance even after leaving New York for her native Paris, as if a mere ocean were no obstacle at all. We owe thanks to all of the writers who contributed to the volume, with special nods to Gilliam gurus David Morgan and Phil Stubbs, our Spanish colleagues Jordi Costa and Sergi Sánchez—who generously provided a copy of their marvelously produced book on Gilliam before we had a chance to plead for it—and Gregory Solman, who volunteered a fuller version of his excellent interview than we had found in our research. It is especially gratifying to include pieces by old friends like Stuart Klawans and Anne Thompson, insightful professionals if ever there were any.

David also thanks the Columbia University Seminar on Cinema and Interdisciplinary Interpretation for tremendous support and collegiality over the years, and Mikita Brottman for her indefatigable work on this volume's index. He dedicates his portion of the work on this project to her, for more reasons than he can count. Lucille dedicates hers to her former colleagues at the C. W. Post Center—including those at the B. Davis Schwartz Memorial Library, who were of marvelous help in researching Gilliam interviews—and to Terry for his longtime encouragement, inspiration, and support.

—David Sterritt and Lucille Rhodes
New York City, July 2003

CHRONOLOGY

1940   Born on November 22 in Medicine Lake, Minnesota.

1951   Family moves to Los Angeles.

1962   Graduates from Occidental College in Los Angeles.

1965   Takes a job at the American humor magazine *Help!* at the invitation of editor Harvey Kurtzman, one of his longtime heroes.

1967   Moves to London, where he contributes to the *Car-Toons* comic book and works as art director of *London Life* magazine.

1968   Begins as an animator for *We Have Ways of Making You Laugh* on London Weekend Television. Also does animated sequences for *Marty* on BBC television and the Christmas program *Do Not Adjust Your Stocking* on Thames Television.

1969   *Monty Python's Flying Circus,* with Gilliam's animations as links between live-action segments, has its premiere in October on British Broadcasting Corporation television. Also does animated sequences for *Do Not Adjust Your Set* on Thames Television.

1970   Designs the title sequence for *Cry of the Banshee,* a Vincent Price thriller for American International Pictures.

1971   Release of Monty Python film *And Now for Something Completely Different,* with Gilliam as cowriter, animator, and performer. *Monty Python's Flying Circus* goes on hiatus. Does animated sequences for the American program *The Marty Feldman Comedy Machine* on ABC-TV.

1972   *Monty Python's Flying Circus* returns to the BBC. Also does sequences for the German episode *Monty Python in Deutschland* and commercials for British Gas.

1973   Marries Maggie Weston, a makeup artist who worked on the Monty Python series. *Monty Python's Flying Circus* ends its run on the BBC. Does sequences for the German episode *Monty Python Blödeln für Deutschland*. Designs the title sequence for *William*, a fall special on ABC television.

1974   A fourth season of *Monty Python's Flying Circus*, with six installments instead of the usual thirteen, airs on the BBC. Installments begin appearing on Public Broadcasting Service channels in the United States.

1975   Release of *Monty Python and the Holy Grail*, with Gilliam as cowriter, animator, performer, and codirector with Terry Jones.

1977   Release of *Jabberwocky*, Gilliam's first film as sole director. Makes acting appearance in *Pleasure at Her Majesty's*, also known as *Monty Python Meets Beyond the Fringe*, with members of the Monty Python and *Beyond the Fringe* troupes. Birth of first daughter, Amy Rainbow.

1978   Publishes the picture book *Animations of Mortality*.

1979   Release of Monty Python film *Life of Brian*, with Gilliam as cowriter, animator, and performer. Assembles the short film *Story Time*, a compilation of animated sequences.

1980   Birth of second daughter, Holly Dubois.

1981   Release of *Time Bandits*, which does extremely well at the box office.

1982   Release of *Monty Python Live at the Hollywood Bowl*, with Gilliam as cowriter and performer.

1983   Release of Monty Python film *The Meaning of Life*, with Gilliam as cowriter, animator, performer, and director of "The Crimson Permanent Assurance," the special sequence that opens the film.

1985   Release of *Brazil,* after it wins awards for best picture, best director, and best screenplay from the Los Angeles Film Critics Association in the wake of Universal Pictures' initial refusal to release it; the script, written by Gilliam with Charles McKeown and some participation by Tom Stoppard, is nominated for the Academy Award for best original screenplay. Makes acting appearance as Dr. Imhaus in John Landis's comedy *Spies Like Us.*

1988   Release of *The Adventures of Baron Munchausen,* after a difficult production period and cuts made at the behest of its distributor. Birth of son, Harry Thunder.

1989   Directs a TV commercial for Orangina, the soft drink.

1991   Release of *The Fisher King,* which earns Mercedes Ruehl the Academy Award for best actress in a supporting role and Robin Williams a nomination for best actor; nominations also go to Richard LaGravenese's original screenplay, George Fenton's music, and the art direction by Mel Bourne and Cindy Carr.

1995   Release of *Twelve Monkeys,* which earns Brad Pitt an Oscar nomination as best supporting actor. Directs a TV commercial for Nike, the sportswear company.

1998   Release of *Fear and Loathing in Las Vegas,* which has its world premiere in the prestigious competition at the Cannes International Film Festival.

2000   Begins production in Madrid of *The Man Who Killed Don Quixote,* inspired by Miguel de Cervantes's novel *Don Quixote,* after two previous attempts and a decade of developing the project with various producers.

2001   Serves as a jury member at the Cannes International Film Festival.

2002   The collapse of the *Man Who Killed Don Quixote* project is chronicled by Keith Fulton and Louis Pepe in their documentary *Lost in La Mancha: The Un-Making of Don Quixote,* which has its world premiere at the Toronto International Film Festival. Gilliam announces that he hopes to restart production of *Quixote* in 2003.

FILMOGRAPHY

D—director; P—producer; S—screenplay; Ph—cinematography; E—editor; M—music; C—principle cast.

1975. *Monty Python and the Holy Grail*. D—Terry Gilliam, Terry Jones; P—Mark Forstater; S—Graham Chapman, John Cleese, Terry Gilliam, Eric Idle, Terry Jones, Michael Palin; Ph—Terry Bedford; E—John Hackney; M—Neil Innes, with De Wolfe; C—Graham Chapman, John Cleese, Terry Gilliam, Eric Idle, Terry Jones, Michael Palin, Carol Cleveland, John Young. Python (Monty) Pictures. 90 min.

1977. *Jabberwocky*. D—Terry Gilliam; P—Sandy Lieberson; S—Charles Alverson, Terry Gilliam; Ph—Terry Bedford; E—Michael Bradsell; M—De Wolfe; C—Michael Palin, Max Wall, Deborah Fallender, John Le Mesurier, Annette Badland, Warren Mitchell, Bernard Bresslaw. Umbrella Entertainment. 101 min.

1981. *Time Bandits*. D—Terry Gilliam; T—Terry Gilliam; S—Michael Palin, Terry Gilliam; Ph—Peter Biziou; E—Julian Doyle; M—Mike Moran; C—John Cleese, Sean Connery, Shelley Duvall, Katherine Helmond, Ian Holm, Michael Palin, Ralph Richardson, Peter Vaughan, David Warner, Kenny Baker, Jim Broadbent, John Young. HandMade Films. 113 min.

1985. *Brazil*. D—Terry Gilliam; P—Arnon Milchan; S—Terry Gilliam, Tom Stoppard, Charles McKeown; Ph—Roger Pratt; E—Julian Doyle; M—Michael

Kamen; C—Jonathan Pryce, Kim Greist, Robert De Niro, Bob Hoskins, Michael Palin, Ian Holm, Katherine Helmond, Ian Richardson, Peter Vaughan, Jim Broadbent, Simon Jones, Charles McKeown. Brazil Productions, 142 min.

1988. *The Adventures of Baron Munchausen.* D—Terry Gilliam; P—Thomas Schühly; S—Charles McKeown, Terry Gilliam; Ph—Giuseppe Rotunno; E—Peter Hollywood; M—Michael Kamen; C—John Neville, Sarah Polley, Eric Idle, Charles McKeown, Winston Dennis, Jack Purvis, Uma Thurman, Valentina Cortese, Oliver Reed, Jonathan Pryce, Bill Paterson, Alison Steadman, Sting, Robin Williams (uncredited). Prominent Features, Laura Films. 126 min.

1991. *The Fisher King.* D—Terry Gilliam; P—Debra Hill, Lynda Obst; S—Richard LaGravenese; Ph—Roger Pratt; E—Leyley Walker; M—George Fenton; C—Jeff Bridges, Robin Williams, Amanda Plummer, Mercedes Ruehl, Warren Olney, Kathy Najimy, Michael Jeter. TriStar Pictures. 137 min.

1995. *Twelve Monkeys.* D—Terry Gilliam; P—Charles Roven; S—David Peoples, Janet Peoples, inspired by Chris Marker's film *La Jetée;* Ph—Roger Pratt; E—Mick Audsley; M—Paul Buckmaster; C—Bruce Willis, Brad Pitt, Madeleine Stowe, Christopher Plummer, Joseph Melito, Simon Jones, Bill Raymond, Frank Gorshin, David Morse. Polygram Filmed Entertainment with Universal Pictures, Atlas/Classico. 129 min.

1998. *Fear and Loathing in Las Vegas.* D—Terry Gilliam; P—Laila Nabulsi, Patrick Cassavetti, Stephen Nemeth; S—Terry Gilliam, Tony Grisoni, Tod Davies, Alex Cox, based on Hunter S. Thompson's book; Ph—Nicola Pecorini; E—Lesley Walker; M—Ray Cooper; C—Johnny Depp, Benicio Del Toro, Christina Ricci, Gary Busey, Ellen Barkin, Michael Jeter, Harry Dean Stanton, Katherine Helmond, Tobey Maguire, Cameron Diaz, Craig Bierko, Penn Jillette, Lyle Lovett. Summit Entertainment, Universal Pictures, Rhino Films/Laila Nabulsi. 118 min.

Special Sequence

1983. "The Crimson Permanent Assurance," in the Monty Python film *The Meaning of Life.* D—Terry Gilliam; P—John Goldstone; S—Terry Gilliam; Ph—

Roger Pratt; E—Julian Doyle; M—John Duprez; C—Sydney Arnold, Ross Davidson, Eric Francis, Russell Kilminster, Peter Merrill, Larry Noble. The Monty Python Partnership. 16 min.

Television animations

1968. "Jimmy Young Puns"; "The History of the Whoopee Cushion"; "Beware the Elephants," for the program *We Have Ways of Making You Laugh*, London Weekend Television.

1968. Sequences for *Marty*, BBC Television.

1968. "The Christmas Card," for *Do Not Adjust Your Stocking*, Thames Television.

1969. "Elephants" and other sequences for *Do Not Adjust Your Set*, Thames Television.

1969–70. Sequences for *Monty Python's Flying Circus*, BBC Television.

1971. "The Miracle of Flight" and other sequences for *The Marty Feldman Comedy Machine*, ABC-TV.

1972. *The Great Gas Gala*, commercials for British Gas.

1972–74. Sequences for *Monty Python's Flying Circus*, BBC Television, and for two German television episodes, *Monty Python in Deutschland* and *Monty Python Blodeln für Deutschland*.

1973. Title sequence for *William*, ABC-TV.

1989. Commercial for Orangina.

1995. Commercial for Nike.

2001. Commercial for Nike.

Films directed by others

1970. *Cry of the Banshee*. D—Gordon Hessler; P—Samuel Z. Arkoff, Gordon Hessler, Louis M. Heyward; S—Christopher Wicking; Ph—John Coquillon;

E—Oswald Hafenrichter; M—Les Baxter, Wilfred Josephs; Title design—Terry Gilliam; C—Vincent Price, Hilary Heath, Carl Rigg, Elisabeth Bergner. American International Pictures. 87 min.

1971. *And Now for Something Completely Different.* D—Ian MacNaughton; P—Patricia Casey; S—Graham Chapman, John Cleese, Terry Gilliam, Eric Idle, Terry Jones, Michael Palin; Ph—David Muir; E—Thom Noble; Animation—Terry Gilliam; C—Graham Chapman, John Cleese, Terry Gilliam, Eric Idle, Terry Jones, Michael Palin, Carol Cleveland. Kettledrum Productions/ Python (Monty) Pictures. 88 min.

1977. *Pleasure at Her Majesty's,* also known as *Monty Python Meets Beyond the Fringe.* D—Jonathan Miller; C—Rowan Atkinson, Alan Bennett, Eleanor Bron, Peter Cook, Jonathan Miller, Graham Chapman, John Cleese, Terry Gilliam, Eric Idle, Terry Jones, Michael Palin.

1979. *Life of Brian.* D—Terry Jones; P—John Goldstone; S—Graham Chapman, John Cleese, Terry Gilliam, Eric Idle, Terry Jones, Michael Palin; Ph—Peter Biziou; E—Julian Doyle; M—Geoffrey Burgon; Animation—Terry Gilliam; C—Graham Chapman, Terry Jones, Michael Palin, John Cleese, Eric Idle, Terry Gilliam, Carol Cleveland, Spike Milligan. HandMade Films. 93 min.

1982. *Monty Python Live at the Hollywood Bowl.* D—Terry Hughes, Ian MacNaughton; P—Terry Hughes; S—Graham Chapman, John Cleese, Terry Gilliam, Eric Idle, Terry Jones, Michael Palin; E—Julian Doyle; M—John Duprez, Ray Cooper; C—Graham Chapman, Terry Jones, Michael Palin, John Cleese, Eric Idle, Terry Gilliam, Carol Cleveland, Neil Innes, Pamela Stephenson. HandMade Films. 80 min.

1983. *The Meaning of Life.* D—Terry Jones; P—John Goldstone; S—Graham Chapman, John Cleese, Terry Gilliam, Eric Idle, Terry Jones, Michael Palin; Ph—Peter Hannan; E—Julian Doyle; Animation and special sequence—Terry Gilliam; C—Graham Chapman, Terry Jones, Michael Palin, John Cleese, Eric Idle, Terry Gilliam, Carol Cleveland, Simon Jones. Celandine Films/The Monty Python Partnership. 90 min.

1985. *Spies Like Us*. D—John Landis; P—George Folsey Jr., Brian Grazer; S—Dan Aykroyd, Lowell Ganz, Babaloo Mandel; Ph—Robert Paynter; E—Malcolm Campbell; M—Elmer Bernstein, with Paul McCartney; C—Chevy Chase, Dan Aykroyd, Bruce Davison, Bernie Casey, Terry Gilliam. 102 min.

1996. *The Hamster Factor and Other Tales of Twelve Monkeys*. D, P, S, Ph, E—Keith Fulton, Louis Pepe; M—John Benskin; C—Terry Gilliam, Bruce Willis, Brad Pitt, Madeleine Stowe, Charles Roven, Keith Fulton (narrator). Universal Pictures with Atlas Entertainment, Poo Poo Pictures. 88 min.

2002. *Lost in La Mancha: The Un-Making of Don Quixote*. D, S—Keith Fulton, Louis Pepe; P—Lucy Darwin; C—Terry Gilliam, Johnny Depp, Jean Rochefort, Jeff Bridges (narrator). IFC Films. 89 min.

Animation compilation

1979. *Story Time*. D—Terry Gilliam. 9 min.

TERRY GILLIAM

INTERVIEWS

Bandit

ANNE THOMPSON/1981

H E   CERTAINLY   LOOKS   E NGLISH :   Cockney face, spiky-cut long
hair, bright corduroys. Sounds English, too, with his speech as smooth and
clipped as an earl's lawn. But Terry Gilliam is an American, born in 1940 in
Minneapolis and raised from age eleven in Los Angeles. Most people assume
he's English because of his work with the Monty Python troupe. Gilliam is
one of several Americans—Stanley Kubrick, Richard Lester, Joseph Losey,
Frederic Raphael—who left for Britain and never came back, in the process
creating films whose tone was more royalist than Kingsley Amis. Gilliam
himself couldn't believe that his own favorite "British" director, Alexander
MacKendrick *(The Man in the White Suit, The Ladykillers)*, was born in Boston.
The fact is, Gilliam doesn't like America much and has no intention of coming back.

But he is here now for a visit, promoting his $5-million *Time Bandits*,
whose rich cast includes Sean Connery, Ralph Richardson, Ian Holm, John
Cleese, Michael Palin, Shelley Duvall, Katherine Helmond, and David Warner, plus dwarfs, ghouls, and a small boy. When Gilliam came up with the
basic story in a fit of inspiration, he ran to fellow Python Michael Palin, who
agreed to write the script with him, then ran to producer Denis O'Brien and
acted it out for him so convincingly that he got his backing on the spot.
O'Brien's enthusiastic response is easy to understand: Gilliam is most ani-

From *Film Comment*, vol. 17, no. 6 (1981): 49–54. Reprinted by permission of Anne
Thompson.

mated when acting out a scene from one of his movies, complete with sound effects.

Time Bandits is a grim—and funny—fairy tale, full of amazing adventures, laughs and scares, good and evil, heroics and befuddlement. The world is a place where anything is likely to pop in or out of the frame. Or into one's bedroom. A scurvy band of dwarfs scoop our young hero up and bear him off to brave the unknown—the only known quantities being the coordinates of the time holes on the map they've stolen from the Supreme Being—their boss. They want to steal and plunder, and Kevin lends his considerable talents to the task. They skip from one century to another and traverse regions too fantastic to describe.

Gilliam possesses the imagination and daring of an animator. He isn't bound by reality, and with his motion picture seasoning (he co-directed *Monty Python and the Holy Grail,* designed *The Life of Brian,* and wrote and directed *Jabberwocky*), he now knows how to make his visual conceits work with live actors operating in earth's gravity. Although Gilliam insists he followed certain rules in *Time Bandits,* Newton's Laws seem truly suspended. Anything can happen.

Like other filmmakers of his generation, young Terry was an avid comic-book reader, especially inspired by the work of Harvey Kurtzman *(Mad, Trump, Humbug,* and *Help!)*. But Gilliam went John Landis, George Romero, and John Waters one better: After college, he joined Kurtzman as assistant editor at *Help!* which specialized in "fumettis"—comic strips using photographed actors instead of cartoon characters. And after *Help!* folded, Gilliam settled in England with two actors he'd hired for *Help!* photo sessions: John Cleese and Graham Chapman. They introduced him to a producer who got him work drawing caricatures for a TV show called *Do Not Adjust Your Set.* He then moved on to *We Have Ways of Making You Laugh* as part of the resident company which included Michael Palin, Terry Jones, and Eric Idle. One week he came up with the idea of animating something. It was, as his subsequent career proved, an excellent idea.

When Cleese, Chapman, Palin, Jones, and Idle formed *Monty Python's Flying Circus* for the BBC series (1969–72), Gilliam provided skit links with his inventive cut-out animations. The series was excerpted for a movie, *And Now for Something Completely Different* (1971), and expanded for a 45-minute TV film, *Pythons in Deutschland.* Their feature films, *Monty Python and the Holy Grail* (1975) and *Monty Python's Life of Brian* (1979), were worldwide hits;

another film is set for next summer, for which Gilliam will again provide animation. He co-directed *Holy Grail* with Jones and didn't like the experience, so he stuck to designing for *Brian*. After a mixed reception for his medieval tale *Jabberwocky*, *Time Bandits* shows his growth as a filmmaker and could repeat its British success here.

Although Gilliam says that he always wanted to make films, that animation was a detour, his animation work, combined with the Python experience, makes him a rich creative resource. *Time Bandits* is visually and aurally stunning, so chock-full of clever detail as to make *Raiders of the Lost Ark* look flat and toneless by comparison. This film is not mechanically propelled—it's a crazy whirligig of a movie, and the closest thing to a delicious fairy tale since *The Wizard of Oz*.

—A.T.

Q: *How did you come up with the* Time Bandits *story? You did it in seven pages?*
A: The legendary seven pages. I wanted to do a kid's film, and all these things came out. They've obviously been storing themselves up in my head for a long time, just looking out for the right outlet. I wanted to work at a kid's level through the whole thing, and the kid would be the main character. But a kid isn't going to sustain a film, so he's surrounded with a gang of interesting characters, but they've got to be the same height as the kid, so we're talking about dwarfs, folks. Step by step, it goes. The first thing was the knight on a horse coming out of the wardrobe. It just hit me one day. Wow, what the hell is that? And the film was very odd in the way it developed because certain things didn't work themselves out until very late in the day—almost to the point of shooting.

But we still didn't have an ending to it at all. And then I remembered that Sean Connery had suggested that he come back as a fireman. I'd already shot the scene with the firemen coming into the room and dragging Kevin out. I had to beg and scream to get Connery for one hour. So we got a fire truck, put it in the parking lot of the studio, and got him in the fireman's outfit. We got the kid down there—"Say, you're a lucky fellow"—he walked and got in the truck and then winked. That was all. He went away, and then about two months after that, we finally got around to writing the end scene and then fitting that in.

The whole film was very much like that. You can really fuck it up. You really don't know what you're doing half the time, but it's quite exciting because you've got to think on your feet. And you can't assume that it's going to sort itself out. There's nobody else to sort it out.

Q : *Do you like working with Michael Palin? Did he write the script out?*
A : The way it works, I actually work the story out, all the scenes, and Mike then writes, because I'm terrible at dialogue, and Mike is not only good at dialogue, but at characterizations. Then we'd talk a lot about it. Then he'd go down and write it. Then I would take it and then rewrite it.

Q : *Did you think of Sean Connery from the very beginning?*
A : No, we put him in the script as a joke, because the script read originally, "Greek warrior takes his helmet off, revealing himself to be none other than Sean Connery, or another actor of heroic stature." That's what it said, and we never really thought about getting Sean Connery at all. Denis O'Brien said, "Terrific idea; let's get Connery." And he went and got him, like that. Connery read the script and said he'd do it. I couldn't believe it. I can't believe he really came to do it. I don't think he gets offered father-type roles very often, and it was a good father role because it's a nice relationship ,and the boy was terrific.

Q : *Is it a classic fairy tale?*
A : I think it's more of a fairy tale than most. Most modern fairy tales are so vulgarized. I think the purpose of the fairy tale is to give a rather frightening experience. Kids come out of it at the other end all right, but it says there are less than wonderful things in the world, that there's evil out there, there's dangerous things, and I think it builds the kid's strength up in an interesting way, rather than *Sesame Street,* which says that everybody's lovely and the world's a wonderful place. I don't believe that.

Q : *You killed off the parents in the end.*
A : Well, they deserved it, didn't they? I don't necessarily take the parents' death as a literal thing. I think it's a good surprise and a good joke. That was the initial thing; but, basically, it's the kid's imagination just going to its logical conclusion, to his surprise as well. They may not have blown up. He may just have imagined that. Connery's wink is saying, "It's okay"; it's saying, "It may not have happened, folks."

Q: *That's* The Wizard of Oz, *too.*

A: And all that stuff. At the end, the pull-back gives the whole thing a sort of cosmic perspective. Whatever has gone on has only been a tiny little tale in the middle of a million-billion-trillion tales. A tiny little grain of sand in a cosmic beach. You really don't do that sort of thing in kids' films. What's happened in this film is that it's down to parents to reassure the kids. We've put the onus on the parents now.

Q: *Would you make a sequel?*

A: There's one scene that was cut out that is very good, a spider women scene. We've got it on film. There's some other scenes that were written, which we never did. We've got pirates in the bedroom, for instance. We've got all these things that we could put into a sequel, but it all depends. At the moment, I wouldn't consider it, but if this film turned out to be a huge success . . . I've got too many things that I want to do at the moment to get tied down into sequels.

Q: *Are you committed to any given project right now?*

A: There's a Python film coming up next summer. In fact, it's really in the way. I've got two other projects I'm keen on. One's about America; it's a cross between Franz Kafka and Walter Mitty. It's got a happy ending, but it involves our hero becoming insane. It's a very black piece that is still quite funny in a very, very, black, dark sense. It's all about paranoia, and it's about America.

Q: *Would you make it here?*

A: I like the idea of somehow being able to continue making films outside the States, thumbing my nose at Hollywood. People say you can't do that.

Q: *What if a major studio makes you an offer?*

A: They have, actually, Disney. They almost took this film. They should have. They offered me something a bit like this one from a kid's imagination. I don't think they'd let me be as unpleasant as I'd like to be.

Q: *You seem to like nastiness.*

A: I don't actually think it's nastiness. I don't think sadism enters into it, which I really don't like, like the current vogue for horror films that are basically about sadism. It's always been, I've found, very unpleasant, except when I'm doing it to somebody.

In the Robin Hood scenes, when the poor are being hit, I don't think that's sadistic. Somebody thought it was really about an American unemployment line. You go there, they give you the thing, and then they just bash you. I wasn't thinking of that consciously, but there it is.

Q: *Tell us about* Jabberwocky. *You wrote it.*

A: Yes, with Chuck Alverson, an old friend of mine. *Jabberwocky* was a reaction to the *Holy Grail* in a sense. There were a lot of things I wanted to do with the Middle Ages, areas that I thought the *Holy Grail* never got into. The approach of Python was slightly different from the way I would approach it, so I wanted to get into those untouched areas with *Jabberwocky*. Unfortunately, I had some problems with it because the distributors said, "It's not as funny." And I said, "Well, it's not meant to be as funny." And so I actually gave in to some pressure, which I'll never do again, and recut the film slightly differently and made it appear to be more of a comedy than it was meant to be.

Q: *What was the story?*

A: Basically, it's a story about a monster ravishing the countryside. The monster is wonderful because you never see him until the end of the film. This monster eats people and all the peasantry have rushed into the walled city for protection. So, it's fairly grisly, but funny. But it's grisly in the same way as Bosch and Brueghel were grisly. It's probably as close to their paintings as any film I've seen, actually.

Q: *What did you think of* Excalibur *[John Boorman, 1981]?*

A: *Excalibur* is a mess. I think *Monty Python's Holy Grail* was a more serious film than *Excalibur,* frankly. I think we were more accurate with our sense of history of the period than he was, and we didn't spend any time being pretentious about it.

Q: *You must do a lot of research on these movies.*

A: Yes, I think it's the thing that's difficult for a lot of people to understand. We're doing a comedy, but people don't expect comedies to be serious in any way. We actually set the scene rather seriously. We want it to look right because, in fact, I think the best comedy comes out of the sense of reality. It's a combination of reality and either surrealism or absurdity mixing.

Q: *You have art directors, you have production designers, costume people. How does it all get put together? Who supervises all this?*
A: Well, it's usually me. I'm the one who sits on all that. I make sure they look like they look. I tend to read lots of books, to delve into everything, find great-looking pictures, and say, "You've got to do that like that and that like that." In a case like *Jabberwocky,* we made it up. I did a lot of serious research on it, and said, "Well, I've done my research and I'm going to ignore it all and just fake it." I'd just steeped myself into the feeling of the period and wasn't interested in accuracy but the feeling of the thing.

Q: *Where do you think all your ideas and inventions come from? Does it filter in somehow and just ferment in your brain?*
A: Yes, it just seems to work that way because I'm rather indiscriminating in my taste. I've always rejected things like good taste, bad taste, concepts like that. I've always just preferred to find other ways of looking at everything. It's more entertaining. You keep from getting bored that way. I really like books a lot because it's a nice way of getting information, at your own pace, in your own way.

Q: *What were you reading when you were young?*
A: *Grimm's Fairy Tales* and Hans Christian Andersen and that nonsense. I used to read the Hardy Boys, Albert Payson Terhune. I'm sure I read Robert Louis Stevenson as well.

Q: *Were you reading comic books?*
A: Ya, I was an avid comic-book reader.

Q: *A lot of people take comic books very seriously.*
A: Well, why not? I don't take them as seriously as the comic fans take them. I think they're terrific. I think it's a great art form. But I don't think they go far. Only a few people have taken them far.

Q: *Who?*
A: Actually, Harvey Kurtzman did. I think *Mad* when it began was wonder-

ful. I think it was just amazing mind-blowing stuff before minds were blown, because it was so fine, so satirical, and intelligent. Kurtzman actually made comics respectable, in a sense, to people like me. But I've always loved comics. I like Superman, Captain Marvel . . . good things, Dick Tracy. It can be very good art work and reasonably intelligent stories. I think it's really quite amazing what you can do in the comic format. At *Help!* I used to do comic strips later on, and it's a very satisfying format because you can do things you can't do any other way. We use a frame, we tell a story, it can be very interesting.

Q : *How did you come up with the cut-out style of animation you used on Monty Python?*
A : There had been cut-out animation going on before. People had always been doing it in one form or another, generally crudely. It was just a pragmatic decision to do something the only way I could do it. Cut-outs are a very cheap and fast way of working. I did it, and it worked and people were amazed because they actually hadn't seen that style. Especially in England, they hadn't. I did it probably neater than people have in the past. I was trying to find a style that fitted what I was willing to do.

Q : *Did you go into these big books full of things, and cut them up and recreate them, or what?*
A : I collect books. I've got tons of books. You blow them up, cut them up, push them around, and photograph them. The sound effects are the other key to it. Always vital, it's always underestimated, the effect of the sound, but it's as much as the picture.

Q : *How did the Python people influence you?*
A : Actually, they loosened me up in a strange way. They let me get away with things easily. It would be hard for me to really know. It's obviously been considerable. What was nice with the shows is that we were all influencing each other incredibly. So that suddenly, John and Graham would write a sketch that was just like Mike and Terry's sketch, or Eric would sort of blend what Mike or Terry were doing with what John and Graham were doing. He would find a middle ground and work in there. They came up with ideas that were cartoon ideas. It was really weird.

Q: *You made the bridges between skits.*
A: That was the main function of my stuff, to get from point A to point B and in a different way.

Q: *You work a lot in scale.*
A: Yes, I've always been impressed with scale. It's a continually fascinating thing. Again, it's another way of looking at things: that something which appears small is, in fact, really large. It keeps things in better perspective. It keeps them in a cosmic perspective as well. I think that almost all these sorts of techniques are to avoid growing old, or, at least, growing into middle age or adulthood, because it seems to me, growing up is about limiting. Someone said that growing up is learning which questions not to ask. You go through life and miss out on a lot in the process.

Q: *Do you regard what you're doing as being in any way surreal?*
A: No, but viewers and interviewers have decided that it's surrealist.

Q: *You've been compared to Dali.*
A: I'd rather be compared to Magritte. I think Magritte's funnier than Dali. Magritte's got a sense of humor. There was a big Magritte exhibition at the Tate ten years ago. Everybody was going around very solemnly, looking at the paintings. Nobody was laughing. It was hysterical stuff—he's a great joke teller, amongst other things. I've also been compared to Max Ernst. I only knew Ernst by name, not by collage. The best thing about reading reviews of yourself is that you discover all the things you missed and so you go out and find kindred spirits. I've got piles of Max Ernst stuff now. His collage work is wonderful.

Q: *Where did the costumes for the ghouls in* Time Bandits *come from?*
A: Hieronymous Bosch was a constant source of inspiration. I don't consciously use others like the designer Diaghilev, but all that stuff is sitting around in the back of my head.

Q: *You were borrowing a lot from Hollywood movies.*
A: Yes, I find this an extremely eclectic movie. There's *Snow White, Alice in Wonderland, The Wizard of Oz.* Every film I've seen and everything I've read is there in one form or another. That's where I find the difference between

this and, say, *Raiders of the Lost Ark,* which is a pastiche of very identifiable things. *Bandits* isn't a pastiche. It takes all that information, stirs it around, and comes up with something different, which to me is more important than making pastiches.

Q : *Do you think you're doing something along the lines of what Lucas is doing, which is bringing back some of the mythology that's been lost to children?*
A : Yes, I think there's something awful with being an American. You're stuck with it. I live out of the country, and I make films out of the country; but I actually do think I'd like to have some effect on the country. I'm well aware of what I'm doing and having Evil being obsessed with technology is very important to me. It's a very dangerous thing, and it isn't the answer to everything, and that's why we've got the Supreme Being obsessed with wooly-minded thinking and rainbows—really nice things. God is British, and Evil is American. There's no question about it.

Q : *Are British children better off?*
A : I think so. They have less, so it gives them a chance to contribute more.

Q : *Do they read more?*
A : Yes, I think they're more literate. England is a richer base of fantasy, intellectual curiosity, individualism. I'm always amazed at America, a country that always prided itself on its individuals. It's the least individual-based country I've ever been in, almost. They talk about it all the time, but people basically do things in mobs. You have to hunt for individuals in America. In England, what's always wonderful is that people, like accountants and little bureaucrats—people you'd think wouldn't have a weird thought in their mind at all—they live much richer lives. They protect their own personal space and flourish in that.

Q : *So the British parents that you paint such a vivid picture of are American parents?*
A : No, they're definitely British. They're the New Britain, which really horrifies me, parents like that who are obsessed with Americans. When America does something, it does it rather spectacularly, England does it on a rather nasty, tacky little level.

Q: *What do you think of Ralph Bakshi? His rotoscope?*
A: It's a mess. I think he's sloppy. I can't stand him. I saw *Lord of the Rings,*
and I was really angry. I thought that was appalling. It's very funny 'cause I
was just talking to Harvey Kurtzman on the phone from L.A. He's talking to
Bakshi about a film. I think he can be quite talented. *Fritz* is good. *Coonskin*
is outrageous, amazing, terrific. And, then, *Lord of the Rings.* He's putting
people in horrible baggy costumes and puts Halloween masks on them. He
runs them around and photographs them, and then paints on top of that. I
hadn't read *Rings* until I saw Bakshi's film. I go so angry. I said, "Tolkien has
got to be better than that."

Q: *Sci-fi and animation are fields where you can do incredible things with the
right amount of intelligence and imagination, and yet neither field has seemed to
reach its promise.*
A: That's what bothers me about Lucas. I think he's probably being very
shrewd, because he's got those mammoth successes, but he's not pushing it
anywhere. He's almost taking it down to television level, except it's done so
technically well. But it's like lowest common denominator. We don't ask
questions. *Raiders* was almost the ultimate in that. I think there were only
two or three major things in the film that really did bother me. You can't
have great stone Egyptian statues that suddenly wobble around and topple
like that. You see, that's breaking the rules. That angers me. The next thing
is that you don't go halfway around the world on a submarine on top of the
water. Then, the ending. You open the Ark. Silly time, folks.

Q: *What was your contribution to the collaborative Python films?*
A: As for the *Holy Grail,* Terry Jones and I codirected it, whatever that means.
I found codirecting a difficult thing because Terry and I are both adrenalin
freaks. We went around shouting our heads off. The crew gets a bit confused
when there's two people shouting orders, especially when the orders don't
necessarily agree with one another. The way we ended up working on *Grail*
after the first couple of weeks is that I ended up working with the camera
and making sure it was looking right and the camera was in the right position. I also spent most of my time in the beginning on the look of the thing,
as usual.

And then when it came to *Brian,* Terry wanted to do a co-direct thing
again. I didn't want to, so I agreed to design it. But it doesn't really work

because you've got to make a film look as good as it can no matter what the sets are, or the costumes. It depends where you put that camera and what you do with it; and, unfortunately, I wasn't around the camera that much for a variety of reasons. So *Brian* doesn't look as good as it could have. It could have looked a lot better. There's a lot more to it than what's on the screen. I don't like that. I find it a waste—in *Time Bandits,* there's nothing that isn't on. I mean, if you look a foot in either direction, the set doesn't exist.

Q : *You drew it all, shot for shot?*
A : It's the only way I can work. It isn't the best way, because you draw a storyboard, and real people don't fit into the frame like a drawing fits into the frame, which can be really painful for real actors when I try to force them into the frame. But that's the thing I've learned a bit about as we've gone on, because *Jabberwocky* was very much like that—the realities of shooting made it very difficult because somebody didn't do what I drew, and it took me a while to get used to that.

Q : *As an animator, you had total control. You could do whatever you wanted.*
A : Yes. It's taken a couple of films to make the transition from animation to working with real people and admitting that they were real people and not just drawings on pieces of paper. I've actually come to enjoy working with live action, particularly because working with good live actors can be really exciting. I have X amount of ideas about what I want the effect to be like, and then you get with Ralph Richardson, Ian Holm, or Sean Connery. Working with those people is great because you really expand. The problem with animation is that you've got total control and you learn less in a strange way because you're not confronted with pieces of recalcitrant paper that make you think.

Q : *How would you describe what you're doing as being different from your work with Monty Python?*
A : I don't think I'm interested in being just funny. *Time Bandits* isn't primarily comedy. It's primarily an adventure spectacular—the comedy is secondary to it. I don't want the comedy to stop, but I could see getting to a point where there is really very little comedy in it. I carry it blacker. It's not great belly laughs, but it's chuckling a lot of the time.

With comedy, the surprise makes you laugh. I'm not always interested in making you laugh. I'd rather just scare the shit out of you. During the cage sequence, I loved watching the audience saying, "Wow! That's great." And the horse coming out of the wardrobe does have just about the best reaction I've seen for a long time. People just leave their seats. They go wild. I'm really happy about that.

I like the idea of amazing and astounding people. That's great, and that's what I do for a living.

Laughs and Deep Themes

DAVID STERRITT/1982

''ACTUALLY, WE'RE PRETTY CHILDISH. It would be nice to say childlike, wouldn't it? But no, childish it is!''

The speaker, with a broad smile on his face, is Terry Gilliam—writer, director, and member of the Monty Python comedy troupe. He's referring to himself and Michael Palin, a fellow Python who teamed with him to create *Time Bandits*, one of the most popular movies of the holiday season.

It's not surprising that a children's film should be successful at this time of year, but *Time Bandits* is no ordinary children's film. On the plus side, it carries its comedy to hilarious heights in a few scenes, while bringing in some unexpectedly deep themes—the nature of reality, the problem of evil, the relationship of God to mankind. Not that any deep conclusions are reached on any of these matters, but it's rare to see them even hinted at in an entertainment film. Indeed, one character (played by Ralph Richardson) is a so-called "Supreme Being" who shows up just in time to vanquish "Evil," slitheringly portrayed by David Warner.

On a less uplifting note, *Time Bandits* contains a share of violence, though it's cartoonish rather than realistic, and there's less of it than in a *Star Wars* or a *Superman II*. Also included are a few moments that kids would describe as "gross" (a hungry hero gnawing on a rat, for instance) that help account for the movie's PG rating. And the ending is downright bizarre for a chil-

From the *Christian Science Monitor* (January 7, 1982): 19. Copyright © 2001 by The Christian Science Monitor. Reprinted by permission of the *Christian Science Monitor*.

dren's film—an unexpected and unsettling twist that may disconcert younger moviegoers.

While these elements have put off some viewers, Gilliam feels they add a kind of weight—comic and otherwise—that speaks to children more than their elders realize. "This isn't really a comedy," he said over lunch recently. "It's an adventure, and the comedy just springs from our approach. What we wanted to make was a decent kids' film, something that hasn't been done for years. Beyond that, we just followed our feelings like we always do."

The trouble with adults, in Gilliam's opinion, is that they don't really look at children. "They look at their own romantic views of their own childhoods," he says. "But actually, kids are very clear-minded. They don't have our prejudices, our structures, our pigeonholed ways of looking at life. And they can be ruthless. Though they have less experience than adults, they are no less intelligent. Their minds are just as active—more so, in fact, because they haven't been limited and defined yet. To them, wonderful things can happen!"

In writing and directing *Time Bandits*, filmmaker Gilliam was reacting against the bowdlerized and "suburbanized" versions of fairy tales he ran across in reading to his own four-and-a-half-year-old daughter. Still, he acknowledges meeting with some studio opposition to the last scene, which has a downbeat feeling.

"There were two arguments against our ending," he says, "the commercial and the paternalistic. The commercial one didn't interest me at all. But the other argument—that children might be disturbed—did concern me. I'm really pro-kid, you know! So we screened it for lots of people before it was released, and we found the kids weren't bothered at all. Anyway, at the very end the camera sweeps back from the action, which puts everything in a cosmic perspective. I like to take the large view. I think it's comforting."

The story of *Time Bandits* concerns a lad named Kevin, who finds a "hole in time" right in his own bedroom. Venturing through this mysterious tunnel, he emerges in different historical periods, teaming up with a band of comical time-traveling outlaws. There are strong echoes of *Snow White and the Seven Dwarfs* and *The Wizard of Oz*, and also of the *Chronicles of Narnia* novels by C. S. Lewis, which are among the few children's books to tackle questions usually regarded as food for philosophers rather than youngsters.

Still, most of the action is blatantly boisterous, with flashes of Python sharpness among the more frivolous jokes and surprises.

Gilliam seems aware that it's an odd duck of a film. But then, cheerful eccentricity has always been a Python stock in trade. According to Gilliam, the troupe's humor is invariably personal. "If it makes us laugh, that's the end of the discussion," he says. "We've never gone chasing after the audience, though we love having them along. The important thing isn't how many people come to see your work. The important thing is having to live with it for the rest of your life."

That's why Python comedy always seems so individualistic: It's based on "nothing but what pleases us," says Gilliam. "In fact," he continues, "it's all about us—or, in this case, about what's left of the kid in us."

Hence the philosophical issues in his latest movie. "The 'big questions' are always there for us. Michael and I had solid religious upbringings, so we grew up believing and thinking about God and religion and good and evil. I can't get those out of my system; they're a part of me. The normal approach in a kids' film is to make the final character a wizard. But why not bring God into it? Why not stop fiddling around, and get right down to things? The cosmic view appeals to me. I like to think I'm not alone, that there's a whole structure around us. . . ."

If his name and approach seem more familiar than his face and voice, it's because Gilliam is the Python behind the scenes—the nonperforming member of the popular troupe, the one who dreamed up the zany animations that filled in between comedy skits on their bygone (but frequently rerun) TV series. When the sextet moved toward the movies, it seemed natural that Gilliam (whose background is in magazine work as well as TV) should turn director. His first feature-filmmaking job was *Monty Python and the Holy Grail*, followed by the less inspired *Jabberwocky*. Though the Python TV show is no more, the troupe remains loosely together, and will be putting a new movie together soon.

Time Bandits is very much Gilliam's work, though it was cowritten by Palin and features a brilliant appearance by Python stalwart John Cleese as a hilarious Robin Hood. As a basically personal project, it reflects Gilliam's views. He leans away from some popular entertainment: "I enjoyed *Raiders of the Lost Ark* while it was on," he recalls, "but I couldn't remember it much afterward." And he favors some older forms of expression, such as classic fairy tales. "They put you through some rough experiences, but you come out a little more confident at the end," he says with emphasis.

His values are visible in many details of *Time Bandits,* such as the fact that the young protagonist is seen as a book reader, while his parents are hooked on TV. "The boy is a throwback," says Gilliam proudly, "while his parents are the wave of the future, and much less attractive." There's even a bit of international satire here, since Gilliam—an American who moved to Britain as a young man—considers the English youth of today (like Kevin in the film) to be more literate than their American counterparts. "British kids still read, and are still uncorrupted by a lot of the Americanization that's going on," he says.

Time Bandits is very much a British film, right down to its incredibly low budget of under $5 million, less than half the Hollywood average. "The [British] have gone through disasters much worse and much more real than the apparent disasters in the States," Gilliam says, "and yet everyone gets along, and seems quite happy! That's why it's better in England, even with all the problems. The people have more sense of history, more perspective, and more resilience."

Which sounds like a list of main ingredients in *Time Bandits,* a flawed and quirky movie, yet one that may be remembered after more expensive and more ephemeral entertainments have faded from the screen for good.

Graham Chapman and Terry Gilliam of Monty Python: What Do the People Want? Who in the Hell Are "The People"?

TONY DESENA / 1982

PUBLICITY TOURS ARE OFTEN a confusing blur of interviews, faces, hotel rooms and seemingly endless questions, but when Graham Chapman and Terry Gilliam hit the circuit to promote their riotous new comedy, *Monty Python Live at the Hollywood Bowl,* they attacked their chore with typical Python aplomb.

The day before the film opened, they arose early to be chauffeured from their posh Parker Meridien suites to beautiful downtown Newark where they taped impromptu segments on *The Uncle Floyd Show,* capped by an out-of-control pie-throwing fight.

They rushed back to Manhattan to record an interview for WNEW-FM, met with a writer from *People* magazine and appeared on *The David Letterman Show.* Between all this activity, they also found time for a working lunch with the *Aquarian* at the hotel's quiet, elegant restaurant—a setting somehow incongruous with Monty Python, yet a setting that permitted the two performers privacy.

"Actually John (Cleese) is probably bothered more than any of us when he goes out," Gilliam states. "He's the most recognizable and people are always asking him to do his 'silly walk' or something."

There's no jealousy in Gilliam's voice over his friend's high public visibility. Although Gilliam, the only American-born member of the troupe, isn't as recognized as his partners, his bizarre animation is as integral to the Monty Python mystique as the many comedy sketches they've performed.

From the *Aquarian* (July 21–28, 1982): 15, 24. Reprinted by permission of Arts Weekly, Inc.

In fact, Monty Python has been unchanged as a six-man team since they first began their BBC-TV series in May 1969, an impressive record in a business known for fragile egos, envious competition, and star-trips.

"Oh, we have our egos," Gilliam quickly points out. "We go off on our own with other projects, but we always come back."

"I think it's a mutual respect for each other," Chapman adds, "and the fact that we all like each other and what we do. It's nice to have a year or two away—time to ourselves. Now I'm really looking forward to starting our next movie soon."

That next film is presumptuously titled *The Meaning of Life* and if the Python's collective ego is facing a test, this film may be it: They've reached the enviable and rare position in their careers when they can call their own shots. That includes garnering financial backing for their film without letting their investors see one page of the script!

"They agreed to go ahead on it just on the fact that it was a new Monty Python film," Gilliam smiles.

"But we write it, perform it, and direct it," Chapman explains, "so it's 'all our fault.' We totally take the blame."

"They like us now because our last thing made money!" Gilliam cracks. "For years we could never get financing for our films because studio people frequently misunderstood our comedy. Thank God pop stars like George Harrison believed in us (a long-time fan of the TV series, Harrison helped finance *Life of Brian, Time Bandits* and now, *Hollywood Bowl*).

"Actually," Chapman cuts in, "I'd be disappointed if the 'greasy eminences' at the studios adored us. It's funny because after we've had a film that's been successful, everybody turns out to be the guy who was pitching for us and supporting us when no one really was, back then."

Not too many folks supported them back in 1969 either, when *Monty Python's Flying Circus* first aired in what Chapman calls "the least favored time period on BBC—Sunday nights at 11."

Those six fellows—Chapman, Gilliam, John Cleese, Eric Idle, Michael Palin, and Terry Jones—were clean-cut young chaps who mixed film and videotape, indoor and outdoor segments, wild animation with cartoons and generally created a sensation in Britain.

Trying to label their whirlwind brand of comedy was as tough as trying to figure out how they got their name. (It was the only suggestion they all agreed they *didn't* like.)

Like most innovators, they were greeted with skepticism, surprise and mis-understanding . . . and that was just from the BBC.

"The BBC was always very lenient with us until our third season when we started to get larger and larger audiences," Gilliam remembers. "Then they started getting more interested. And most censors have distorted viewpoints, reading things into a sketch that aren't there.

"Once John was in a sketch where he thrusts a severed leg through a door to ask for a receipt—just a silly leg—and they saw it as a huge penis."

"There was even a foot on it," Chapman says with a pained smile. "It showed how *their* minds worked, not ours." Terry Gilliam recalls another battle he waged with a censor on this side of the Atlantic.

"I was working with Marty Feldman on his ABC series *Marty Feldman's Comedy Machine* and I was doing this thing on 'fat' and I wanted a Rubens nude to illustrate fat. There was this censor at ABC at the time; she was about twenty-seven and she weighed twelve or thirteen stone (about 180 lbs.), and I don't think she was a sexually happy lady.

"Larry Gelbart was producing it and he wanted to check the nude. I said, 'Why? It's a famous painting.' But she said no frontal nudity so I found a Boucher painting which was even better, with a huge reclining fat ass! Then I was told I could only use it if I covered up the offending area—the crack in her bum. First they said no frontal, now they've changed their mind.

"So," Gilliam continues with a long sigh, "I got a Victorian nude with her legs crossed and cut holes out at the breasts and a fan-shaped cut-out at the crotch, so you could see through to the background. Then I was told that I was calling *too much* attention to them by cutting them out! It was a losing argument."

"There was a rule at the BBC," Chapman solemnly intones, "only one 'shit' per program. No more. I mean, what's the difference if you say it just once or repeat it? You've already let the cat out of the bag in the shit department. Why not just 'shit, shit, shit'? And you were only allowed one 'bug-ger,' too. I remember in *Holy Grail* we traded off a few 'Jesus Christs' for some 'shit' with the censors."

"Another time," Gilliam cuts in, "we talked about a man in a bath wash-ing his arms, legs, chest and naughty bits and they cut out the naughty bits!"

"Of course masturbation was definitely out," Chapman nods with a casual draw on his pipe. "Once I did a character whose hobbies were golf, strangling small animals, and masturbation. The strangling of small animals was okay, but the masturbation was out. You can talk it to death in great explicit detail on serious talk shows, boring people with it day after day, but try to get just one laugh out of it and—whoosh—right out."

Obviously, they don't worry about that problem anymore. Their *Hollywood Bowl* film concludes not with the familiar "The End" logo, but a pointedly rude "Piss Off."

"There's nothing we consider bad taste," Chapman asserts. "I think there's a way to get a laugh out of almost anything."

"It's all in how you do it," Gilliam agrees. "We have no self-imposed restrictions, but making cheap jokes offends me . . . a 'We-are-cleverer-than-you attitude.' I thought that Mel Brooks's character of the governor in *Blazing Saddles* having crossed eyes was a cheap joke, like he couldn't think of anything else funny to do. I think you can joke about people with crossed eyes, but it has to be cleverer than that."

There were many folks who thought *Life of Brian*, the Pythons' 1979 farcical interpretation of biblical history, was one long cheap joke, bordering on blasphemy, with homosexual inferences.

"The original title was *Jesus Christ: Lust for Glory*," Gilliam recalls. "But we changed it to *Life of Brian*, which was really rather dull. It's odd that the American reaction to the film was just not to go see it but in England, the controversy fueled the flames. *Brian* made almost as much money in England as in America. Of course it was also banned in nine southern states."

One minor restriction the Pythons do observe is to avoid topical, particularly political, jokes.

"Too transient," Chapman shrugs. "It dates the material. We're political but not overtly. We poke fun at the institutions and get down to the nub of things."

Because of that reason, *Monty Python Live at the Hollywood Bowl* is loaded with the classic sketches of their TV series, including "The Lumberjack Song," "Nudge, Nudge," "The Ministry of Silly Walks," and "The Argument Clinic." It's the first time Python fans have been able to see these routines since the series' PBS run ended in 1980, where it enjoyed the highest ratings ever on any non-commercial television station.

Because of the series' exacting demands, one BBC season consisted of thirteen weeks, rather than the twenty-six used as a guideline in American television.

Although Terry Gilliam was not often seen in the TV series he appears in a number of sketches in *Hollywood Bowl,* and plans to keep up with his behind-the-camera duties as well as some new ones in front of the camera.

"Yes, and he should, too!" Chapman praises. "He's really quite funny."

"Actually," Gilliam corrects, "I was in a lot of the TV shows, but always under a lot of heavy makeup. I always found I could do a little bit of performing when I was heavily disguised."

Chapman's recurring characterizations as buffoonish Bobbies or military men grew out of his childhood. "I used to hang around police stations when I was young," he jokes. Then after a pause: "Because my father was a policeman." This revelation is new to Gilliam. "Really?" he says. "I didn't know that. Aren't these interviewers wonderful?"

Chapman once incorporated another personal experience into a sketch. While vacationing in Paris, some years ago, he boldly called up Jean-Paul Sartre to arrange a meeting with the famous French existentialist. But the eighty-five-year-old writer-philosopher was out that day handing out leaflets on a street corner!

"I was so taken with the man's verve," Chapman whispers, "I had to include it in a skit."

After *The Meaning of Life,* the Pythons plan to pursue more individual projects (Gilliam is supervising a rerelease of his *Jabberwocky,* definitely NOT a Python film, but mistakenly sold as one) before touching base again.

"I think there's an advantage to the six of us being together," Gilliam muses. "People on their own are very vulnerable and often have to put up facades. We're a group of people who give *each other* a bad time. We take care not to allow each other to think too highly of himself, so we're reasonably confident and not worried about exposing ourselves."

"That's why we liked the idea of doing a show like the Hollywood Bowl," Chapman concurs. Their four-night stint in 1980 was the group's first live performance in America since a three-week engagement at New York City's City Center in 1976. "It's a nice venue," he continues, "and it was also easy, because we had all performed the sketches before!"

In an era of market surveys and demographic analyses, Monty Python presses on with its own eclectic tastes—tastes that don't conform to any show-business formula. Both Gilliam and Chapman admit to having no real conception of who an "average" Monty Python fan might be.

"And we don't really care," Chapman remarks half-seriously. "It sounds arrogant but it's also honest. We don't know or care about demographics.

We write totally for ourselves, what *we* think is funny. We never take into consideration anyone else."

"We've tested out film sections to see what works best with audiences," Gilliam clarifies, "but the initial writing stage is done just to please ourselves."

What about the old show-biz maxim, "Give the People What They Want?"

"Who are 'They'?" Gilliam and Chapman ask in unison. Obviously they're both on the same wavelength.

"I don't know who 'They' are or what 'They' want," Gilliam laughs, with his partner nodding in agreement. "All you can ever do is something you like and something you believe in and hope it works. And if it doesn't. . . ." He shoots Chapman a wry smile and is repaid with a similar grin. ". . . Then we'll have to start rethinking what we're doing for a living."

A Zany Guy Has a Serious Rave Movie

RICK LYMAN / 1986

TERRY GILLIAM IS GAME for just about anything. He'll climb up a tree. He'll hang off a big rock. He'll even pretend to fall asleep on a Central Park bench. *Anything.*

Go ahead, name it: Pretend that knobby tree over there is a woman and give it a great big hug. *OK.* Go straddle that bush. *Sure!*

Whether he's jaunting through a Central Park photography session or relaxing in his Hotel Westbury suite in the first of three weeks of interviews, Gilliam's energy is infectious. He is one happy buckaroo.

And why not?

After almost a year of beating his head against a brick wall trying to get Sid Sheinberg, president of Universal Pictures, to release his macabre, futuristic fantasy, *Brazil,* director Gilliam is finally seeing the film released. It opened Friday in Philadelphia and has been snaking its way around the country since mid-January, getting reviews that range from good to ecstatic. Playing now at a theater near you: the grim, comic saga of a faceless bureaucrat who reaches for love, only to be squashed by the brutal, inept system.

"Yes, sir," Gilliam says. "This is the fun part."

When he tosses his scarf over his shoulder and narrows his eyes with malevolent glee, Gilliam, forty-five, resembles an evil leprechaun. For the first time in who-knows-how-many awful, endless months, the mention of Sheinberg's name elicits not a grimace but a grin from Gilliam's square face.

From the *Philadelphia Inquirer* (February 9, 1986): 1-J, 12-J. Reprinted by permission of the *Philadelphia Inquirer.*

"I am not bitter, really. And I suppose it was a victory, but I don't think I'm gloating. I'm just glad that the movie is going to be released—my movie, the movie I made, not somebody else's version of it."

Gilliam was born in Minneapolis and spent his youth there and in Southern California, where he went to high school in the San Fernando Valley and to college in Pasadena. (His father was a carpenter who did a lot of work for the movie studios.)

While in college, the young Gilliam worked on the student satire magazine; he later used his experience to land a job at a struggling satirical magazine in New York called *Help!* There he earned $50 a week and in his spare time tried to teach himself how to be a film animator with a 16 mm camera— just about his only possession.

"I tried attending evening classes at City College, but it didn't take long to realize that I really wasn't learning anything there," he says.

In the early '70s, Gilliam used his life savings on a now-or-never trip through Europe, spending several months bumming around the continent and landing eventually in London. It was there that he met a group of young British satiric writers and performers. Collectively they were hired by the British Broadcasting Corp. to put together a loosely structured satiric television series that became *Monty Python's Flying Circus.*

Though Gilliam appeared in a handful of the skits, his chief contribution was in the weird animated sequences in the series. His work was always set in a surreal universe mixing classical antiquity, Victorian bric-a-brac, and drab London urbanscapes. The sequence that began both the television series and the group's best movie, *Life of Brian* (1970), showed a winged figure (a recurring image that Gilliam calls his "Icarus fantasy") flying heavenward through a peaceful sky, only to be squashed—with a grotesque *splursh*—by a giant foot.

"After a while, I just started to get bored with animation," Gilliam says. "I decided that I wanted to do the things on film that I was doing in animation."

The saga of *Brazil* begins four years ago, just after the 1981 release of Gilliam's *Time Bandits,* his second directorial effort (the first was the medieval farce *Jabberwocky* in 1977). *Time Bandits,* an erratic, episodic fantasy, was a surprise hit in U.S. theaters, suddenly making him a bankable director. A chance meeting at a London cocktail party with producer Arnon Milchan resulted in a partnership to make the movie that Gilliam had been dreaming about for almost a decade: a fantasy about a drab Everyman caught in the gears of a comically imperfect totalitarian state—*1984* on acid.

Financing was obtained from two Hollywood studios that agreed to share the burden, Universal pledging $9 million and Twentieth Century Fox $6 million (in the film's final financing plan, Fox's share entitled it only to the film's distribution overseas).

"From the very beginning, everyone at Universal knew what the movie was about," Gilliam says. "They knew how much it would cost. They knew how it was going to end."

Gilliam banged out a first draft of the screenplay with playwright Tom *(The Real Thing)* Stoppard but found it an unsatisfying collaboration. "Really, Tom was not all that comfortable with collaborating," he says. A more polished final draft was completed by Gilliam and actor-writer Charles McKeown, who also plays a small role in the film as a weaselly bureaucrat. That screenplay was nominated Wednesday for an Academy Award.

Gilliam shot the film at various locations in and around London. Welsh actor Jonathan Pryce was hired to play Sam Lowry, Gilliam's futuristic Everyman, backed up by an impressive cast of international performers including Robert De Niro, Michael Palin, Katherine Helmond, and Bob Hoskins.

The finished film, which ran 142 minutes, opened in the spring in Europe to positive reviews and good business. But by that time, Universal was growing nervous. The film was a comedy, but a *gruesome* comedy. It tended to be cluttered, rambling. And the ending was decidedly downbeat.

"This should not have come as a surprise to anybody," Gilliam says. "It was right there in the script. But all of a sudden they started invoking a clause in the contract in which we were supposed to turn in a movie no longer than 125 minutes."

The real problem, though, was never the length of the movie, Gilliam says. It was the ending. "As I understand it, they were talking about using two or three different endings, one more ridiculous than the next. There are points toward the end of the movie where it could possibly end. You can see them when you're watching the film. But none of them are the right ending, none of them are what the movie is about."

Sheinberg has told reporters that Universal wasn't so much interested in a happy ending as a "satisfying ending." He said that although the movie "has brilliance in many portions of it," its commercial potential was "something close to zero."

Universal's plan, he said, was to edit the movie itself and then show test audiences both cuts to see which one would go over better.

Gilliam tried to placate Sheinberg by cutting the European print of the film. He trimmed out eleven minutes. But it wasn't enough. And it didn't alter the ending.

Gilliam refused to cut any more. Sheinberg yanked *Brazil* from Universal's calendar of releases—indefinitely.

So Gilliam and Milchan took the audacious route of a renegade publicity campaign in the Hollywood trade papers: an "open letter" to Sheinberg, begging him to release *Brazil*. In addition, Milchan offered to pay the expenses of any American movie critic who wanted to travel to Canada to see the film (many major publications, including the *Philadelphia Inquirer*, have rules forbidding staff members from accepting such free trips).

The film had been tentatively set for spring '85 release, then yanked. After Gilliam made his cuts, it was reset for fall '85 release, then yanked. Finally Sheinberg said there was no way he was going to release the movie in 1985, negating its chances for Academy Award nominations. At one point, he offered to sell the movie to anyone who would cover Universal's original expenditure, $9 million.

But somehow, in late November, Milchan was able to show a print of the film (minus the eleven minutes Gilliam had already cut) to the members of the Los Angeles Film Critics Association. And when that group announced its year-end awards, Gilliam's *Brazil*, a movie that had never been released in America, was the surprise choice for best movie of the year.

"It was the most amazing thing, the most incredible turnaround," Gilliam says. "One day we were nowhere, fighting for every inch, and the next day, all of a sudden, we're victorious. We had absolutely no warning that it was going to happen."

Universal hurriedly made plans to give *Brazil* a weeklong booking in Los Angeles and New York in late December to qualify it for the Oscars, and then announced plans for a series of bookings all over the country beginning in mid-January.

"Something happens to people when they become movie-studio executives," Gilliam says, sipping a glass of water and contemplating the onset of a long publicity tour that had until recently been only a feeble dream. "I'm not sure exactly what it is. They're businessmen who have risen to the top because they are very good businessmen, but when they find themselves running a movie studio, they suddenly want to be filmmakers. They think they *are* filmmakers.

"But you know what? They're not."

The Life of Terry

OWEN GLEIBERMAN/1986

EVERY SO OFTEN ON *Monty Python's Flying Circus,* you can catch a glimpse of Terry Gilliam playing the village idiot or a mute torturer's assistant; he can usually be spotted in the corner of a sketch, grimacing into the camera and looking blissfully at home amidst the usual Python madness. Monty Python is nearly twenty years old now (the show débuted in 1969), but at forty-five, Gilliam, who began his career as the troupe's animator, creating those surrealist cutout cartoons in which dumpling-cheeked figures fall down pipes and sprout flowers from their heads and get chomped on by buildings, still looks every bit the overgrown imp, with a big, broad, cherubic face that's always breaking into a feverish grin. Born in Minnesota in 1940, he moved to Los Angeles with his family when he was eleven and then, in the late '60s, settled in England to work with the Python crew. After codirecting its first feature, *Monty Python and the Holy Grail,* he knew he'd found his calling, going on to direct *Jabberwocky* (1977), *Time Bandits* (1981)—a surprise hit that ended up netting more than $40 million—and now *Brazil.* Gilliam, who lives with his wife and two children in Britain, has been called "an Englishman in an American's body"—a description borne out by his pancontinental accent, which smooths over a home-grown drawl with rolling English cadences, and by his effortlessly clever, devilish-yet-polite style. He seems, well, like a guy from Minnesota who has spent the better part of his life hanging out with madcap-intellectual English comedians. I talked with him about *Brazil,* Monty Python, surrealism, technology, America, and, of

From *Boston Phoenix* (November 21, 1986): 2, 12. Reprinted by permission of *Boston Phoenix.*

course, fantasy and reality—two concepts that, by Gilliam's own admission, he often has trouble distinguishing.

Q: *How did you dream up* Brazil?
A: Nineteen-eighty-four was approaching and I thought it was time to do the cautionary tale, to do *1984* for 1984. I haven't actually read Orwell. But, I mean, I know the book. It was more Kafka than Orwell I was thinking of; the atmosphere of Kafka intrigues me more, the inability to get hold of this thing that seems to be controlling or determining your life. It was interesting that the thing ended up being as close to the story of *1984,* because I didn't plan it that way. It just seemed to be the natural course of events. I had a script that no one was interested in giving me any money for, so I wrote *Time Bandits* with Michael [Palin], and after the success of that, people said, "Well, now you can really do all sorts of things." They were saying I ought to do something like a follow-up, that it would work well to do another romp. And I figured it was time to do the one that no one would give me any money for.

Q: *How did you collaborate with Tom Stoppard on the script?*
A: We didn't. I mean, that ultimately is why it wasn't satisfying. Because Tom likes working on his own and I like collaborating. At the end, after I'd given him the script a number of times and he'd gone off and worked on it, I thought that it was now quite clever. There were some neat dialogues, but I felt the world still wasn't complete and there wasn't enough anguish in the thing, enough *muck* in it. So I started mucking it up, making it just a bit messier. I don't like just having people walk into a room and do their dialogue. I want the chair to be a character, you know? I want the knife and fork to somehow be part of the scenery. It's pantheism.

Q: *Where did you come up with the mask Michael Palin wears at the end?*
A: It was a doll that some kid had left in my parents' backyard. I said, "I've got to remember that face," and I had a photograph taken of it sitting in a little wagon. It was *awful,* because the hair was all pulled out and the thing was rotting and . . . that face! That strange mongoloid face on that doll. And I just kept it pinned on my wall for a long time. I liked the face because it had a certain Buddha-like quality; it was Eastern, it was very enigmatic—it could be taken in many ways.

Q: *Is your imagination always working?*
A: Yeah, and I don't try to control it. I do everything in my power to keep things from falling into neat little slots. And that includes reality or fantasy, which sometimes start slipping. There's a point where, I must admit, I used to dream a lot about flying—not way up in the air but just a couple of feet off the ground. You'd lay on the ground and just sort of float up. And there was one day, years ago, when I was with a friend, and I couldn't remember whether I really could fly or whether I'd just dreamed I could. My body and everything I knew told me I could except the fact that you can't fly. And I had to get down on the floor and try it. That's how my brain works. The terrible thing is that I've never even taken acid.

Q: *I was going to ask you about that.*
A: Yeah, I've never been a druggie. When Python began in the late '60s, we were always being interviewed and people would just assume we were acid-heads. But it's all been . . . a natural high. John Denver and me.

Q: *In* Brazil, *when Robert De Niro, as Tuttle, opens up the wall to reveal all that tubing, it reminded me of those Monty Python cartoons where a guy would slide through miles of pipes. What is it with you and inner pipes?*
A: The inner workings of things have always fascinated me. For most people, life seems to be organized to try to cover up all of that. There's this hotel in San Sebastian, in Spain, it's wonderful—a massive, monumental place. The walls are very thick, and on the side there'd be little doors going into the walls, and there are people inside them who are really running the place. Basically, there's a life going on behind the scenes—people in the kitchen, the maintenance men. The way things work always intrigued me, and the people who make things work. That's why you get Tuttle as a hero.

Q: *What's going on behind those walls has taken on a life of its own.*
A: Well, it does. My feeling about it is that there is a price to pay for all of these Central Services, for the world we have. To switch on the light isn't as simple as it looks, because you've got to pay the man who works for the company that goes back to the power station and then to central grids and the government. By taking part in that process, the price you pay is a more complicated society, and one you're dependent on. I've got a house in the country, and we had it for years before we put in electricity. I was very loath

to put it in, because there's something about having a house without it. And there's also a very sensual enjoyment, or at least a visually sensual enjoyment, in walking around at night with a lantern. Shadows move—the whole thing becomes exciting, changing.

Q: *So when you make this movie in which technology appears as monstrous, it's almost a way of keeping your sanity.*
A: If you can visualize it, name it, point a finger at it, you destroy the beast that way. That's how you destroy death: you laugh at it. Because it's going to get ya, so you might as well laugh it away as long as possible.

Q: *You were doing cutout animations fifteen years ago, and now you're a major filmmaker. How much of that was by design?*
A: Since college I wanted to be a filmmaker, but none of it was by design—it was all by default. I knew I loved films, and I think I sensed I would be good at it, because it uses most of my skills and interests. But I had no ability to work my way up through anything, because I don't like most systems. I was doing the animation for Monty Python, and then eventually it came time to do *Holy Grail,* and Terry Jones and I were both obsessed about making films, and became film directors.

Q: *Was it a tough leap?*
A: No, because it was, like, anybody named Terry could direct. And in five weeks we made that film for $400,000. I don't know how we did it. I look back now and think, "Who were those guys who did that?" In *Holy Grail* we did the shell thing because we *couldn't* have horses; we wanted horses desperately. Given enough money, we would have been totally mediocre.

Q: *Could you see yourself making serious fantasy epics, without the humor?*
A: I don't want to, because I think other people can do that. The next film is less angry than *Brazil,* though—it's more sentimental. Do you know *The Adventures of Baron Munchausen?* Munchausen is an eighteenth-century gentleman, soldier, adventurer, and liar; he basically tells fantastic tall tales that are done totally straight-faced. It's the Age of Reason when everything is starting to be perceived, but Munchausen is of another age, he's a fantasist, an extravagance.

Q: *Were you born in the wrong century?*

A: [laughing] I think from this perspective it's a rather nice one to go on journeys from, the twentieth century. I mean, I keep thinking I'd love to be Bruegel, or Bosch. But then maybe I wouldn't. Maybe the reality would be far too oppressive. I think I am happier as a pre-Freudian, though. Freud, in a way, has made some things banal. I like the idea of actual demons sucking your brains out—envy and greed, these things being tangible. It's somehow, on a common level, a more sensible way of dealing with the world, rather than an idea. Ideas and concepts—they're labels. Whether "libido" describes something better than this great thing with horny hooves and all that—that seems to me as good a description, if not a better one.

Q: *You were born and raised in America, yet you've lived in England for almost twenty years. Did you move away to escape the "quality of life" here?*

A: It was partly that, yeah. Living here, I couldn't distinguish my dreams from the dreams that were being sold to me. I couldn't even experience reality without questioning whether I was really experiencing reality or somebody else's idea of reality. A simple thing like walking down the beach—sun setting, birds flying, waves lapping, the sand beneath your feet: was I enjoying it because it was genuinely enjoyable to walk along the beach with the sun setting, or because I'd seen it in ten hundred commercials telling me, "*This* is what life is all about"? And I couldn't tell. I had to get out.

Q: *Do you think of yourself as a surrealist?*

A: I think so. Except that I'm such a cheap . . . *comic.* I mean, there aren't many surrealists who deal in pratfalls and farts. But I love Magritte and all those great surrealists. Dali's a con man, I'm convinced. De Chirico impresses me but he's lacking the liveliness of Magritte. I mean, Magritte tells jokes.

Q: *I think of the archetypal Terry Gilliam image—it's there in both* Brazil *and* Time Bandits—*as a peaceful, tranquil setting suddenly disrupted by a force of great violence. What is that all about?*

A: It's the big foot coming down in the Monty Python opening. It's my fear of reality—my fear of violence, of the unreasonable violence that seems to permeate every part of our lives. It's the bus hitting you as you cross the street. It's all of those things you can't control; they frighten me because I love beautiful things. And in a way that's what happens to Sam Lowry. He allows himself to become vulnerable by falling in love and becoming obsessed, and he gets stomped on. It's me seeing things I love so much, and knowing that they're not permanent, that they're going to get destroyed one day. And it's sort of preparing myself for it, in a strange way, by doing it. The ridiculous thing is that I've had such a good life. *Nothing has happened!* I'm waiting for it to happen. And it terrifies me every day of my life—that it's going to end tomorrow, that it's all going to be over and I'm going to be so *pissed off!*

The Mad Adventures of Terry Gilliam

DAVID MORGAN/1988

''I GET THE FEELING THAT, a bit like *Brazil,* the making of the film is going to be like the film itself. Where *Brazil* was about a nightmare, this one is about impossibility and overcoming it, and trying to push through a lot of things and a lot of people who don't think they can do it, because they are realistic.''

Terry Gilliam obviously knew, perhaps better than anyone, the impossibility of creating his new film, *The Adventures of Baron Munchausen.* Just before shooting began in September last year, the director admitted what everyone has been trying to tell him ever since: the film cannot be done. But Gilliam went ahead and did it anyway. What his ultimate vision of *Munchausen* will be is anyone's guess, including Gilliam's own. He has spoken of making this film for years. But the processes by which it has been evolving, growing, shrinking, and being cast into the cold public spotlight before its time have proved bigger than anything he has experienced before. Gilliam has stood apart, feeling protected from the "factory" aspects of filmmaking. Now he is caught up in the largest movie to shoot in Europe since *Cleopatra.*

Though born in Minneapolis, the forty-seven-year-old writer-director grew up in Hollywood's backyard, an environment which fuelled both his desire to enter films and his dislike of the film community itself. "A lot of it came from the fact that I wanted desperately to get into movies and didn't have any idea how one got into it. And I didn't like the rules of the game, if

From *Sight and Sound,* vol. 57 (August 1988): 238–42. Reprinted by permission of *Sight and Sound.*

you were going to work your way up from the bottom. The majority of people in the movie business in Hollywood are there for the money and the power, and if you are working there you have to talk to them, and if you do that you are going to be influenced by their attitudes. I don't want to talk to them about anything: hand over the loot and let me get on with the work. And what I like in England is that the film industry is not a very healthy thing, so that those involved with it are there because they love film. I really just spend my time working in a very useful way, as opposed to meetings with a lot of inane discussion. . . ."

Baron Munchausen's estimated budget of nearly $25 million made it one of the largest independent productions in history. Earmarked as a co-production between Laura Film (the film's production office headed by Thomas Schuhly) and Prominent Features (a division of Prominent Pictures, the Monty Python organization), *Munchausen* was picked up by David Puttnam and Columbia, which signed a distribution deal for worldwide theatrical and video rights (excluding Italy and Germany, territories already signed for by other investors). The $20.5 million which Columbia promised upon delivery of the completed film (making it a "negative pick-up") was used as collateral to obtain a bond from Film Finance, Inc., a Los Angeles-based company. . . . Delays in the preproduction period only foreshadowed the greater financial and logistical difficulties once the film started shooting at Cinecittà in Rome, and later during location work in Spain. Because *Munchausen* is an independent production—caught without the built-in safety net of an in-house studio film—Gilliam found himself struggling to complete his dream project, while up against the same Hollywood bureaucracy he has repeatedly criticized since before his much publicized battle to save his cut of *Brazil* from that film's U.S. distributors. And the film's problems, already bad enough, were made to seem even worse because of the press reports they generated.

The insurance company wanted no part of a runaway production, which was what *Munchausen* appeared to be. They sought financial assistance from Columbia, but by that time the upheaval of management which marked the departure of David Puttnam as head of the studio left no one willing to address the film's troubles: *Munchausen* was an independent feature and therefore on its own. "Basically you do a film in a certain atmosphere," Thomas Schuhly said. "Columbia just said, 'Okay, we changed our management, the guys who set up this atmosphere are out; therefore there is no more atmosphere—there is just a deal.' It's like getting married. You marry

because your intention is to get along, and beside your legal obligations there
are many other obligations you don't put on paper. Here there was no
divorce, but the marriage was different suddenly."

In November 1987, Film Finance halted shooting for two weeks in order to
rein in the spiralling budget and shooting schedule. Gilliam and Schuhly
were threatened with dismissal. Rather than have his film taken away from
him, Gilliam found himself forced to make drastic cuts in the screenplay, to
eliminate or pare down the more expensive sequences. Even given the slicing
and hacking, which couldn't totally prevent a budget overage projected at
about $10 million, Gilliam is convinced that *Munchausen* still stands as a film
far more elaborate, more difficult, and more uncommon than anything he
has ever experienced or imagined.

It is certainly far removed from the quick, frenzied shoots to which he has
accustomed himself, having to work with new talent not used to dealing
with special effects—or, for that matter, with Gilliam himself. It was Gilliam's association with Thomas Schuhly which brought the production to
Rome, where Schuhly hoped to foster a special working relationship between
Gilliam and the artists at Cinecittà. "The English character for me is a very
dark one," Schuhly said. "Italians are very light, very sensual. And I thought
that the film should get the feel of a very light atmosphere. You see it on the
screen—it's totally different from *Brazil*." Director of photography Giuseppe
Rotunno, art director Dante Ferretti and costume designer Gabriella Pescucci
were signed up. Gilliam's enthusiasm for working in Rome soared.

One of the painful truths of this arduous shoot, however, is that Gilliam's
working habits do not travel well. Though he is thorough in preparing films
down to the most minute detail, the time it takes to carry those details onto
film never matches his hopes. Even when the shooting schedule approaches
anywhere near normal, he feels "Normal isn't fast enough." And while his
other pictures have helped him establish a team of people who apparently
satisfy his demands, few Gilliam veterans are in Rome to take part in this
adventure. An apt example of the problems the production has faced is the
difficulty of communication on the set, which sometimes finds Gilliam on
one side and the Italian crew on the other, with a harried interpreter in the
middle.

On the set of Vulcan's arms factory during the last week of shooting before
the 1987 Christmas break, the smoke-filled atmosphere lit by the fiery yellow
and orange glow of the furnaces is deceptively arctic, as Gilliam tries to get a

single take to his satisfaction. John Neville, as the Baron, is sprawled in front of the camera, being pushed along a track toward a pool of water. While they run through the shot, Gilliam watches a TV monitor which shows the camera's POV. After calling action, his eyes are glued to the screen. He silently mouths the dialogue as Neville speaks. His eyes are wide and gleeful; he looks like a child watching his favorite Saturday morning cartoon show. But his happiness turns to dismay as the take continues, and the camera moves just don't match what he wants to see. He huddles again with the camera crew, his frustration obvious.

The shot is run through over and over again. As Gilliam examines the monitor on each take, his happiness with Neville's reading begins to evaporate. He goes back to the crew. "It's nothing like in rehearsal," he yells. "I want the shot done right here as it was done. It is now 11 o'clock in the morning. You don't have a director. You don't want to turn over? I go home!" Gilliam storms off the set, with the actors sitting nearby looking somewhat shocked, though not too surprised.

"He knows just what he wants," says Winston Dennis, a huge, cuddly giant playing Albrecht (he also appeared in *Time Bandits* and *Brazil*). "It's the first time I've seen Terry blow his top." Neville's stand-in has taken the Baron's place, as the crew reviews the moves they're supposed to make. "Of course, on the set, *we're* two little angels," says Dennis, nodding toward Oliver Reed. Reed rolls his eyes in amusement.

Outside the soundstage next day Moo Moo, a cow, is tethered to a tree, awaiting her appearance on the set. Her genial keeper shoos people away, but there's no need; the cow is quite unfriendly to anyone passing by. "It was actually written as a herd of cows," remarks Gilliam. "It comes from Gabriel García Márquez's book *Autumn of the Patriarch,* where he has this scene of a cow on a balcony. I don't know, cows are on my mind. I made the mistake of having animals all over the place on this film." As he walks toward the Cinecittà lunchroom, for the only hour of peace he seems to have each day, he talks spiritedly and enthusiastically, even of events he might prefer to forget. His infectious giggle makes him sound like a tenor Woody Woodpecker.

Q: DAVID MORGAN: *How have you had to adjust your working habits since coming to Rome?*
TERRY GILLIAM: For people here the concept of the maestro is very impor-

tant—this one man, from whom all knowledge and wisdom flows—and I don't like to work that way. I really like being part of a team, but people here aren't used to working that way—or at least the people on this film aren't. I think it's a Catholic thing. If the director can be made God, then people can be popes and cardinals and bishops, and so the greater the director, the greater your popehood or your bishopric. It really is like that. So they elevate the director.

It's more of a team in England; it's the nature of the society. They all squawk, and they go at each other, but basically people have an attitude that they are more or less equal. They come up and say, "Why are you doing that?" or "What about doing this or that?" I get a lot of feedback, a lot of information, and they give me ideas that are better than my own ideas. I become a filter for a lot of ideas, and that give and take is the way it works. Here I have to place the camera *exactly,* and if I don't say something it doesn't generally happen.

After working for years with the same people, they got used to me, so that you could communicate in Neanderthal grunts. But here, because everyone is new, it's a big problem that I didn't really worry about early enough. You see, I get very impatient. I want to do things fast, explain things fast. When you do that, no one knows what you're talking about, and because people are not used to complicated ways of making special effects, they're worried. They want to work slowly until they understand. That slows the process down and I get frustrated. I only control my madness with a lot of feedback on how the world really is, and if nobody tells me what *they* think the world is, I have no idea what it is.

We're in a strange situation. The film has gone way over budget, all sorts of political problems. Also, the studio isn't a problem, because they made a contract and they are going to stick to it. They have the *best* deal, of this year or many years to come. We have cut the film a lot, even before we started shooting. We've been trimming it down and trimming it down. And up to now I have really avoided looking at the film. For the first time in my life, I have never gone to the rushes. I go to the cutting room and see it on the editing machine, and we go through it in little sections. But I am trying to stay away from it for some reason. I don't know why.

D.M.: *Is it that you are afraid you will want to reshoot things?*
T.G.: Yes, I think so. The most frightening thing is when you actually get

close to doing something good. You can just make a little mistake then and it's destroyed. [The story already] exists in a lot of people's minds, and I worry that I will disappoint those people, because they have their idea of *Munchausen* and mine is different. I worried about it for a long time, and now I just ignore it. We invented most of this film. He's Munchausen, but I'm using him for my own purposes. It was too restrictive just to do the original, because there was no shape to the whole thing, other than this incredible liar telling these amazing tales. But I'm beginning to think that everybody is getting a little bored with science fiction and the same creatures that keep popping up all over the place. What is nice about *Munchausen* is that it is eighteenth-century science fiction, so it has a different attitude. The imagery is quite unlike what people are used to at the moment. It gets a bit closer to something like *The Thief of Bagdad,* where it isn't about machinery—it's about people and gods and mythological things.

I just got hooked again on my same old theme, Fantasy/Reality. Lies and truth is an extension of that, and it's about age and youth. Also death, birth, all those things. I *think* that's what it's about. . . . *Time Bandits* was a story about a boy going through space and time and history, and never knowing whether it was real or a dream; *Brazil* was about a man who refused to take his responsibility in the real world and spent his time dreaming, ultimately escaping in madness; and *Munchausen* is really the happy ending, the triumph of fantasy.

D.M.: *Do you think there will be more cuts in the script?*

T.G.: I don't know. We had another session this weekend where we had to give another bit away because the film is being taken over by the completion company, and they need their little pound of flesh to go back and show that they're on top of it. And so we keep giving them flesh. We're down to the bones now. It's weightier in a strange way. It's not as fantastic. Luckily we started with such an extravagant piece, there's room to trim, but the terrible thing is that the stories I was most interested in were lost very early on. There was a whole thing about a horse being cut in half that's *wonderful*. It's a great sequence. That was one of the main reasons I wanted to make this film—it's not there. It's still the same film somehow. We've been having "crisis meetings" where we've got forty-eight hours to come up with the answer, and thirty-six hours later there's no answer. So, "That's it! Call the lawyers, it's all over, the film is dead, the Baron is finally buried." And then, Bingo! At the last minute we've found an answer every time. I have never seen a film so determined to keep going.

D.M.: *When you storyboard and design a film, do you take into consideration how much something might cost, how difficult it might be to film? Or do you let your imagination take you away and worry about logistics later?*

T.G.: I sit there and I really think about it and I work out, "It'll only take me a day to do that," and then I think I know what I'm doing. And I've always been wrong. And each time I can convince myself that, "No, I am right *this* time despite the past." Strangely enough, because I believe it's possible, I am able to convince other people that it's possible. So we venture forth on these adventures that are just totally impossible. But it's too late by the time people have discovered the truth.

We have on the film now David Tomblin, the associate producer. He is one of the most experienced first assistant directors in the world. He did *Empire of the Sun, Gandhi, Cry Freedom, Star Wars, Raiders of the Lost Ark.* He came late to the film, which is a pity, because he is the one that knows better. I have to try to convince him; he's what I need.

One of our problems is that we spend so long on trying to deal with some of the special effects and the set-ups that the actors don't have time to work. John Neville has been here every day for months and he has worked only in little bits. And this is really depressing, because he is an extraordinary character: he runs the Stratford Festival Company [in Ontario], he has a hundred actors and they do fifteen productions a season, and he directs, he acts, he's an incredibly organized man. Now he is caught in this nightmare where he has to sit in make-up for hours and then doesn't get to work. And he sees around him disorganization, inefficiency and just chaos, day after day. He has stayed away from films for years, he has concentrated on theater. Finally we lure him back and it's like the Nightmare Come True. I don't even know what to say to him anymore, because I can't justify it.

I really like actors. This started on *Jabberwocky,* right after *Holy Grail,* working with Python. I went and did my first film on my own with actors, and suddenly discovered how wonderful they were. I like working with British actors particularly because they are technically wonderful and less "Methody" than American actors. You can be sitting chatting about the last football game and then say, "All right, here we go," and Boom! They are right immediately into the character. They do the scene, it might be a fairly emotional scene, and then it's over and we're back to talking about football.

On the Vulcan dining-room set, they are filming Uma Thurman's entrance as the goddess Venus. Standing naked on a giant clamshell, posed to mimic Botticelli's painting, the young actress is understandably nervous about her scene. In between takes, she keeps her composure by dancing a silly little dance on the shell. Her surreal act resembles a Monty Python cartoon, and the connection of this image is not lost on Gilliam, who stands dumbfounded, watching Uma Thurman inadvertently recreate a piece he had animated before she was even born.

D.M.: *How did you get involved with filmmaking in the first place, in particular with animation?*
T.G.: That was really a fluke. I was on a program [*We Have Ways of Making You Laugh*] doing caricatures of the guests, and they had some material they didn't know how to present. I suggested I might make an animated film and they let me; and overnight I was an animator. And then when *Holy Grail* came along, Terry Jones and I decided to be film directors. We had never done *that* before. We make these quantum leaps and once your name is up there with the credits, people believe it.

I always drew when I was a kid. I did cartoons because it's easiest to impress people if you draw a funny picture, and I think that was a sort of passport through much of my early life. The only art training I had was in college where I majored in political science. I took several art courses, drawing and sculpture classes. My training has actually been fairly sloppy and I've been learning about art in retrospect. But I've always kept my eyes open, and things that I like I am influenced by.

D.M.: *How is your work with Dante Ferretti?*
T.G.: It's great. This is one reason that I came to Italy, just the artistic side of things. I don't think the film would look nearly so good if we were back in England, because everybody here has such a sense of color and form. That's one of the good things about being here, that the film has been influenced by being in Rome.

Something was bothering me about the physical location of the dining-room, where the Baron and Vulcan are supposed to be sitting at the table with goblets of wine; it wasn't quite right. So Vulcan is now in a room that is like an eighteenth-century salon, and it's very delicate. This is partly because of this location we were sitting at. We changed it round, having him drink out of these little demitasse cups. Here's this rough, crude, brutish man having to behave in a civilized eighteenth-century manner. It starts getting better and more interesting. And that's the result of a physical place. You are sitting there and you're trying to force the place to behave as you originally conceived the scene, and it doesn't quite fit. You fight this for a long time, and you eventually give in and let the place dictate a few ideas.

Dante is an incredibly hard worker, he never stops. At first of course it was difficult because he wants to do his job and *I* want to do his job. But we reached a really good working relationship. He has excellent ideas; he's funny. It would be nice if we spoke the same language. No, we actually do speak the same language. It's not Italian or English: it's images.

D.M.: *And your relationship with Giuseppe Rotunno?*

T.G.: His sense of light is fantastic. He has reached the stage where he's so good that he concentrates on fine points like one-tenth of one percent difference. I don't think he is used to someone like me, unfortunately. He has worked with more controlled directors. On the other hand, he has worked with Fellini, but Fellini plays in a different way. Fellini does have total control of the thing and I keep wanting just to be one of the team members. And Peppino wants me to be God.

D.M.: *Is one influencing the other more?*

T.G.: No, because he is making it as beautiful as I want it to be. I get frustrated because I want it to be beautiful, but I also want it to be fast. And Peppino gets frustrated because he wants it to be beautiful and he will hold out to get it the way he feels it should be. So in a way he benefits me enormously because he is holding out for what I really want, but how this actually works with the schedule is something else. On the one hand, I have to get the thing done in the time and money available, and on the other hand, I want it to be an incredibly beautiful thing. Much of the time, what we are doing is telling cheap jokes, but they are dressed so beautifully they don't look like cheap jokes anymore.

There's one scene in the destroyed city, and the little girl's father in the film is a theater manager and he wears this great long blue dressing-gown. Standing in front of the theater, he is desperate because she has disappeared.

There are bombs falling everywhere, and the group of actors is around him and the little girl appears and he rushes out to get her. Now what happens, one of the actors steps on his robe. It's sort of a cheap comic thing, but somehow because everything is so beautiful and stunning-looking, it's *wonderfully* funny, whereas it would only be a titter otherwise. I quite like that. I think that's what a lot of it is about. You can tell the same joke, and if it's done like *Revenge of the Nerds,* nobody will think it's funny, it's just crummy. But if you actually surround it with beautiful costumes and sets, brilliant lighting, you set this stage and then you have this silly little thing happen; it moves up to another level. It's very strange, the way it works.

You lead the audience in one direction, their expectation is going, "It's beautiful," and then suddenly, whoops, somebody trips. Slips on a banana skin. It's the same old thing except you have been raised into a different world where it happens. It's funnier when it happens to the gods than when it happens to the man in the street. I think all Greek myths were based on this.

D.M.: *The post-production and effects work is going to be handled in England?*
T.G.: Yes, I'm bringing the model shooting back to England, though in a way I am going to miss Rome. But we will put it all in one place, so that I can keep working with the editor and keep an eye on the models. That's the part I really like, doing that. It'll be a smaller group of people, we'll have more control. David Tomblin, the Experienced One, said that it was one of the most complicated films he had ever seen. And to choose to come to Italy is a very bizarre thing to do. The Americans and the British are really the only ones with the necessary experience to make this sort of film. Trying to make a difficult film, plus trying to invent a new system, plus trying to work with new people . . . I don't know what possessed me.

D.M.: *Do you have anything to look forward to after* Munchausen?
T.G.: Death. Always an optimist.
It's the first time I never actually had another thought in my head about what to do next. This may cure me of filmmaking, for all I know.

D.M.: *What else would you pursue?*
T.G.: I think it would be nice just to do something smaller with a group of people that I feel close to. But my real problem is that I am caught with these

images that I want to put on film, and they're very complicated, expensive things.

Actually, one of the things that came out of this is that we have been doing a lot on this stage with sets that are just painted sets, and it looks wonderful. I keep thinking that I want to make a film which is like that—everything painted. It's totally artificial and yet totally credible. So it will really be my animation and live action put together. On this film, I wanted to do the things that Disney did on his big cartoons for real. And we're still doing it in a sense; it has a bit of that feel to it. The stuff we did on the stage was interesting because it was so effective, so magical in a way I haven't seen very often. And it would be nice because it could be done cheaply. You just paint things, you do false perspective things.

D.M.: *That's similar to what Méliès did.*

T.G.: It would really be exactly what he did in that sense, only a modern version of it. It bridges theater and cinema because it's artificial and yet believable. And people are so literal now and so into naturalism or realism. Theater and cartoons have always been abstract things. Films are abstract but people *think* they're realistic or naturalistic; people seem to think you have to have things that look real to be real.

I think that might be the next way to work. Really cheap. The cheapest film ever made.

Birth of *Baron* Was Tough on Gilliam

STEVEN REA/1989

IN *THE ADVENTURES OF BARON MUNCHAUSEN*, the
Baron—a crusty, glinty-eyed windbag fabulist—faces death square in the
face.

He is swallowed whole by a monstrous whale. He hurtles through the sky
clinging to a cannonball. And, on several occasions, his head, dandified coif-
fure and all, is laid on the chopping block (once over a wager about the
merits of a Viennese empress's wine stock).

In the adventures of Terry Gilliam, the filmmaker—a blustery, glinty-eyed
windbag fantasist—has looked down death's maw a few times himself. More
than once his film required near-divine intervention to save it from disaster.

There was a week that was lost during *Baron Munchausen* location shooting
when the lead actors' costumes were left behind in Rome. The hot-air balloon (a giant patchwork of fanciful female undergarments) that wouldn't fly
in the right direction. And the lawsuit from a German producer who said he
owned the rights to the mythic yarns of the eighteenth-century German cav-
alry officer, Karl Friedrich Hieronymous von Munchausen.

Not to mention the day that Gilliam was directing a battle scene in Belch-
ite, Spain, when he found himself interrupted by a call from Lloyds of London. It seemed that the insurance company that controlled the production's
purse strings had suddenly decided said purse was shut.

No more moolah. No more movie. *Finado.*

From the *Philadelphia Inquirer* (March 19, 1989): 1-L, 10-L. Reprinted by permission of the
Philadelphia Inquirer.

"Making the film was exactly *like* the film," says Gilliam about his $40 million-plus adventure epic.

"The Baron is almost dying all the time, and he somehow makes it at the last minute. And the production was like that: Just when we thought it was finished, that there was no way of going any further, something would occur and we'd be alive again, and off we'd go!

"It was a total nightmare," he concedes. "It was the worst thing I've ever had to do in my life. I felt like I was being punished for something I had done in the past. I wasn't sure what the crime was, but revenge was being wreaked on me."

Tumultuous and heart-stopping as the making of *Baron Munchausen* was for its English-Spanish-Italian crew, the result is nothing short of spectacular.

The slightly-more-than-two-hour film, starring John Neville as the legendary liar Munchausen (his motto: "Through lies, truth"), is a prodigious invention incorporating many of the themes and motifs of previous Gilliam endeavors, *Time Bandits* and *Brazil*.

Heaped on top of this story, adapted by Gilliam and Charles McKeown from German author Rudolf Erich Raspe's popular eighteenth-century *Baron Munchausen* books, is a crinkum-crankum of cross-cultural references: the films of Victor Fleming *(Treasure Island, The Wizard of Oz),* Michael Powell *(The Thief of Bagdad)* and Federico Fellini *(Satyricon, Juliet of the Spirits);* the paintings of Botticelli (Gilliam re-creates, in living color, the artist's *The Birth of Venus*), Gustave Doré and Bruegel; the poetry of Shelley; the tales of the Grimm brothers; the sheer velocity of the Road Runner cartoons; the loony, lunar comedy of Robin Williams (in an uncredited extended cameo as the Man in the Moon—"the King of Everything, *Rei di Tutto;* but you may call me Ray"); and, of course, the Anglophilic anarchy of Gilliam's alma mater, *Monty Python's Flying Circus.*

Although a few have faulted Gilliam for over-the-top excess, most critics have bombarded *Baron Munchausen* with a hailstorm of praise ("Everything about *Munchausen* deserves exclamation points," gushed Richard Corliss in *Time*). It is, in the immortal words of surly beatnik comic Brother Theodore (who was talking about something else altogether), "a delicious metaphysical goulash of all the human emotions."

"I just wanted to play around with some things," understates Gilliam, the forty-eight-year-old American expatriate responsible for Monty Python's surreal animation (he co-wrote and co-directed *Monty Python and the Holy Grail* before embarking on his own oddball first feature, the slogging-through-the-Middle Ages, Lewis Carroll-inspired *Jabberwocky*).

"There are some cartoony things in *Baron Munchausen*," he says. In the *Python* series, "I would've done it with my cutout animations. I would have gotten a photograph of a building and then I would have taken my felt pen markers and done something very strong and graphic on top of it."

But in *Baron Munchausen*, Gilliam has done all that with *real* actors, on *real* sets. Aided by the estimable troika of cinematographer Giuseppe Rotunno, production designer Dante Ferretti and costume designer Gabriella Pescucci—all collaborators on films by Fellini—Gilliam has conjured up a go-for-baroque world: leviathan men hurling ornate galleons through the air; cherubs fluttering their wings like hummingbirds; disembodied heads of the Man and Woman (Fellini alum Valentina Cortese) in the Moon, sailing off into a galactic dreamscape.

"It's weird," says Gilliam, a deadpan man with big meaty features. "Some people come out [of the theater] saying it's just too rich, but if it was a cartoon, a Disney cartoon, it could be that rich and nobody would comment on it. You'd accept it in that form. And that was what I was trying to do: to see how far you can push filmmaking with live people, real things. All the things that would have happened in *Cinderella*, or *Pinocchio*, or *Snow White*—but it's real this time.

"That was the experiment," he says, chuckling. "All the films I make are me just testing out some questionable theories, and finding out whether they work."

The test now is finding out whether this idiosyncratic, mega-dollar movie will find an audience. Essentially a children's story (it costars Sarah Polley as the ten-year-old waif Sally Salt, who accompanies the Baron on his journeys), the film nonetheless has the sumptuous look of an art-house film. Its cast boasts the aforementioned Italian star Cortese and Canadian stage actor Neville, plus Oliver Reed (as the squat volcanic god Vulcan), Uma Thurman from *Dangerous Liaisons* (as Venus, goddess of love), former Pythonite Eric Idle, and pop star Sting (in a daft one-line cameo).

And while Gilliam says *Baron Munchausen* represents the final part of a trilogy begun with *Time Bandits* and *Brazil*, its tone and mood are different from those of its predecessors: It is more sophisticated than *Time Bandits*, more upbeat and optimistic than the doomed Orwellian world of *Brazil*.

"*Brazil*, in some circles, was perceived as this serious political statement," says the director, "whereas this is a lot of frippery. This isn't a serious political statement at all. It's a joyous film for children of all ages."

Baron Munchausen also, in Gilliam's words, bears "the Mark of Putt-nam"—it was commissioned by the controversial former Columbia Pictures chief and has been singled out by David Puttnam's (many) detractors as a prime example of the expelled executive's anti-Hollywood follies.

But the new Columbia regime, Gilliam says, seems "to be really behind the whole thing, which is encouraging. . . . There are no original parents anymore, and the adoptive ones are eager to see it succeed."

Columbia's marketing strategy is to "platform" *Baron Munchausen's* release: It opened in eight U.S. markets on March 10, and this Friday the film opens in an additional sixteen cities across the country—cities where *Brazil* and the Python flicks have demonstrated considerable drawing power. After that, say Columbia execs, it all depends. If *Baron Munchausen* performs up to expectations, the movie will move into wider release. If not, the studio and the movie's investors have a $40 million pill to swallow.

That cost is $16.5 million over the original budget. Gilliam cites "total chaos" for the movie's monetary overruns, which have made it the most expensive film shot in Italy since the 1963 Dick-and-Liz opus *Cleopatra*. Production, which began in September 1987, was based on six soundstages at Rome's sprawling Cinecittà Studios, with additional shooting in Spain and forty-five days of miniature work at London's Pinewood Studios. Filming ended in March 1988, while the rest of the year was consumed with elaborate post-production work.

Early on, Gilliam felt the whole thing getting away from him.

"There was no real production on this film," he reports. "It was helter-skelter, the production side of the thing. I mean, it was getting like that before we started shooting. You could see that we were in real trouble.

"Because it's a really complicated film, it required incredible planning. And what was in the original script was even more complex than what's on film; the end result is about two-thirds of what we planned. And there was no proper organization.

"You'd say, 'OK, we're going to shoot this scene in this location.' And they'd say 'No problem.' And then you'd spend a couple of months designing and preparing, all for that location. And then after these couple of months, somebody would say, 'Oh, we can't get permission.' So you start all over again. We remade the film several times before we even started shooting.

"I kept writing notes to myself, and I think when the budget hit about $36 million I said, 'If only somebody'd give me $36 million, I could make a really great film.'" The money, says Gilliam, was just being frittered away.

But "once you set a thing like that in motion, it's a real juggernaut," he says. "We set the style of the film and the scale that we were working on months before we started shooting. And then you can't stop. Everybody just holds on for dear life and somehow you hope you get through it. And we got through it. But there were bodies lying all over the place."

He laughs. "We were actually going to build a monument to the fallen."

Instead, Gilliam has built a monument to the imagination.

"Here it is, kids," he offers, his hands outstretched. "What do you think?"

Gilliam, Gotham, God

DAVID MORGAN/1991

TERRY GILLIAM CANNOT BE mundane, no matter how hard he tries.

It is the director's grand visual style which most audiences take away with them; because the images on screen are so dense, the stories cover so much territory, many of the subtleties that he draws out from his actors are only glimpsed on a second, third, or fourth viewing, peeking out from behind a curtain of fireworks.

Yet even at their most simple levels, Gilliam's films reveal a sensibility that likes to ridicule, and condemn what might be seen as crimes against the natural order of the universe: hypocrisy, aggression, and Man's prideful arrogance over all with whom he shares the planet.

"I'm just bothered by the basic attitudes about the way people deal with the world," he says. "It's out there ticking away really nicely, and providing all sorts of goodies that people seem to ignore—they're too busy building things, so that they can say, '*I* did this!'"

The drive to build is partly what makes a city, yet a Gilliam city is often defined by how it is destroyed, or rebuilt against its original design. His urban settings reflect the deepest desires and fears of their inhabitants. They are themselves major players in his stories, shaping—sometimes threatening to obliterate—the central characters, even occasionally steering the narrative. At times these cities and the events that take place within them may be at

From *Metropolis* (September 1991): 42–43, 56–57, 59. Copyright © 1991 by Bellerophon Publications, Inc. Reprinted by permission of *Metropolis*.

odds with logic and the demands of physical laws, but they always speak truths—usually unsettling ones.

While his humor may be either broad or biting, Gilliam's worlds are never simple. A recurring theme is humankind's vain attempt to subjugate Nature with destructive machines and repressive regimes—an endeavor, in Gilliam's opinion, always destined to backfire. His set designs express his viewpoint with tongue planted firmly in cheek: an elegant restaurant is infiltrated by massive, Stalinesque heating ducts; a Gothic hall is constructed from giant Lego blocks; sleek, postmodern furnishings look more like prison furniture than the trappings of wealth.

One of Gilliam's talents in constructing cities is his agility at finding sources or references in other artists' works and incorporating them into his own. In his early animations, his creative pilferings were quite literal: bits and pieces of paintings, statues and photographs performed strangely accentuated comic routines—the hallucinations of a museumgoer on acid. He feeds upon the contributions of his collaborators—writers, cameramen, designers, actors—until he hits upon the truth of a situation, how a particular setting should be in relation to its inhabitants. This was most successfully done in *Brazil*, set in what the director described as "the flip side of now," a totalitarian society whose entire apparatus crushes its citizens in so many ways, leaving flights of fantasy as the only means of escape.

Part of the results of Gilliam's working method, what he calls a magpie approach ("Having a central idea works like a magnet; things just start sticking to it"), are messy, intentionally so. His worlds are not sterile; a clean white corridor would not exist in a Gilliam film unless it were stained with a drop of blood. And of course it may be taken to extremes: *Jabberwocky*'s collapsing medieval castle—thick with dust and excrement, and burdened with overcrowding, ineffectual leaders, and unscrupulous businessmen—could stand for the modern world, which has forsaken Nature's beauty for profit and left in its wake an infrastructure too weak to support itself; likewise *Brazil*'s messy, bureaucratically suffocating society, where nothing works properly, and aesthetics have lost a war of attrition to the functions of plumbing and pneumatic tubes.

But his attacks on technology are also a cry for Nature, and against the abuse which is heaped upon the earth by those who should be safeguarding it. In the dream sequences of *Brazil* massive windowless skyscrapers thrust out of a serene countryside and blot out the sun. But the "real," waking

world of the film's protagonist is no less forgiving of Nature: miles of advertising billboards along a highway hide the desolate landscape beyond from
one's view, or cheerfully prescribe feel-good messages amidst destitute or
condemned surroundings.

Even his Baroque epic, *The Adventures of Baron Munchausen,* contains the
same passions about the man-made mentality. When the Baron flies to a
lunar city ruled by an egocentric, calculating intellectual King who is convinced that all of the universe is the creation of his own feverishly active
mind, we find the place to be cold, empty, artificial, and flat.

These settings are not always destructive of the central characters, but
they leave their marks on them, and often steer the narrative—not always
where the characters wish it to go.

Born in 1940, Gilliam grew up in a rural community in Minnesota before
being transplanted to Los Angeles as a teenager. After fluttering between New
York, Europe, and California, working on magazines and at ad agencies, Gilliam finally settled in London in the late sixties, at which time he forged ties
with his future partners in *Monty Python's Flying Circus.*

He provided animated sequences for the troupe's TV series and films, and
codirected with Terry Jones *Monty Python and the Holy Grail* (perhaps the
most authentic-looking film of Arthurian England, even though it was a
farce). He also designed *Life of Brian,* and for the Pythons' last film together,
The Meaning of Life, he contributed an outrageous short film about ancient
insurance clerks battling like pirates against corporate financiers.

While Gilliam's films away from Python—*Jabberwocky, Time Bandits, Brazil,* and *Munchausen*—are noted for their wild designs and special effects, the
stories each hinge on clashes between unyielding or oppressive social orders
and the efforts by a visionary few to break through calcified modes of behavior and thinking.

This attitude clearly infiltrates his life as well as his work, since Gilliam
has often painted himself as one of the visionary few battling the unyielding
or oppressive constraints of the Hollywood studio system. Despite his track
record, which had accorded both mainstream success (*Time Bandits* is one of
the most successful independently-produced films ever) and critical acco-
lades (*Brazil* was included in *American Film* magazine's list of the decade's top
movies), Gilliam is only now winning over nervous studio executives who
confuse his elaborate visual style with overindulgence—a sin in Hollywood,
though a widely practiced one.

Gilliam's latest film, *The Fisher King,* has provided the expatriate his first excuse to work in the States since moving to England over twenty years ago. Underneath the fairy-tale romance is a familiar tale of clashes, this one of two worlds sharing Manhattan Island but in point of fact miles apart. Jack Lucas, a successful, brash radio deejay (played by Jeff Bridges), suffers a spectacular fall from his high-profile life at the top, bringing him into association with fellow street denizen Parry (Robin Williams). A disturbed homeless man, Parry is given to visions of a New York both idyllic (as a medieval setting filled with magical, heraldic romance) and horrendous (as a battleground against a ghoulish phantom on horseback).

Parry's unrequited love affair with wallflower Lydia (Amanda Plummer), and Jack's unsure relationship with Anne (Mercedes Ruehl), are played out in more intimate fashion than has been evidenced in Gilliam's previous work; there are more close-ups of actors, and the deeply detailed backgrounds are not kept on screen as long as in, say, *Munchausen.* But New York is clearly depicted in an unusually eccentric way, playing up the city's architectural diversity and capturing it with disorienting or intrusive camera angles and lighting. Capitalizing on medieval elements in Manhattan architecture, Gilliam's locations, sets, and costumes appear deeply influenced by the works of Bosch, Goya, Piranesi, Dante, Dürer, Claes Oldenburg and anonymous manuscript illuminators.

Exuberant, elegant, perverse and scatalogical, *The Fisher King* as envisioned by Gilliam celebrates New York at the same time that it kicks it in the ass.

MORGAN: *As you've come back and visited the States over the years, what changes have you seen in New York?*

GILLIAM: I actually thought New York had gotten to be quite a jolly place. I don't know if that's a product of having money now, rather than being poor in New York, where I can actually stay in nice hotels, go to nice restaurants and see the good sides of the city. That may have a lot to do with it, because when I lived there, I had no money at all. You feel you're at the bottom of all those great towers the whole time, and everybody else is up there having a good time except you. The streets were where you were left.

I didn't actually like the streets because I in my heart of hearts wanted to be up in the top of the towers. The streets, I mean they were lively, but when you're trying to get away from them they're not as interesting as when you just submit to them and allow them to take over. When you aspire to those towers, once you get up there, it's the world that Jack's inhabiting on many occasions; you've lost yourself in the process.

M :   *So you have to clamor back down onto the streets.*
G :   Yeah, that's where I feel happier now. At least there are people down there, 'cause it's all about humanity. And the higher you get, the more iso-lated you get, the more separate from humanity you become. And again you get lost in yourself, you become isolated within yourself. And that's a part of what *Fisher King* is certainly about.

M :   *You have portrayed the modern aspects of a city as being antithetical to social interactions. For example, in* Time Bandits, *in ancient Greece we see a very social place: people meeting and talking at markets, craftspeople making things, activities, banquets. But in* Brazil *you hardly ever see people in social situations, and when you do, they behave terribly awkward and evasive—they barely acknowledge one another on the street. They're almost hiding from other human beings.*
G :   In the case of *Brazil* it's because it's a terrorized society, and whatever that terror is, whether it's terrorists or just the complexity of a system that just blows up in your face the whole time, the best way to survive it is just staying in your own little cubby hole.

M :   *And even that can be terrifying because your own home might revolt against you, as Sam Lowry's does.*
G :   Yeah, I know, that's the problem with it. Modern life is designed to sepa-rate us much more than it used to; it's not the village any more. We all have our little boxes we live in, and we've got the television that is our communi-cator. Television sits there and tells us what's going on in the world, what the world's like out there. We walk out on the streets with all these ideas presented from television, and it colors your perception of the world and your reaction to it.

   That's one of the reasons I live in Europe; I think that European cities—because their civilization is an older one—they've held on to more direct communications, a more direct way of working and dealing with people. The cities haven't become totally dominated by these great monoliths. It's funny that man builds these things. I don't know if he builds them because he's aspiring to get higher and higher and closer to God, or more like God but not closer to Him; it's probably direct competition to Him.

M : *Trying to beat God at his own game.*
G : Yeah, your basic hubris. Towers of Babel, Icarus, all of that. I think they want to find out not what God is like; they want to compete: "I'm as big as you, buster!"

M : *That's very American.*
G : Yeah. I think it's man, it's always been going on. I think other, older societies have built their Towers of Babel and then fallen on their face, and they've gotten used to it. And America, being a twentieth-century nation, a place where modern technology can do its most work—or damage, which-ever—it gives man incredible powers he never had before, and that's the way it goes; he builds faster, taller, everything. He's got more ways to keep every-body at bay. And it really worries me.

One thing I do like about New York, you're in the life on the streets. But I used to like it when you got down to [Greenwich] Village, places like that where it wasn't a grid—the grid drives me crazy. With a grid of streets there aren't surprises, you've got a vista that goes forever. When you're down in the Village you've got curves and twists and so on, your view doesn't go further; it turns the corner and there's a building there that stops you.

M : *And if you're on 43rd Street, you* know *the next street up is going to be 44th.*
G : That also, yes. You're victim to the limitations of numbers. Everything is defined. I hate this idea of numbering the streets like that. Streets have *got* to have names.

Getting from A to B [in Europe] is not as simple as getting from A to B in the States. A to B in the States is a straight line. One of the things I like about Europe, is going from A to B you have to meander—the quickest way from A to B is meandering. And if you're meandering, things happen.

I think the meandering approach of Europe is much healthier. The way Los Angeles works, it's a series of oases, and people rush from one to another and try to get through the bits in between as quickly as possible and have nothing to do with the bits in between. So you get on the freeway, *zip, boom,* they're there. They miss out on chance encounters or something that diverts you from your immediate goal. I mean, L.A. even got rid of the streets!

M : *You just drive right over the streets now.*

G : You get in your car, your capsule and *zip!* As fast as you can to the next thing where you know somebody.

I've got a place in the country in France, a little farmhouse which I really love. And I hardly ever get there, but the fact that it's there is really important to me. I know I can get there, I know I can always escape back to the country. But unfortunately I find that the city fuels me all the time, and I think just so much of what I do is based on anger and frustration and confusion and trying to deal with these conflicting things, you know; when I get out to the country I get very placid and calm and boring and noncreative.

M : *How long a stretch can you go in the country?*

G : I don't know, a few weeks. But it refuels me in a different way; that's what I think is important, is that if I just was within the city the whole time it would drive me crazy. I think it means just dropping back to something much more basic and simple.

We didn't have electricity for years, 'cause I didn't want electricity. In the end we got it because I wanted a fridge to keep the drinks colder. But what I loved without electricity, at night walking around the house with lanterns, the shadows are shifting all the time; the place becomes really wonderful. Wherever you go the light's shifting and the shadows, everything's twisting and turning; it makes the place a *moving* kind of place; it's not a fixed, rigid house. And with electricity it is. The light sources don't move, and there it is: a rigid thing. And I find in France I sit and watch the fire, and it's infinitely interesting.

These are ancient things, but the thing about them is they *work*; it's not that anybody was very clever, it's just that our cleverness creates all these other forms of entertainment and distraction, but it's hard to beat a fire.

I'm trying to work on a thing on the gods of the city. Because at least the old gods were streams, rivers, lakes, trees, stones, all the things that make up the world. And we've created these cities, which are all man-made, and I'm not sure what you worship there; I suppose you end up worshipping money, another creation of man, because you've got to have one god or another to deal with. So it becomes money, and position, and career. And then there are those who worship at the altars of culture: theater, abstract expressionism, whatever. And these are things you can then dedicate your life to, but they are all basically man-made, and so they're all insular in that sense, rather than just going back to the things, the earth itself, which is the thing that really does support us.

It's this constant fight that's been going on for millennia, of man trying to establish his dominance over nature rather than the other way around. I think most other animals don't spend their time doing that, they just get on with it. That's why I think we're, maybe we're just one of those unfortunate dead-ends of evolution: Nice try, but it didn't work.

M : *Well, you have shown revolution in reverse, in* The Crimson Permanent Assurance, *where an old, Edwardian-era building filled with ancient insurance clerks sails to the glass towers of Wall Street to lay waste upon them.*
G : It's a romantic idea that these little old guys can take on these modern monsters. It's a bit like Saddam Hussein taking on America; it's a foolish, romantic idea. And I sort of give them their moment, and they defeat them, but in the end it's a silly idea and they fall off the edge of the earth! Because it doesn't really work that way in the real world.

M : *What do you get the most out of living in London? And has that changed over the years from when you first moved there?*
G : I love architectural diversity. I like architecture that gives me a sense of a very long continuum. I like reducing my role in the world to being some-thing just on a long pathway, rather than being the center of everything, which I think happens here. And when you're in a place like London, around you constantly are seventeenth-century buildings, sixteenth-century build-ings, twelfth-century buildings! You know it's been going on for a really long time. People have been doing things and building things, and then I look at what *I* have done, and it seems to be, you know, a little pin prick compared to what other people have done over the centuries. And I like that; it keeps putting me in my place. And I love the juxtapositions of twelfth-century buildings next to an eighteenth-century building next to a twentieth-century building.

M : *Or in Rome, where there are buildings older than rocks.*
G : I love Rome even more than London possibly. That's what was great about making *Munchausen*; I wanted to be able to spend time in Rome. And I'm right now in the process of trying to buy a house in Italy. I keep moving further east. Unlike "Go west, young man," I've been going east all my life.

Mister perverse! And I keep heading back for older and older cultures because I think there's a lot to be learned. America has done the terrible deed of getting rid of history, I really think it has.

M :   *They refuse to acknowledge history.*
G :   Uh-hmm. America has gotten rid of it. They just knock it down, put up something new. And it drives me crazy. I mean in London again, when you walk past these places, you're really affected by the aesthetics—it's all around you all the time, and this affects you in a very healthy way. And it just reminds you that there have been a lot of people out there before me!

M :   *What is the history of the seventeenth-century house you live in, The Old Hall?*
G :   Actually the fifteenth century originally, and in the seventeenth century the house, where Francis Bacon died, was divided, part of it moved to High-gate Village and reassembled there. Then in the eighteenth century it was refaced with a Georgian front. And then at the turn of this century an addition was made; the ground floor room that had been originally in a house in Great Yarmouth that was used by Oliver Cromwell was dismantled and reassembled in this house. It's a room that's dated 1595; wonderful Tudor-panelled rooms, incredible plaster ceilings, very ornate vines and fruits dangling off the ceiling, and it's got this amazing overmantel piece. It's just amazing, just sort of figures wrapped in wooden shields. It's really sort of a display of the carver's skill, not for any other reason other than showing off. Then another room up above that came from another Jacobean room from a manor in Yorkshire. People like Margaret Rutherford used to live there.

And then we moved in, and what did we do to it? I hope we put it back to something beautiful. I mean, I came in there with lots of bright ideas that I was going to do this, that and the other thing, and be very clever with the adapting of the house, and in the end, you have to listen to the house. You can come in there and say, "Wow, this is what I'm gonna do," and get yourself some smart architect and together you design something very clever and witty using the old and the new, or you let the house talk to you a bit. And we ended up doing a lot less clever work than we originally planned because I think it was in violation of the place.

M :   *The people who were there before you spoke to you?*
G :   Well, they spoke through the house, whatever they'd done to the house;

it had been sort of an organic growth rather than a *wham-bam* approach, and I like that. That's probably why I've always liked medieval cities in particular, places like Rome. They're just a series of accretions; things growing on other things, being altered rather than being torn down and replaced with something new. That kind of organic growth of a city is what I really like, 'cause it's both totally surprising and utterly human, because you can see each time somebody's gotten a hold of something and done a little more fiddling with it.

M : *There is clearly a conflict between a modern world imposing itself upon people, and the history of a city trying to be remembered. In* The Fisher King, *in the early scenes which show Jack in his disk-jockey environment, modern New York looks extremely oppressive—very sleek, cold, monochromatic, and he seems trapped wherever he goes. And it's only when he can get out and breathe the air down on the Lower East Side when he's with Parry that he can actually become a human being and associate more with other humans.*

G : Yeah, this is pretty consistent through all my stuff; it springs from the fact that I lived in New York after college for three years. Most of the attitudes I put in my films are based on that period. I find it's a strange place, New York—I mean, all cities are strange, but New York in particular—because it's more of an extreme version of what a city can be. And I'm always torn by them, because on one hand they're this center of incredible activity and energy and massed humanity and I get a real buzz off of that; but then at the same time it seems to crush people. It reduces people to cogs in the machine or molecules within a system, whatever, and that part just drives me crazy, when individuals get lost to be aspects of the machinery.

I remember my first view of New York was getting out of the subway at 42nd Street, coming from the airport, and that was just *Whooah!* There you are at the bottom of these monoliths and there is this dichotomy because it's exhilarating *and* terrifying at the same time, and so I try to deal with that.

M : *That dichotomy is represented by Jack, who's really a product of the times, because he can be both exhilarating and terrifying to listen to on the radio.*

G : I made Jack the product of magazines like *Metropolis—oops!* His world is all about design and it is very photogenic, everything is minimalist. It's reduced to the bare bones. And everything he's in is a cage of one sort or another. He's isolated from the world totally, by all these man-made things.

So we've got his radio studio, there are no windows, that's one box he'd be in. We actually put all those little shadows around to make it look like a cage. And he's on his own, he's not even in direct communication with his crew, who are on the other side of this glass barrier. And his only contact with the world is through machines, the telephone—it's nothing that's direct; every-thing is distanced and made safe in a sense that he doesn't have to get dirty, he doesn't have to rub shoulders. He's in his agent's limo and the world is knocking at his window and he won't open the window.

M :   *And it's one-way glass; the world can't even see in to him.*
G :   Yeah, that's right. And then there's his apartment, which again we made a bit cagelike. The apartment is actually based on the metropolitan Tower, which is on 57th Street next to Carnegie Hall, which we used for the outside. I looked up and said, That's where I want Jack to live, the point where the razor-edge wedge slopes back, and it turned out that apartment is owned by Mike Ovitz, whose agency [CAA] I just joined. A very bizarre moment!

I mean, I gave Jack all the best clothes; everthing he's got is the best the modern material world offers. But there's a tendency for it to lead to isola-tion, losing touch with anything natural or God-made as opposed to man-made. It's a barren environment he lives in; he's a prisoner of his desire for success. It's the kind of success that I'm afraid love of the modern world aspires to, and in a sense encourages. It's like all those stylish magazines where people pose in the best clothes and the sleekest environments; there's nothing *alive* in there. There's *nothing*; everthing is very anal, it's all con-trolled. Jack's controlled his life—he thinks—but by controlling it he's allowed nothing to get into it. And it becomes a very empty life.

So that's what all that was: pretty obvious stuff!

M :   *The locations chosen, such as the Armory at Hunter College or beneath the Manhattan Bridge where Jack meets Parry and the other bums, and the way they're photographed, certainly don't look the way you generally see New York in movies.*
G :   Yeah, you normally see New York through Woody Allen's eyes, or Rob Reiner trying to be like Woody Allen. I'm amazed because New York is an extraordinary, phenomenally visual city. I always try to use architecture and the sets as a character in the film.

I was really doing it like a fairy tale on many levels, when I was designing the thing. So under the Manhattan Bridge when the bums are there, or where Jack's about to commit suicide, it's like the moat of a castle or of a kingdom, the river that surrounds it. And these bridges come from foreign lands and cross into this very restrictive kingdom where everything is thrust together.

Jack's living in the great castle with all the money and power the world offers. And then when he falls from grace, the first place he falls is to Anne's video shop, [which is] like the peasant cottage in the forest. That's the way I've always seen the thing. And Anne's very earthy; her tastes are pretty eclectic and awful really, but [her home's] full of life and color and mess, clutter. And she's a live creature there, a love of flesh and blood. And then they go even further down—that's just ground level—then we sort of go below ground level, under things. Under bridges, in the basement with Parry, where it gets really ripe and smelly. A potentially rich ground. I mean, there's a lot of manure down there, a lot of fertilizer for seeds of life.

And what I liked about under the bridge was those arches, it's like Piranesi. It's the closest I could come to Piranesi in New York—these very massive classical arches, buttresses, and I quite like that. It's like moving back in history to an earlier time which is now where the homeless and bums live. They live in this, well, literally they're living in a Piranesi world, as opposed to the modern world.

M : *Parry certainly fits right in, because he is of that world.*
G : He happens to be sort of fixed in the Middle Ages. I was being very broad about where there was new and there was old. And Parry has in part invented this older world which is medieval, and that's why I liked Carmichael's [the millionaire's home which Parry believes houses the Holy Grail], which was originally just a townhouse. I found this armory up on Madison Avenue and 94th Street and it *was* a medieval castle.

If you've got the eyes to see, New York can be anything you want it to be. It can be any world, any time, and Parry has chosen an ancient world, and he's peopled it with castles and princesses.

Lydia's office building, I put her in the Metropolitan Life building. It's a Deco building, a great stone building as opposed to a modern building which is steel and glass, because a stone building seemed more like a tower that a princess might be held captive in. And it's really heavily fortified that way—it's got great thick walls, huge blocks of stone.

M: *And a revolving door that she can't past through safely.*

G: Then you've got this modern problem that adds to it. I mean, I never try to be a *purist* about anything.

Then the next time we get back to something modern is when Jack's going into the TV executive's office, and we're back into the sleek glass and hard edges. There's a lot just to do with texture—there are things that are smooth and there are things that are rough, and I like things that are rougher because there's a little more chance for things to cling to him.

M: *What did production designer Mel Bourne bring to the film?*

G: I wanted Mel because he is very experienced in New York [*his credits include several Woody Allen pictures and* Reversal of Fortune], and I wanted somebody who would constantly double-check my choices so that I wasn't forcing too many foreign ideas upon New York. I really felt *Fisher King* had to feel real; I didn't want it to turn into my normal "Escape from Reality" designs. So everything had to be a real place, especially on interiors and things which we built. I wanted Mel to be able to choose with the kind of security that you have when you've spent your whole life in New York. Because I didn't trust mine; I haven't been in the States enough over the years to really know all the details of what some of these places were going to be like.

M: *What are your plans after* Fisher King?

G: Richard LaGravanese and I are working on a thing called *The Defective Detective.* I think it's a nice idea. I keep thinking it's kind of like *Brazil* meets *Time Bandits*—with a little bit of *Fisher King* thrown in. And maybe *Baron Munchausen.* I keep doing the same kind of things, I keep rolling . . .

M: *It's a sign of accretion!*

G: Yeah, well, that's it, I mean, none of these things are big leaps; every time I *think* I'm making a big leap I realize I haven't; I've only just gone around the corner a bit.

M: *But it's like building one century's architecture on top of another's.*

G: Oh it is, it's exactly that. It all starts from one sort of personality disorder and keeps growing.

Terry Gilliam

PAUL WARDLE / 1995

TERRY GILLIAM HAS had one of the most varied and interesting careers in the entertainment industry.

In his youth, he served as art director for the ground-breaking black-and-white humor magazine *Help!*, working for his idol, Harvey Kurtzman. It was during this period that he chanced to meet John Cleese, then touring in New York City with the British satirical revue *Cambridge Circus*. When *Help!* folded in 1965, Gilliam began selling comic strips and panel cartoons to a variety of magazines such as *Drag Cartoons, Car-Toons,* and *Cavalier.*

It was a soul-destroying job at an advertising agency and the outrage he felt witnessing the 1967 Los Angeles police riot that finally soured Gilliam on remaining in the United States. Arriving in England, he contacted the afore-mentioned Cleese who had since become a popular writer/performer on BBC radio and television, and through him was introduced to Humphrey Barclay. Barclay liked the young American cartoonist and gave him work on two Brit-ish television shows where he would meet Eric Idle, Terry Jones, Michael Palin, and Neil Innes. With the addition of Cleese and his writing partner Graham Chapman, this group would form the crux of the landmark BBC series *Monty Python's Flying Circus*. Python would forever change the face of television comedy, and Gilliam's crazy animated links became one of the show's most recognizable trademarks, the style of which is still being ripped off today in TV commercials.

From *The Comics Journal,* no. 182 (November 1995): 65–92. Reprinted by permission of Paul Wardle.

In the fourth season, with John Cleese absent, Gilliam began to do more performing on the show as well as animation. When Cleese returned for the group's feature films, Gilliam continued to play bit parts, characterized by grotesque make-up and costumes, such as the Keeper of the Bridge of Death in *Monty Python and the Holy Grail* and the jailer in *Monty Python's Life of Brian*. With *Holy Grail*, Gilliam first tried his hand at live-action directing along with co-director Terry Jones.

From then on, he found his niche in life and has since become one of the most critically-acclaimed fantasist directors of recent years, making such films as *Jabberwocky, Time Bandits, Brazil, The Adventures of Baron Munchausen,* and *The Fisher King*. His new film is tentatively titled *Twelve Monkeys* and will star Bruce Willis, Brad Pitt, and Madeleine Stowe. It is scheduled for Christmas release.

I interviewed Terry Gilliam on June 2 and 5, 1995, at the film's postproduction office in London's Soho district. I had not slept the previous night on the flight, and was greeted by two of Gilliam's cutting room assistants who offered me a cup of coffee and asked why I wanted to interview Terry anyway. This I attempted to explain while sipping my coffee and trying to stay awake. Gilliam arrived about an hour later, and after being introduced to him by his right-hand woman, Lucy Darwin, we proceeded to go across the street to the Groucho Club, where Mr. Gilliam has a membership. This seemed to be the first time he had taken advantage of the facilities for which he pays dues, and there was some confusion about where we would be able to conduct the interview. After I rejected the crowded, noisy bar, we were finally allowed an upstairs boardroom which was vacant at the time.

Soon to be fifty-five, Terry Gilliam looks surprisingly young. His long hair is only slightly streaked with gray and he is still unaffected by his success, though frustrated that he will never have time to make all the films and finish the other projects that he would like.

In addition to the charming Mr. Gilliam, my thanks must also go out to Lucy Darwin, a former film student who had written her thesis on a comparison between Gilliam's *Brazil* and Michael Radford's version of *1984*. She is very protective of her boss/mentor and was careful to ensure that his privacy was maintained and that I didn't keep him any longer than was absolutely necessary. Nevertheless, it was with her help that this project came to fruition.

He is far from being the noncommunicative member of the old Python troupe, as is often assumed. I wish it were possible to duplicate on paper the enthusiasm, visual mannerisms, and infectious giggle that accompanied the following words. I could have talked to him all day.

PAUL WARDLE: *What was your first job as an artist?*
TERRY GILLIAM: First job . . . Jesus, I'm tryin' to remember.

WARDLE: *And how old were you?*
GILLIAM: That's what I'm trying to work out. I'm thinking there was something I did in college that actually earned me money as an artist. I can't remember. I may not have been an artist, but I was certainly a male model for the local menswear shop in Panorama City. I must've been about sixteen.

WARDLE: *I read somewhere that you worked for an advertising agency.*
GILLIAM: Yeah, but that was all much later. I mean, *Help!* was the first real job I had in the art field. Before that I had jobs in the Chevrolet assembly plant . . .

WARDLE: *Odd jobs and stuff.*
GILLIAM: Yeah. I mean, these were jobs to get through college. You know, butcher shops and things like that.

WARDLE: *Where did you go to college?*
GILLIAM: Occidental College, outside Los Angeles. Eagle Rock, California. It was in my junior year, when I was working in the Chevrolet assembly plant. Night shift. That's when I said, "I quit. I'm never going to do this again." I got a job in a children's theater, building sets and painting myself green and being an ogre and all that. I said I'd never, *never* work for money again in my life. So maybe that was my first job as an artist [giggles], but I wasn't paid. It was really going to New York and meeting Harvey [Kurtzman] that got me a proper job.

WARDLE: *So what made you decide to do that in the first place? How did you just suddenly show up in New York?*
GILLIAM: Well, Harvey was the great idol of my generation. *Mad* comics inspired everything we ever did. Then when he began *Help!* magazine, I was in college at the time and started the college humor magazine and copied a

lot of the kinds of things that Harvey was doing in *Help!* Basically, we turned
what was originally a high-class art and poetry magazine into a cheap comic.

WARDLE: *What was the name of it?*
GILLIAM: The magazine was called *Fang*. We were the Occidental Tigers,
you see. I was the editor. I took over the magazine and converted it into this
silly comic book. It used to come out about three times a year. We took it
over and put it out six times in a semester. It was good fun. We were cartooning, writing, editing, everything, and I was sending copies of it to Harvey. He
wrote me a nice letter back saying, "Terrific! Well done!" And that was it, so,
having graduated from college with no idea what I was going to do, I decided
to go to New York. In fact, it was funny because I was counseling up at a
summer camp in the Sierras, and I was reading *Act One,* which was Moss
Hart's autobiography. George S. Kaufman and Hart wrote great plays in the
1940s and 1950s, and Hart was writing about how he met his great hero,
George Kaufman, and became his assistant.

WARDLE: *George S. Kaufman used to write for the Marx Brothers, right?*
GILLIAM: Yeah, and so I'm reading this book about a guy who goes to the
Big Apple, meets his idol, and ends up working for him. And since I had
nothing better to do, I decided to go to New York.

WARDLE: *You just packed up everything and moved to New York without knowing what you were going to do when you got there?*
GILLIAM: Yeah, basically. I'd written Harvey that I was going to come to
New York and he wrote me a letter saying, "Stay put, kid. It's a big city, blah,
blah, blah, blah, blah. Don't bother." And I just said, "Fuck it. I'm going to
go." So I went off to New York and made an appointment to meet him. He
was at the Algonquin Hotel.

WARDLE: *Another Groucho Marx hang-out.*
GILLIAM: There you go! The mighty round table of the Algonquin. I just
couldn't believe it. So, I went up to this room for this meeting and knocked
on the door. The door opens, and it's Arnold Roth. The whole room was full
of all these great cartoonists! Al Jaffee, Arnold Roth, Willy Elder. They were
all there, and they were doing the first ever *Little Annie Fanny.* This was the
end of Harvey's career, as far as I was concerned. But there they all were, and

the only way he could get them to all work was to stick them in this hotel room, lock the door, and keep 'em in there until this thing was done. So eventually Harvey turns up, we started talking, and it turned out that Chuck Alverson, who was the assistant editor of *Help!*, was quitting, and they were looking for somebody to take his place. I got the job.

WARDLE: *What was it like working for Harvey? Was he a tough guy to work for, or was he very easygoing?*
GILLIAM: It was easy 'cause he was a really sweet man, and basically *Help!* magazine consisted of Harvey and me as the editorial staff. Harry Chester was the production guy. He had his own production outfit and he would handle *Help!* production, and I was earning two dollars a week less than I would've earned on the dole.

WARDLE: *But you were doing what you wanted.*
GILLIAM: Right. So I was getting $50 a week basically, working for Harvey, and the magazine was coming out bimonthly at the time, which left me a lot of time to do other things.

WARDLE: *Gloria Steinem worked there too, didn't she?*
GILLIAM: No, she was the first assistant editor of *Help!* She sort of hid this part of her career, which is a great pity because she was brilliant. The early *Help!*s always had famous people on the cover, and that was Gloria who would get them on. Except I got Woody Allen. Gloria didn't get him, but she did get Dick Van Dyke.

WARDLE: *You got John Cleese.*
GILLIAM: Yeah, and Gloria was brilliant at getting famous people to be in *Help!* magazine. She was also brilliant at doing the caption pictures. Very funny lady.

WARDLE: *How did you run into John Cleese and get him to be in that fumetti* [photo story with word balloons], *"Christopher's Punctured Romance," about the man who falls in lust with a Barbie doll?*
GILLIAM: Well, the thing with fumettis is that we paid actors the giant sum of $15 a day to appear in these little photo stories. So we were very good at getting out-of-work actors, and John was appearing in *Cambridge Circus*,

which had arrived in New York on the coattails of *Beyond the Fringe.*[1] Now, unlike *Beyond the Fringe,* which was a big success, *Cambridge Circus* was not, and ended up in [Greenwich] Village Square East or one of those kinds of places, and I went and saw it. I thought it was wonderful, brilliant stuff, and John, as usual, just stood out from the crowd 'cause he was so grotesque.

WARDLE: *So you've always had an affinity for British humor even before you came to England?*
GILLIAM: Oh yeah. I was a big Anglophile. It was all the Ealing comedies with Terry-Thomas, Peter Sellers, Alistair Sim.

WARDLE: *Were you a fan of* The Goon Show[2] *as well?*
GILLIAM: Yeah. *The Goon Show* you could only get on record. There were some discs going around. And then there was this short the Goons made that Richard Lester directed, which is the *Running, Jumping, Standing Still Film,* which again, I saw somewhere in New York and went, "*Wow!* This is great stuff!" It really just set me off. I don't know why I was such a fan of British humor. Maybe it was just sillier.

WARDLE: *When I was in high school, I was exposed to it and just thought, "Wow, somebody who has the same sort of sense of humor that I have."*
GILLIAM: I mean, what was funny was that before I left the States, the people I was working with were people like Joel Siegel, who's now a famous critic . . .

WARDLE: *He'll be interviewing you in a couple of weeks, I hear.*
GILLIAM: Yeah. [laughs] . . . and Harry Shearer.

WARDLE: *He's doing pretty well these days.*
GILLIAM: Oh yeah, and we'd all come out of college humor magazines. So did Gilbert Shelton. What was amazing about *Help!*, although we didn't know it at the time, was that it was really the only national humor magazine that provided an outlet for all these cartoonists. So they were all coming through New York and invariably staying at my place 'cause I at least had a bed. So there would be Gilbert Shelton, Bob Crumb. I mean, the guys I never met were people like Jay Lynch and Skip Williamson. I never met them. They

were sending stuff in. Paul Merta, who used to do great cartoons for *Help!*, ended up working for the defense department, building missiles.

WARDLE: *That's kind of a conflict of interest, when you think of it.*
GILLIAM: [laughter] No, I think he had a good sense of humor in whatever he did, whether it was bombing Laos or drawing cartoons.

WARDLE: *So, a couple of years after your tenure on* Help!, *you decided to move to England, and because you knew John Cleese, he helped you make contacts and you got a job as a TV cartoonist on a show called* We Have Ways of Making You Laugh. *How did all that progress?*
GILLIAM: What basically happened was that I was still in magazines when I got over there, art directing and drawing cartoons. That's how I was keeping myself alive, was these things in the States.

WARDLE: *Were there other underground comics or anthologies you were in besides these* Car-Toons *magazines and such?*
GILLIAM: Yeah, well there were some tit and bum magazines like *Cavalier.* Also, do you know *Pilotte,* the French magazine? I was doing stuff for them, and the London magazines. I wasn't doing so much cartoons. I was doing illustrations. That's what was so irritating. I had come to England, and all my friends from *Help!* were now the great famous underground comix artists.

WARDLE: *And you weren't.*
GILLIAM: And I wasn't. I was stuck over here, and I went, "Wait a minute. What's going on here?"

WARDLE: *You got a lot of work, though.*
GILLIAM: I got enough to keep going, but then John [Cleese] had established himself in television, and he introduced me to a guy named Humphrey Barclay, who was a producer. What he was producing at the time was a show called *Do Not Adjust Your Set,* a children's show that Michael Palin, Terry Jones, and Eric Idle were writing and performing. The great thing was that Humphrey was an amateur cartoonist. What he liked more than the written material I was offering him were my cartoons. So he took pity on me and bought a couple of my written sketches, and forced them on Mike, Terry, and Eric, much to their chagrin, because it was their show. Then this loud-

mouthed, loud-dressing American turns up and starts invading their pitch. What happened at the end of that series was that Humphrey went to London Weekend Television, which was a new television station, and he had a show, *We Have Ways of Making You Laugh,* and he dragged me along with Eric Idle. There was a group that used to sit there, in the format of some of the television satire shows of the time, where there would be a group consisting of Benny Green, who was a jazzman and a good writer; Katherine Whitehorn, who has gone on to be a columnist; Dick Vosburgh, who was a great comedy writer. This group of people would sit around and talk and I was the silent one who would draw caricatures of the guests that were on the show. The camera would dolly in over my shoulder as I finished the drawing.

WARDLE: *There was an American show where Sergio Aragones did the same thing called* Speak Up America. *The first time I read about* We Have Ways of Making You Laugh, *I realized that they had stolen the idea from you guys.*
GILLIAM: Well, most of the American shows were being stolen from the British. Britain was a far more free place. American television in the 1960s was stagnant. It was completely dominated by Standards and Practices people [censors], and trying to be as middle-brow as they could, whereas the BBC was this great institution with this laissez-faire attitude.

WARDLE: *You mentioned* Do Not Adjust Your Set. *That was the show where you first did your animation, wasn't it?*
GILLIAM: No, it was *We Have Ways of Making You Laugh.* Dick Vosburgh had spent three months taping off the radio the "links" on this guy named Jimmy Young's radio show. He had these terrible punning links between the records. They were awful! You'd groan. So, Dick had three months' worth of this material and he didn't know what to do with it, so I suggested that I make an animated film.

WARDLE: *What was the budget for the first piece of animation?*
GILLIAM: Four hundred pounds, and I had two weeks to do it. That was to produce about two and a half minutes of film.

WARDLE: *In those days the pound was worth more. What would it be in U .S. dollars?*
GILLIAM: You're lookin' at $1,000, and two weeks to do something. So the

only way to work on that budget in that amount of time was to do cut-outs, cutting out his picture and . . .

WARDLE: *You just answered my next question.*

GILLIAM: [laughs] I just did it basically out of necessity, the old mother of invention.

WARDLE: *You use a lot of famous paintings and photos. How did you decide what to use as the cut-outs?*

GILLIAM: I remembered that there was an underground cartoon I had seen in America by Stan Vanderbeek a couple of years earlier in New York around '63, '64. That's where I first saw cut-out animation. I remember he had a picture of Nixon with his foot in his mouth.

WARDLE: *Appropriate.*

GILLIAM: Yeah, so basically that's what I relied on. In this case it was Jimmy Young, so I got a lot of stills of him and cut them out and drew other bits. So when it came later to doing Python, the problem was there's one side of me that was very lazy. I didn't have the patience to draw frame after frame after frame. . . . But somehow, just by using pictures, I could do it quickly. I didn't have a team of artists. It was just me, so I just started cutting out all the things I liked, whether it was photographs, engravings, famous paintings. Things I liked, I used. Strangely enough, I think it really freed me up as a cartoonist.

WARDLE: *Also it sort of gave you a new medium in which to work, one that hadn't been walked all over already.*

GILLIAM: That's right, and the thing is, it was always the speed that was important, so that dictated things. There was always a way out, because I'd find myself so easily trapped in my own level of excellence, or at least what I'm striving for, and sometimes that can take very silly turns where I think what I define as excellent is not necessarily excellent. . . . It's just the way I think I should be working, so I get myself into these traps. By having the pressure taken off me to do something wonderful and to only have to do something to fill up the time, it freed me up.

WARDLE: *So after* We Have Ways of Making You Laugh, *you did the same kind of animation on* Do Not Adjust Your Set. *What was the response to that*

*show? I hear it was a kids' show that adults used to skip off work early to get home
to see.*

GILLIAM: Do you remember Soupy Sales? It was very silly stuff, but at the
same time it was very intelligent. It was a children's show in America and
that's what was interesting. It was on when I was in college, which was 1960,
'61, '62, and all the college kids would gather round and watch this stuff,
because it was surreal, it was outrageous. It was disguising itself as children's
fare, but it was much stronger. I never saw *Pee Wee's Playhouse*, but I had a
feeling it was the same kind of thing.

The trick is, and this is what I learned from Soupy Sales, you do children's
shows because nobody's paying any attention. You can do whatever you
want. Back in the 1950s and 1960s, that's what it was like. It was only in the
1970s that it changed. Jim Henson ruined it for everybody. [laughter] He
brought everybody's attention to it, and it brought a lot of well-meaning
people in to work on children's shows and that blew it. That's what *Do Not
Adjust Your Set* was like. It was ostensibly a kids' show, but it was the same
kind of material we were doing in *Python* a couple of years later. It also had
the Bonzo Dog Doo Dah Band on it [Neil Innes]. The Bonzos have a great
following even now.

WARDLE: *I have their box set. I think a lot of that stuff is hilarious.*
GILLIAM: It's great! It's really intelligent, and yet, because it seems so silly,
adult television didn't want this stuff around.

WARDLE: *Was their hit, "I'm an Urban Spaceman," out while the show was still
playing?*
GILLIAM: Yeah.

WARDLE: *Did that increase the popularity of the show?*
GILLIAM: Probably the two things were totally linked [laughs], because *Do
Not Adjust Your Set* had an audience and the Bonzos were on that show. One
must keep reminding oneself how powerful television is, how many millions
of people watch it. It was like doing *Python,* where ten million people watch
it in one night, and then doing films where, if you're lucky, 100,000 people
go to see it in a year. The difference is phenomenal!

WARDLE: *If* Do Not Adjust Your Set *was so popular, why didn't it keep going?*
GILLIAM: Because we started *Python,* basically [laughter]

WARDLE: *So you thought, "Hey! We're successful! We're going to do something for real money now."*

GILLIAM: No, it wasn't even that. It was children's television. Even then, while doing children's television, knowing we were getting away with murder, nobody wanted to get stuck in children's television. The second [season] ended, and Eric [Idle], Mike [Palin], Terry [Jones], and I said, "Well, let's do something else together." One of the things that happened on *Do Not Adjust Your Set* was that there were two other people, David Jason and Denise Coffey, who were also part of the team. It wasn't just the four of us. It was a bigger crowd and everybody decided that they didn't want to work with that crowd, but the four of us wanted to work together.

WARDLE: *Yet, as you were saying, when you first came over they sort of viewed you as . . . "Oh, who's this guy, and why do we have to do his material now?" How did that friendship develop?*

GILLIAM: It was really Eric, who was on *We Have Ways of Making You Laugh*, and so when I started doing animation, he really got excited by that. He asked me to do animation on the second season of *Do Not Adjust Your Set*. That's really how that connection was created. The two sketches that I had written for the show didn't interest them too much, but Terry, in particular, has a very good eye for visual, graphic, conceptual things, and liked what I was doing. Plus I was no longer intruding on their territory. We all had our area of expertise.

WARDLE: *Who of the Python group would you say you are closest to as a friend?*

GILLIAM: It works in different ways. I suppose Mike. It's partly because Mike is everybody's best friend. There's something about Mike that becomes the cement that always kept us together. He's the one that, no matter how much we hate the others at any given point, everybody likes.

WARDLE: *He's like the Ringo Starr of the group.*

GILLIAM: [laughs] It's a strange one, and Terry and I have always felt very close on ideas.

WARDLE: *Visual things.*

GILLIAM: Yeah, and Eric and I stay very close because we were the ones that worked on our own during the show. The others, Mike and Terry, worked together, and John and Graham worked together, but Eric did his things and I did my things, so there is a bond between Eric and me. Also, Eric is the most American of the group. [laughter]

WARDLE: *He's got a pretty thick English accent. How do you mean that?*
GILLIAM: [giggles] I think he's the most keen on success. He's drawn to it. He likes the flash and glamour of America.

WARDLE: *He even did an American sitcom.*
GILLIAM: Well, that's it. That's why he's the most American. [giggles]

WARDLE: *When the* Monty Python *show started to get popular, how did that fame change your personal life?*
GILLIAM: I don't think it did. That was the great thing about the group, because it was a gang of six, and no matter how big any individual head got, there were always five others to knock it off. That's what kind of kept us in our places as individuals. As a group, we're pretty arrogant. [giggles] I just remember the moment when it happened, in a sense, and I panicked. It was at the end of the first [season] of shows, and there was a program called *Late-Night Line-Up* that went out at 11:00 at night. It was an interview show, and we were on it, being interviewed on television! Even though we had been doing a television series, this was too much to take. Suddenly I knew we were successful! We were famous! I remember grabbing my knapsack and rushing away from England to go down to Morocco, and really roughed it for a couple of weeks.

WARDLE: *Just to put things in perspective?*
GILLIAM: Yeah, because I thought, "This is getting to me."

WARDLE: *How does it get to you now when it's much more so?*
GILLIAM: It doesn't. Now it's just something I accept. I don't really think about it unless I'm doing interviews. But what's interesting is, while I was in Philadelphia filming *Twelve Monkeys,* I was getting recognized more than I ever have before because the [*Monty Python*] shows are on daily, and they kept running that twentieth-anniversary compilation, *Parrot Sketch Not Included: Twenty Years of Monty Python.* That came on several times and so I

was visible. My face was on TV a lot. I was surprised by how often I was recognized.

WARDLE: *Several documentaries came right at the end of Graham [Chapman]'s life—that's another thing I was going to ask you. Not meaning to bring you down, but . . .*
GILLIAM: Is he still alive?

WARDLE: [laughing] *No, no, no.*
GILLIAM: Is he still gay?

WARDLE: [laughing] *No! Will you let me ask the question?! When he was in the group, he said he had a real problem with alcoholism. He drank sixty ounces of gin a day. Did that ever cause problems between him and other members of the group?*
GILLIAM: *Rampant!* [laughter] Yeah, I mean, he was wonderful. If you were the target of the attack, it was awful, but if you were on the sidelines, it was brilliant! [laughter] It kept things going.

WARDLE: *It's like when Groucho complained later in life that he couldn't insult anyone anymore because no matter how mean he was, the person would laugh and be honored that Groucho Marx had insulted them.*
GILLIAM: Yeah. I mean, Graham kept things adventurous, because he was always a wild card. You didn't know what to expect. Sometimes it was outrageous and funny, sometimes it was just mean and nasty and uncalled for, and it would leave different members in terrible states. I think it was good, because it actually kept the pot stirring, and I think that was great.

WARDLE: *You mean the checks and balances of all these different personalities together.*
GILLIAM: Yeah. That's what was always interesting. Graham was driving John [Cleese] crazy, because he wasn't carrying his weight as a writing partner.

WARDLE: *It's strange that they worked so well together for so long, because they seem to be such different types of people.*
GILLIAM: But that was the strength of the group in some ways. The differ-

ences were greater than the similarities. It kept a really strong internal tension pulling in different directions. When it stopped being like that, I think it lost a lot of its zing.

WARDLE: *How did Graham's death affect you?*

GILLIAM: What was so weird about it was that it came so quickly. On one hand there was Graham looking like shit and I thought he was dying, but then I'd see him in the hospital and he would say it was all gone.

We were convinced it was just an act and he was going to outlive us all. [laughter]

WARDLE: *It was a massive sketch he was writing.*

GILLIAM: He was just asking for our sympathy and pity, because he wasn't doing other things well. Then suddenly there was this call that Graham was going into the hospital and they didn't think he was going to come out, and we said, "*What?!*" I mean, a couple of weeks earlier, everything had seemed dandy. I mean, he was really fucking weak, but he was a doctor and, being the doctor, he was just saying, "I'll take the tablets and everything will be fine." He was telling all of us that and he was telling himself that as well. I think he was surprised by it, because I think he thought he was going to pull through. I mean, he had just sold his story to the *Sun*: "How I kicked the Big C!" I don't know if they asked for the money back at the end of it, but they should have. [laughter] I mean, his timing was brilliant, to do it on the eve of the twentieth anniversary of the first *Monty Python* show. As Mike said, "It was the first time he got his timing right." [laughter]

WARDLE: [laughing] *I have a great quote from Graham Chapman about you. In 1987, he did a lecture tour, and I saw him at the Ryerson Theater in Toronto. At the end they had a question period and someone asked about you. Chapman said, [I may be paraphrasing, but this is the way I remember it]: "Terry Gilliam is a very good visual person, but he's not very good at expressing himself verbally. He basically has two stock phrases that he uses for every occasion. Things are either 'Really great!' or else, they 'Really piss him off!'"*

GILLIAM: [laughing all through quote] There we go. It was very important to be the token American and the token nonverbal one, because they felt better. I really pretended to be nonverbal, so they felt superior.

WARDLE: *Having sat with you even for these few minutes, I can see that it's not the case.*

GILLIAM: It's very funny, in fact, with them I was always . . . I don't think I was intimidated, but I was always impressed by them, and they were better verbally. It was very hard to beat the Pythons verbally, so I never even tried to compete with them. As we first flew to Canada on the very first Python stage tour, I'm supposed to have said, "There's a whole bunch of water down there," as we were flying over the Great Lakes, and I didn't actually say that, but it just got built up into a running gag. It went on and on and on. It was very funny.

What was so bizarre about Graham was that he was very destructive, and he actually destroyed a lot of other people along the way. There was a point, a few years before he died, that I had completely gone off Graham. He was like Dorian Gray, and there was a portrait hanging in his house, but it wasn't a portrait. It was a real person, John Tomiczek, his ward, who was getting more and more scarred as Graham floated through life. What was good about him was that there was an incredible mixture of total selfishness and total generosity. There were extremes to Graham, and in the midst of it there was this man who just sort of sat there and puffed on his pipe. Sometimes Graham was the person that we could all agree was a total waste of time. "He's totally useless! He's not doing anything, and he's fucking up the sketches!" But then he would be brilliant. The moment that was interesting was when we discovered that Graham was the great lead man in the group, because we used to think that Mike was going to be the lead man in the group, like in *Life of Brian* and *Holy Grail,* as a lead actor.

WARDLE: *And he did a great job in both films.*

GILLIAM: Yeah. He was brilliant! But that's what was good. We actually spent a lot of time just going at each other, complaining about each other, not talking to each other, and yet the common respect that everybody held for each other held this thing together. That and Mike. [giggles] We were six people doing exactly what we wanted to do [with no interference].

WARDLE: *Until the undertaker sketch.*[3]

Do you ever wish that you'd been allowed to do more performing on the early shows?

GILLIAM: No, not really. Again, I never felt up to their standards as a performer, to be honest. I'd done a lot of performing in college, but then you leave all that. They went straight from university to performing nonstop on shows with David Frost, Marty Feldman. They never stopped. These guys were really good. I never felt that's what I was about. The cartoons were what I did well, but I'd be there on the days of the show, and I needed something to do, so I'd start playing bit parts in sketches. What I've always liked from the beginning was disguise, makeup, costumes, all that stuff. So I would start doing these weirder and weirder costumes and enjoying it.

WARDLE: *Especially in the films. You seem to play all the ugly parts.*
GILLIAM: The grotesque. Always, because nobody else would go through the business of being made up for it.

WARDLE: *Like the jailer in* Life of Brian, *and the prophet with mud all over his face.*
GILLIAM: Yeah, I happen to like those kinds of characters, period, but they also gave texture to the film, I thought. Whereas John wouldn't wear anything uncomfortable, he wouldn't put a beard on, I said, "Fuck this!" We were trying to make period films and they had to be peopled with great characters.

WARDLE: *Is it true that Eric Idle once broke into your place and stole some of your animation cels because you refused to contribute to the Python books?*
GILLIAM: What?

WARDLE: *In one of the books about Monty Python, Idle says that you wouldn't contribute to the books because you claimed, "Funny books don't sell." So he claims that he actually had to break into your house and steal some of your cut-outs.*
GILLIAM: I might have been hesitant about how successful the book would be, but I do know that Eric is very good at starting things and is less good at finishing things. With *Monty Python's Big Red Book,* what happened was that Eric was away on holiday and I was finishing off the book.

WARDLE: *So he never stole your cut-outs?*
GILLIAM: No, it might be more interesting as a story, but it's not true.

WARDLE: *I guess that's just a legend that he's built up.*
GILLIAM: I think it's good to build up legends. It's always more interesting

than reality. The reality was, Eric gets these things going, and people like Terry, Mike, or I finish them off.

WARDLE: *What about [John Cleese's] assertion that "Terry Gilliam has had a falling out with everyone he's ever met and not talked to them for three years"?*
GILLIAM: When did he say that? [laughter]

WARDLE: *On that* Life of George *documentary.*
GILLIAM: I think he's probably right. There seems to be one side of me that has to break things up. I don't think I've had a falling out with *everybody.* I just get intense. [laughs]

WARDLE: *Underneath it all you're still friends with all of them?*
GILLIAM: Yeah. That's the important thing. All that shit, it just happens. I just get so convinced of my rightness over certain things, I can't see that there can be another way of looking at it. In fact, that's actually died down a bit as I've gotten older. It's really taken the fun out of life.

WARDLE: *You're not as angry as you once were?*
GILLIAM: Yeah. I'm not so certain, either.

WARDLE: Monty Python and the Holy Grail *was your first stab at directing live-action sequences. Was it difficult working with a budget of only $460,000?*
GILLIAM: No, that wasn't the problem. In fact it was one of those things that probably made for a better film.

WARDLE: *Using the coconut shells instead of horses . . .*
GILLIAM: I mean, our ambition was to make a great medieval epic with horses and all that, and we couldn't afford it. We made what we made. We were screaming nonstop about not having what we needed, yet at every point, we always managed to come up with a solution that solved the problem.

WARDLE: *Is it true that Pink Floyd and Led Zeppelin put up the money?*
GILLIAM: It was Pink Floyd, Led Zeppelin, Elton John, Crysalis Records and either Island or Charisma Records. At that time, in England, you were liable for almost 90 percent tax if you made enough money. Either pop stars were

leaving the country, or they were trying to find tax losses. Python was always No. 1 with pop groups.

WARDLE: *So Floyd and Zeppelin were fans . . .*

GILLIAM: And their management thought this was a good way of investing money. If it makes money, great. If it doesn't, you've got tax laws. For our first four films, basically that's what it was. *Jabberwocky* was the same financing, and then when it came to *Life of Brian* and *Time Bandits,* it was George Harrison who put up the money. Our initial impetus was always pop groups . . . and impossible taxation in England.

WARDLE: *You were credited as codirector of* Holy Grail *along with Terry Jones. What was your directorial input, beyond the animated sequences?*

GILLIAM: That's what's so hard to remember. The look of the thing, I think. That's again where my strength was. "Let's do this, let's do that, let's choose that place." Terry and I were in general agreement about most things on it. At least at the start. Then it becomes more difficult when you're directing, and I say, "That's what I think we ought to be doing," and Terry says, "Yes, but I think we should. . . ." That's where it became more and more complicated, because there's a crew waiting to know what to do. Then we tried working with a single voice, that of the assistant director, but it turned out he was also a director in the making, and he started not translating what we were saying accurately. Instead, he was doing *his* film. So it became a bit silly. The way it eventually evolved was that Terry spent his time with the guys, and I was in back of the camera. That worked reasonably well. I was in a rather bad frame of mind because, having worked for years with pieces of paper that never talked back, suddenly I was dealing with the rest of the guys in the group who were pissing and moaning the whole time. In one scene, they didn't see why they had to be wearing armor for this shot where the camera was in a hole, shooting up at the Trojan rabbit being flung at them. They were pissing and moaning and complaining the whole time, and I finally said, "Well, fuck the lot of you! I'm off!" I was very petulant in those days. I would say, "Fuck it! Direct it yourself! I'm not going to deal with this."

WARDLE: *So you walked out a few times?*

GILLIAM: Yeah. There was a lot of that. I remember at one point, after the first week—which had been like a nightmare 'cause everything that could possibly go wrong, went wrong. The National Trust threw us out of all the castles we had chosen. The first shot, the camera breaks down. I mean, it was just a nightmare, and in the thick of all this, while we were just scraping our way through it, and just as we were getting somewhere, Graham, one drunken evening, just went berserk against Terry and myself: "You arrogant little assholes! What makes you think you can direct? Why shouldn't Ian MacNaughton (who had done the TV shows) be directing? You guys are fucking everything up!" That's all we needed at that point—Graham going on one of his tirades.

WARDLE: *Still, when you look at* Holy Grail, *it holds up so well.* Holy Grail *was the first film I saw that showed medieval England as it probably really was, with shit and mud and plague victims . . .*
GILLIAM: It was Pasolini who was inspiring us at that point, because he had made *The Canterbury Tales* and others which, for better or worse, have a great sense of the place and the atmosphere, and Terry and I were obsessed with that. A lot of the humor came out of the reality. . . . Shit, mud, and attitudes. That was really important to me that we make the thing smell and stink and feel right. Again, there was a lot of trouble from John, who didn't want to deal with all this crap, and Eric, who didn't really like it either. Graham put up with it only some days. It was Mike, Terry and I who really were serious about re-creating a time and a place. Before *Holy Grail,* comedy was always shot light, bright, airy, clean, and we decided to be as serious as Pasolini or any of the other great filmmakers at re-creating an era. If it had just been the silliness without the atmosphere, I don't think it would've been as funny. We had huge fights on the TV show, trying to make it look darker, and have shadows. You can do that in drama, but not in comedy. We never succeeded in making it darker, because Ian [MacNaughton] never quite got it and the budget was never there or the technicians didn't want to know about it. So, the way we approached the film was to try to get all of that, so it was dark and it was dingy and it was dirty and it was smelly and it was painful and it was cold. Get all of that stuff on film and out of that, the comedy springs.

WARDLE: [laugher] *Mind you, sounds pretty unpleasant to film that.*
GILLIAM: [laughter] It would be interesting to see if we were the first to [show England that way].

WARDLE: *Where did you get the idea for the short* [The Crimson Permanent Assurance] *that opens* Monty Python's The Meaning of Life?

GILLIAM: I had been drawing some buildings with sails on them and I kept thinking about that, and I wanted to use them somewhere, so I sat down and wrote that. It was written as a cartoon originally, and I thought, "Fuck, let's just do it!" 'cause I was fed up with animation by the time of *The Meaning of Life*. I didn't want to be stuck being the animator of the group. I was bored with it, so I said I would make a little film [giggles]. It was kind of a bargain: "You do the animation, and then you can do this film." It was supposed to plug itself into the film, two-thirds of the way through, and we shot it. I had my own soundstage, my own cast and crew and everything. Then we put it into the film and it didn't work. There was this pressure to cut it shorter. It was never going to work in the film. It was a different rhythm. It didn't have anything to do with the world of *The Meaning of Life*. The pace was very different. Terry kept pressuring me to cut it shorter and I suggested pulling it out of the film and sticking it in as a short at the front. Bingo! It just worked as a treat up-front on its own.

WARDLE: *I heard you directed a TV commercial that was only shown in Europe.*

GILLIAM: Yeah. I did this after *Brazil,* when I didn't think *Brazil* was ever going to come out. I was at a really low point and this French company (Orangina was the product) wanted me to do it. It was very funny and I said I'd do it on the condition that they can't show it anywhere but France. I didn't want it shown in England. I didn't want people to know I was doing commercials. That was the deal. It was a really good commercial. I actually did a commercial at the beginning of last year, for Nike. Again, it was a really nice script, and I hadn't been behind a camera for almost four years, and I had to do something. Every time I do one, it keeps me from wanting to do another one for about ten years. I do a commercial every ten years.

WARDLE: *That's a strict regimen you put yourself through.*

GILLIAM: Exactly. Don't make too much money, you see?

WARDLE: *I've read the books* The Battle of Brazil *and* Losing the Light, *which relate in minute detail your problems with the studios over two very unique films. Did this give you a bad reputation with the studios and force you to do more main-stream films to regain their confidence?*

GILLIAM: Not really. It was a healthy bad reputation. It's very good to have a bad reputation in Hollywood, I've decided. What it does is chase away a lot of the idiots that come running because you've made a good film. Most of them stay away. The braver ones come in, and usually they're more intelligent as well. On *Fisher King,* it was great because all the studio people had read *The Battle of Brazil,* and they were waiting for me to behave in some outrageous, explosive way. I never raised my voice once. I just smiled and was very polite. That was very useful, because they were constantly terrified of what might happen, so they tip-toed around me, and that's good.

WARDLE: *From what I read in those books, it wasn't your fault in either case that the films didn't do well at the box office.*
GILLIAM: If you don't release a film properly, you don't make money. It's never bothered me if they don't make money. It's pathetic at the moment the way America has become obsessed with money-making films. Every week in the newspapers—even the *New York Times*—are the grosses. That bothers me. On one hand, we're in a business. Films need to make money, or they shouldn't lose *big* money. But the perception is really skewed because the numbers aren't right. People don't understand what the numbers really mean. When we did the early Python films, we didn't have any reputation in Hollywood, even though we were making big money off the films. We made them for very little money, and they did very good business. Also we owned them. Yet by Hollywood standards, they were not making big money, so we had no status in Hollywood. They weren't interested in us, but I couldn't think of anything better than being completely free to do whatever we wanted to do, making films that we liked making, and making money on them. Where it then gets interesting is that after I made *Time Bandits,* which made a fortune in the States, then by Hollywood standards I was now a money-maker. Then they wanted me to do Hollywood films, which I've never been interested in. The advantage of *Time Bandits* making a lot of money was that it got *Brazil* off the ground. The American people have been trained to believe that money means quality, and that's what really scares me about printing box-office grosses in the newspapers.

WARDLE: *Don't people realize that a lot of the all-time classic films like* Citizen Kane *and* It's a Wonderful Life *were not box-office successes when they were first released?*

GILLIAM: *The Wizard of Oz* and *Singin' in the Rain* were not successes when they first came out.

WARDLE: *Maybe in twenty years,* Baron Munchausen *will be considered a classic.*
GILLIAM: The basic problem with *Munchausen* was that they didn't release the film. They made 117 prints of the film. An art-house film goes out with 400 prints. The film wasn't released. Then I end up with this reputation of, "Oh, this guy makes these big, out-of-control films and then they make no money." I made one film that went over budget and that was it. I'd make it again.

WARDLE: *From reading the book, it seems that very little of that was your fault.*
GILLIAM: My fault, because I went into a situation that was doomed, maybe [laughter]. The whole thing was a big mess. It was badly produced. We had a nightmare making it. We managed to make a film that was almost as good as I set out to make, and then, in order to win over the new studio people, I made cuts to save money. I made the choice. Nobody forced me. I made them to win over these people so that they would be behind the film, and then they don't release it. That's the only thing that ultimately drove me crazy. I think there would be a slightly better film there with a few more minutes added in. I think the thing is a bit rushed and frenzied and tiresome.

WARDLE: *I get nervous just reading that book. It was like you'd all been through a war together.*
GILLIAM: That's exactly what it was. It did leave some pretty deep scars.

WARDLE: *But it brings people together, I guess.*
GILLIAM: Yeah, people you would never choose to spend time with. The worst thing about it was that it was really hard to get going again. That's why when *Fisher King* came along, I thought, "Here's a nice script. It's easy, it's quick. They want me to do it. I'll do it." It has no special effects in it, by my standard.

WARDLE: *When that film premiered at the Toronto Festival of Festivals, you were quoted as saying, "Thank you for justifying my decision to sell out." Is that the way you really felt?*

GILLIAM: [laughter] No, it was just something to say. [laughs again] It was the first studio film I did, so by my standards, it was selling out. It was somebody else's script. I still had complete control of it, and made the film I wanted to make. So by those standards, it was great. The whole point in saying things is to keep stirring things up, and if people want to take it seriously, they can. Some people probably did think that. It's like when Bob Dylan went electric. If I had made a film that I wasn't happy with, that was dictated by other people, and made cuts that I didn't want to make, then that would be different. I had total control of it. I thought it would kick-start me, get me going again, which it did. It was the first film I'd ever done that I didn't have final cut. I was also the completion guarantor. If it went over budget, it came out of my pocket. This was all to show what a good boy he is. Whatever you think he is, you're wrong. I walked right in there, my head in the lion's mouth. "Nothing up my sleeve. Here we go!" Then we finish it under budget, it's my cut, and it's successful. "What more do you guys want?" [giggles] There's a side of me that is practical and pragmatic. I sit there and say, "These are the soldiers I've got. These are the soldiers they've got. Will it work or will it not?" Let's go into battle and see what happens. [giggles] At the end, we got into a situation where they thought the film was too long . . .

WARDLE: . . . *which they always do with your films.*
GILLIAM: Yeah, always. I said, "That's fine, but I don't know how to cut it down to two hours." They wanted to cut fourteen minutes out of this film. We were getting great ratings from test audiences early on. We were in the top two brackets. Eighty percent liked it. They kept pushing and pushing and pushing for me to make cuts. We eventually sat down at the Polo Lounge. All the studio guys were there. I said to them, "All right. What do you want me to cut?" I suggested we do one more screening. I said, "You tell me what cuts you want, and if there is a significant difference in the cards after the second version, I will *consider* making the cuts." I was being as equivocal as possible. They came up with about four-and-a-half minutes of cuts. I knew what they were going to be anyway, so we had them all prepared. So we made the cuts, and it was a terrible screening. From the moment the audience for the cut version walked in, it was a better audience than the previous screening. You could feel it. I thought, "I'm fucked! I'm so fucked! It's going to play 100 percent better and I'm going to be stuck with these cuts that I

don't want to make." And of course, they had a feeding frenzy. "Well, let's cut some more things out!" Suddenly, they were coming up with the most stupid, impossible, ridiculous cuts. Then when I showed my version again, the cards were the same as the cut version. It was a draw, but I said, "If my name goes on the film, I'm not going to do it." They said, "*What?!*" I said, "You forced this fucking system down my throat! The cards are the same. My name is on it. The cuts go back in." And they went ape-shit. They wrote me this letter saying that I was totally selfish, I was not a team player, blah, blah, blah, I hadn't made the cuts and I would hurt the financial possibilities of the film. I wasn't taking their calls. I said it was total bullshit. To me the films are the length they play best at. I wasn't trying to make a long film, but if you start taking things out, then the whole thing starts collapsing on itself. I think it's better to be too long than too short.

WARDLE: *Do you ever think there'll come a time when you'll be able to make a film your way and not have to make any concessions to the studio?*
GILLIAM: I hope it doesn't. I have no idea what would happen. I can't work in that kind of vacuum. I need things to fight against. You need walls. You need parameters to bang your head against. You have to have people to say, "You can't go that way!" Then you say, "I can't go down that way? Fuck it! I'll go down this way." Sometimes it becomes a better way out.

WARDLE: *It seemed when I was reading about this stuff that you hated these studio people and didn't want anything to do with them.*
GILLIAM: Oh, I do. There's no question about that, but I don't want to have a situation with no parameters. I don't know how to work like that. Films are products of specific times and places and combinations of people.

WARDLE: *So you think the destiny of a film makes it come out the way it was meant to come out?*
GILLIAM: Well, there's a bit of that. Certainly, when I'm making a film, I get very fatalistic about these things. I seriously believe the film is making itself. I'm not making it, I'm just the hand that writes. I think any artist, whether you're a sculptor or whatever, a thing starts to form itself. Either you respond to it, respond to the materials you're given, or you fight against them. You do both things, in fact. Given complete freedom, I don't know what I'd do. I would probably just spin off in a million directions and make

a formless mass. Films are weird, and that's the reason I like making them. Drawing a cartoon is one thing. It's just me and that piece of paper. But in the films, you have to deal with so many things, so many different kinds of people: money, talent, time. It's the closest thing to being in the real world, and it's a totally false world. That's what I like about it, and I also hate it for that same reason. You're so divided in a million different directions, you begin to lose yourself in it. You're supposed to be the calm eye of the hurricane, and everybody's coming to you. It's like you're the Wizard of Oz. As long as they believe in you, and the power of the Wizard of Oz, then the film gets made. The minute you lose their confidence, the film starts falling apart. Then you become an actor, playing the role of the director.

WARDLE: *I can't imagine a film where more things went wrong making it than in* Munchausen, *yet it seems like everyone stuck around and really wanted to get it right, just for you.*

GILLIAM: What I do know is that people who have worked on my films in the end feel satisfied, however awful it is, because their work is up on the screen. As a director, I'm interested in all the aspects of film, so people respond to the fact that I come to the costume department.

WARDLE: *You just answered another of my questions: Do you enjoy getting involved in the technical side of filmmaking, or would you rather be the dreamweaver and let other people handle their own departments?*

GILLIAM: A lot of directors get away with murder, because their intelligence and skill lies in hiring good people and letting them do what they do. That's their skill. I want to hire really good people, but I want to then create a leap-frog situation where they come up with an idea, I come up with a better idea. Then they come up with an even better idea, and we all leap forward and excite each other. If I'm going to be a good director, then I've got to be good in all of those areas. I've got to be able to design a costume. I've got to be able to design a set. I've got to know about lighting. Unless I can do all those things, I don't feel I'm doing my job. The point is, I don't think I can do those jobs *better* than the people I hire. That's a dangerous thing. Sometimes I can do it better, but most times I like knowing that person is doing it better than I could.

WARDLE: *That's why you hired him, right?* [laughter]
GILLIAM: Yeah. Sometimes I think, "Well, I could do that better." But I

won't, because I don't want that feeling to creep into the group that, "Oh, Mr. Know-it-all is doing everything." Actually, as I get older, I get more tired, to the point where I *don't* want to do it all. Thank God someone is choosing pink as the color of this costume, because I don't want to make this decision. People know what kind of films I make. Your reputation and your work precede you, which is very useful because they know I have an eye for detail. Even the details I'm *not* concerned about, people think I am, because they've seen the work I do. Once upon a time I *was* interested in every detail. But now I'm more interested in delegating those things. All those people are thinking I'm watching everything, so they work twice as hard and that's good.

WARDLE: *It sounds like, during the filming of* The Adventures of Baron Munchausen, *Eric Idle really kept you going with moral support during the darkest days.*
GILLIAM: Eric was great. Those are the moments when I really like Eric. For all of his selfishness and pigheadedness and awfulness, Eric was really great. He was putting up with a lot of shit, everybody was, and he stuck it out. I think he really felt that we were making something worthwhile.

WARDLE: *When I first saw it at the theater, I thought, "I take my hat off to anyone who could direct this film and stay sane."*
GILLIAM: The staying sane part was questionable. [laughter] It's hard for me to judge, because I made it and all the things that went wrong are still in the forefront of my mind when I'm viewing it, but I think it's a pretty extraordinary fucking film. What's interesting is how it seems to be disliked by so many people. I get very strong responses from critics, which I'm happy to have. At times it gets tiresome, but I really love the fact that they either love it or they hate it. *Fisher King,* for me, of all my films is the easiest to take. Yet, two thumbs down from Siskel and Ebert. Alexander Walker, who's one of the big, big critics here, just vomited all over it. That's very interesting that one gets that kind of response. To get that kind of venom is . . .

WARDLE: *At least you got a reaction out of them. They didn't fall asleep during the film.*
GILLIAM: What I want to know is what gets them that angry?

WARDLE: *Maybe the fact that they want you to be a one-trick pony and do more films that are dark and disturbing, like* Brazil. Fisher King *had a happy ending.*

GILLIAM: The happy ending was in the script. *Munchausen* had a happy ending, so did *Time Bandits*. *Brazil* had an ending that was right for that piece. You can't invent a world like that . . .

WARDLE: *. . . and not be consistent.*
GILLIAM: Yeah. It's the lack of consistency that drives me crazy. *Brazil* was a reaction to a lot of Hollywood films, especially *Blade Runner*. It was a wonderful film, and then at the end it just says, "Fuck all of you. We're going to have a happy ending." The ending was appalling! You create an android, and tell the viewer that they all have limited life spans, and then at the end, it's, "Oh, but this is one that doesn't." That's the kind of thing that drives me crazy. Let's at least be consistent or true to the piece. That's what I was trying to do with *Brazil*. Yet when it came out, Rex Reed tore it to pieces.

WARDLE: *When* Brazil *first came out, a lot of people had different ideas about what it meant. What does it really mean, from your perspective?*
GILLIAM: It was originally going to be called *The Ministry*. It was really about how organizations become self-serving organisms and will do anything to keep themselves alive. That's how it really started, and then you mix into that things like the Peter Principle, which is that people are promoted to a position above their capabilities and there they stay. Therefore, organizations are always peopled by employees that are bad at the job they're doing. I was keen on Sam being a character who was wise, who avoided being promoted beyond his capabilities, because it bought him lots of free time to dream and fantasize, not taking responsibility for the organization.

WARDLE: *In a lot of jobs, employees are even told they're working too fast. They're going to make everybody look bad.*
GILLIAM: Well, that's what Tuttle is. He makes everybody look bad because he's good at his job. He's good at fixing things. It was really all about the way organizations work, and the people within them. In the midst of that is this guy, the smart one, who chooses not to get involved, and unfortunately, gets involved by falling in love. Falling in love humanizes him, and ultimately destroys him. Sam is actually tortured at the end because he chose not to take responsibility for his actions.

WARDLE: *Just like in the corporate world. Nobody wants to admit they made a mistake, nobody wants to take the blame.*

GILLIAM: They want to blame the system. They want to blame somebody else. You get all the goodies from the system, the technology and the toys, but you're attached by these great umbilical ducts to the system. There was an image that I didn't get in the film, the Buttles' home. It was way out in this desolate countryside, but it had this huge umbilical cable line, about four feet wide, extending across the desert. It was this thing about people being connected to a system. I remember being in Chicago, at the University there, giving a lecture, and all these kids were asking why there was so much wiring and ducts. Don't they realize that room they're sitting in is completely surrounded by cables and wires? All that you see is just a thin facade. The other side is this very complicated bit of wiring and ducting, hooking you into the network. It was very funny because we were talking about the explosions, and I said, it isn't just dynamite. Systems go bang. They didn't quite buy all that. We walked out, and what was on the television? The Challenger exploding. I said, "that's what I'm talking about, folks." Sam is a real interesting character. He becomes a hero at the end by killing his girl, by killing her, as far as the system is concerned. He doesn't have a sword and wings, but he can operate computers. Her character was originally supposed to be much more elaborate, larger. Again, she was smart. Rather than taking a job at an office, she had chosen to drive a truck, because she's free most of the time, in her truck, on her own. She was a very isolated person, because she didn't want to get involved either. They were both living in their own worlds and they came together. In the finished film, she's basically cut down to looking like a figment of his imagination, but that wasn't supposed to be that way, it just worked out that way.

WARDLE: *Your new film is called* Twelve Monkeys *and it stars:*
GILLIAM: Bruce [Willis], Brad [Pitt], and Madeleine Stowe.

WARDLE: *What's the film about?*
GILLIAM: That's the trouble. I don't know. Until we see it on Wednesday, I really don't know what it's going to be like. I know all the bits and pieces are all good in themselves. It's how they all string together. It was written by Dave and Jan Peoples. Dave wrote *Unforgiven* and *Blade Runner,* and it was inspired by this French film made in the 1960s. It was twenty-seven minutes long, and all black-and-white stills. Basically, we've got a guy who may have come back from the future to find a virus before it mutates. This virus wiped

out the planet in 1996, and the few survivors went underground and eventually made a life for themselves underground.

WARDLE: *So, does this have anything to do with that monkey virus that they're talking about now?*

GILLIAM: Well, it all managed to match very nicely. I actually think all the big virus stuff is part of a Universal marketing strategy that they have infected people out there so it will be advertising for the film. The question then becomes whether this character is mad, or else it's true. And then there's a psychiatrist whom he kidnaps, who keeps trying to convince him that it's all in his mind.

WARDLE: *Universal is putting this out? Don't you hate those people after what happened with* Brazil?

GILLIAM: Yeah, but it gets even more ironic, because the producer is married to Dawn Steele, who was at Columbia when we did *Munchausen*.

WARDLE: *Why do these people want to keep working with you when they think you're such trouble?*

GILLIAM: I keep saying, "What do you have to do to burn bridges in Hollywood?" Seems to be a difficult thing to achieve. Studio heads change. The guy who's now president, a guy named Casey Silver, is a big fan. He did a very brave thing, letting the beast back into the enclosure.

WARDLE: *Was it your idea to use Bruce Willis and Brad Pitt?*

GILLIAM: Those were not my first choices. I kept walking away from the film, because I thought it wasn't going to go anywhere. For a while, it didn't look like it was going to get made. The producer was very tenacious, and he just wouldn't let go. It reached a point where the studio was pushing for a star, because they think it's an art movie. They're desperate to have a big name in it, and Bruce's name came up. I thought it was a possibility, because I met him on *Fisher King* and I quite liked him. He's a better actor than he seems, on the screen.

WARDLE: *When people back home who heard I was going to be doing this asked what you are doing these days, and I told them you were doing a film with Bruce Willis and Brad Pitt, they all went, "What . . . ?"*

GILLIAM: They don't understand the perverseness. That's the great thing. That's also a reason to do it, it seems to me. If all the fans think I shouldn't be doing it, well, fuck 'em! This is exactly what I should be doing. Constantly shifting perception is really important to me.

WARDLE: *Reinvent yourself?*

GILLIAM: Yeah, and reinvent people's perceptions of who Bruce and Brad are, as well. That's what intrigues me, because they're actually playing parts that are the opposite of anything they've ever played before. The ultimate trigger on this whole thing was that it had been four years since I'd been behind a camera. *Fisher King* was finished in 1990, and I was getting really twitchy, because the projects that I had been working on were all going nowhere, for a variety of reasons. I was getting more and more depressed, and I just wanted to do something. This was a script that I really liked, because it's very complicated. It's not a Hollywood movie by any standards. Bruce is really keen to change his career, because the action stuff is a real dead end. In the last few years you see him turning up in lots of little parts, playing a variety of character roles. Brad was begging to do it, and I wasn't so sure whether I wanted him. In the end, his enthusiasm sort of won me over. I'm always a sucker for that, getting someone like Brad to do something that's way beyond anything he's done before. If someone really wants to do it, and shows a lot of enthusiasm, I'll gamble on it.

It's like, "Do you want to be an actor or a 'star'?" Bruce is one of those guys who became a star very quickly. He leapt from television to film, and *bingo!* He was trapped. Brad, on the other hand, was not yet "the sexiest man in America" when we signed him on. The studio couldn't believe their luck!

One of the big problems was, since we were shooting in the winter, we had to decide whether or not we should go with or without snow on the ground, because there were a lot of exteriors, and you've got to make a choice. I decided that whatever the ground looks like on the first weekend of shooting, we'll go with that. So, there was this beautiful snow and I decided we'd go with snow, and of course, that was the last time it snowed.

WARDLE: *So, did you have to use fake snow?*

GILLIAM: Yeah, all through it, which costs a lot of money and takes time.

WARDLE: *Does it look real enough to compare with the real snow?*

GILLIAM: Well, you've got to see the film and tell me. No, it's not as good as I wanted it. There was a lot of stuff that was very frustrating. It was a club-footed crew, limping along. It was a mixture of really good people and really lame people. This wasn't the problem on *Munchausen*. I had really good people, but there were the English and the Italians and they didn't get along. The Italians were brilliant! The production was what was appalling. The actual coordination, organization of the thing was a disaster, and we also had a brilliant but very slow lighting cameraman, Peppino [Giuseppe] Rotunno. He could only work at his pace and I couldn't change that. I almost left. At one point, I said, "It's him or me," but the idea of firing him is like firing the godfather. You can't do that. That's what films are like. You get into these situations, and they're not just simple little things. It doesn't work that way. You have to cast and crew the film very carefully. If you don't, you pay the price.

One of the reasons for doing *Fisher King* after *Munchausen* was to show everybody I was responsible. We went into it without final cut and putting up my fee as the completion guarantor. Then I had to do it again on this one [*Twelve Monkeys*], because the insurance company wanted a ridiculous percentage as a contingency. They said this was because all my films go over budget. Only one film went over budget, and the next film we did after that was back on budget. They said, "That doesn't count. That was a studio production. This one is an independent production." I have to prove myself again. So, this film is on budget, and that'd better be the end of that shit. If I hear it again, I'm going to kill someone. There are only a couple of insurance companies out there, and the other one is the one who insured me on *Munchausen.* They're not going to insure me!

WARDLE: [laughing] *Yet you're working with Universal again.*
GILLIAM: On *Fisher King,* the producers were going around saying that they were the ones that contained the wild beast. They like being the one who can take this unruly talent and bring it into line.

WARDLE: *Do you really think that you're unruly?*
GILLIAM: No. I'm determined, and I do what I say. I always say things and they never believe me. On *Fisher King*, I sat down with the studio people and the producers and I said, "Here's how it works. You [the studio] have the film. You give it to the producers. They then give it to me and I give it to the actors and we shoot. Then, at the end of the shoot, I take it back from the

actors, and then you're going to try to take it back from me and I'm not going to let you." I said this at the beginning of the film. Then, when it happens, they go crazy! I said, "I told you." [laughs]

WARDLE: *Because you've been through it before. You've worked with yourself before.* [laughter]

GILLIAM: You're right. Now you've got it. I've actually made a Terry Gilliam film before. [giggles] When I'm working I become very depressed because I know how complicated it's going to get.

WARDLE: *Why are you always stigmatized with supposedly making films that are "too British"?* Time Bandits *was a hit in the U.S.*

GILLIAM: That's just the standard litany in Hollywood. "It's too British. They won't understand that word." They probably would have said *Four Weddings and a Funeral* was too British, or *The Crying Game* is too British. They don't get it. They are really very nervous, very conservative, worried people. They're terrified of leaping. You watch people in Hollywood rise through the system. They start out fresh and full of ideas, and as they rise, it's all just cut away.

WARDLE: *A lot of the films you made came out of your head. Are you going to go back to doing that?*

GILLIAM: Yeah, I'm trying to get back to that. I'm working on doing *Don Quixote*. It's not my story, but it's my adaptation, the way I want to do it. There's another one, which is the one I really should be doing, called *The Defective Detective*. That's really mine, it was written by myself and Richard LaGravenese. It's about a middle-aged detective who is effectively having a nervous breakdown and ends up in a kid's fantasy world. It's very autobiographical. We've been trying to get it off the ground, but everybody's afraid, because it's so expensive.

WARDLE: *Another film you were supposed to be doing at one time was the film version of Alan Moore's comic book,* Watchmen. *What happened to that?*

GILLIAM: Joel Silver, who produced *Die Hard* and *Lethal Weapon,* said he had a project for me right after *Munchausen,* called *Watchmen.*

WARDLE: *Had you read the comic book at all?*

GILLIAM: No, not at that point. When he gave it to me, I thought it was amazing. The *War and Peace* of comics.

What happened was that Sam Hamm wrote the script. In many ways it had missed the point of the book. It had condensed it. Then Charles McKeown and I rewrote it. The problem with condensing it is, once you pull all the detail out, all the idiosyncratic, quirky elements, it's just a bunch of superheroes. At the time, Joel had done *Die Hard 2,* which had gone way over budget, I had done *Munchausen.* We were both bad guys dragging this very dark story around. They thought *Batman* was dark. *Batman* was bright and breezy compared to *Watchmen.* We couldn't get the money, so the whole thing just fell apart.

I've got some doubt about how well you can translate comic books.

WARDLE: *You would think because it's the only visual medium besides film that uses words and pictures together, that it would be a smooth translation, but it rarely is.*

GILLIAM: Some of the alternative comics are really harsh and violent. If you did that on the screen for two hours, the audience would probably be puking by the end of it. It's controlled on a page. You can wallow in it or not. With some comics, you suddenly realize how silly the dialogue is when you put it in real, moving people.

WARDLE: *It's the same as when you put real people in the costumes.*

GILLIAM: That's what was interesting about Schwarzenegger coming along. He looked like the drawings in a Marvel comic. He had the muscles. There was no great surprise to me that there was this great renaissance of comics on the screen and at the same time the emergence of the Schwarzeneggers of this world. Bruce Willis was in there too. I really think *Die Hard* is a comic book translated. *The Shadow* just laid there and died, and *Dick Tracy* was lame. They were done by people who were far too cultured. Comic books have got to be raw and rough and nasty. My training as a cartoonist is why my films look like that. I was looking at my seven-year-old, Harry, watching *Brazil* with the sound off. It's a comic book. I use wide-angle lenses like the way comic books are drawn. There are lots of shadows and they're fast and furious. *Watchmen* is interesting because it's drawn rather flatly. The drawing style didn't interest me at first, but the more you got into it, it was spot on.

Graphically, it's really good. It's not flashy, but boy, it tells the story. Ultimately with the film, I was worried that if we cut it down to two hours, we'd lose it. I mean, we had to lose the Comedian! Robin Williams wanted to play Rorshach.

WARDLE: *I don't know if that would work.*
GILLIAM: No, I didn't think it would.

WARDLE: *Do you still do any cartooning?*
GILLIAM: No, not seriously, not professionally. I'm always drawing birthday cards, Valentine cards. The walls are covered with them. I do it for the family. I doodle all the time, but I don't draw any real cartoons like I used to. There's always somebody wanting a drawing or a birthday card. I keep thinking I want to be like Will Elder, doing oil painting.

WARDLE: *Do you do it therapeutically? Does it relax you to draw? You're shaking your head.*
GILLIAM: I like drawing, but I would really have to get back into it. I can still draw well. At the end of every film, I do a cartoon about the film and sign it for everyone in the crew. That's what I do.

WARDLE: *What other films are you planning to work on in the near future?*
GILLIAM: Another thing I've been working on is Dickens's *A Tale of Two Cities*. It's ruthless in what it's chosen to show. It's a great script, but it ended up being *Gone with the Wind* by Charles Dickens, which is fine, a good, sweeping epic.

WARDLE: *What other filmmakers have been an influence on your work?*
GILLIAM: I'm very eclectic. Kurosawa, Fellini, Bergman, Buñuel, Walt Disney. Walt Disney! I love those films. *Pinocchio* and things like that. Orson Welles, like everybody. Kubrick was my great hero for a long time. I didn't discover films as films until I was about sixteen or seventeen. I just went to the movies. When we made *Fisher King* I went to the Sundance Institute, this thing Robert Redford runs. We showed *Fisher King* to film students, and one of the other pros there was Stanley Donen who had done *Seven Brides for Seven Brothers, Funny Face, Singin' in the Rain,* and all those great musicals. I looked at a lot of these clips and I realized I should have dedicated *Fisher King*

to him, because he had this huge influence on me. I just never recognized it, because those were just "the movies" that I went to. I loved them, but I had just dismissed them, because by the time I was discovering movies . . .

WARDLE: *They were fluff.*
GILLIAM: That's right, and I was into *The Seventh Seal,* you know, black-and-white European jobs. Those were the films I thought were a big influence, but these other ones were too. Harvey Kurtzman and Willy Elder taught me about filmmaking with their cartoons. I loved Willy's sightgags. I think I'm kind of like all those guys put together, because one side of me is very much like Harvey, trying to control it, define it clearly. Harvey was a genius. I'm torn between the two. The other side of me is like Elder. "Throw everything in it! Fuck it! This makes me laugh." Harvey was an extraordinarily unimpressive person to be this god. [laughter] He was a sweet man.

WARDLE: *Besides the* Mad *guys, what other cartoonists or animators influenced you when you were just starting out as a cartoonist?*
GILLIAM: Tex Avery, Chuck Jones, all that stuff. You can't beat that.

WARDLE: *I couldn't imagine you* not *being a Tex Avery fan.*
GILLIAM: I didn't know who Tex Avery or Chuck Jones was at first. I just knew the cartoons. What's great now is the laserdiscs. You can get the complete Tex Avery collection. My son loves them. It was more surreal than what half of the surreal artists were doing.

WARDLE: *And, just like with your films, the heads of the cartoon units at the studios had no sense of humor and didn't understand the Averys and the Clampetts.*
GILLIAM: The main thing is getting the work up there. Like on this film, [*Twelve Monkeys*] to work at Universal, I said I'd do it, but I get final cut. They don't do that very often, but I said, "We have a history of your interference, so I only do it if I get final cut. When you go to the cinema, sometimes you go to be entertained, sometimes you go to have your perceptions altered, sometimes you want to be elevated. There's a million reasons for going, but the fact is that most people go just to be entertained, because they work their asses off all week. I have no problem with that.

All I ask of the studio system is that it do what the publishing industry does. You have people like Stephen King who sell tons of books, but the publishers also print books by small-time poets and such. Make your *Die Hards* and *Jurassic Parks*, but save a place for the poets and people who are doing something different.

WARDLE: *What about Hand-Made Films? I haven't heard anything about them in a while.*

GILLIAM: It's dead now. Hand-Made was originally George Harrison and his manager, Denis O'Brien, and Python. It was created to do *Life of Brian* and Dennis was running the show. He was the accountant/lawyer/manager and he became our [the Python troupe's] manager. We made *Life of Brian* and *Time Bandits* and then a pile of other films. What often happens in these cases is you've got a guy like Dennis, who is incredibly talented at business and he seems even clearer in his thinking than we do. Us talented guys are not certain what we want to do, what's right or wrong, and are crashing around, but we have certain skills, and he looks around and says, "I'm as talented as they are. I can make better decisions than they can." So, he just started interfering more and more in the films. Python walked away from it basically. Mike Palin did a couple of films there, but it was really a separate operation.

WARDLE: *It doesn't seem like they had a real financial success since* Time Bandits.

GILLIAM: *Time Bandits* was the biggest success that company had. Dennis was interfering and fucking things up. I didn't want to be around it, and it was a real pity because it could've been a good operation. It only collapsed in the last two or three years. Now it's gotten very messy. George is now suing Dennis.

WARDLE: *But George didn't lose a lot of his own money, did he?*

GILLIAM: That's what he's suing about. He thinks he's been ripped off.

WARDLE: *Are you planning any new projects with any of your old Python cohorts?*

GILLIAM: If I was doing a film and there was a part for Mike or John or Terry or Eric, sure, get 'em in there, because they're great. Terry Jones is making *Wind in the Willows* at the moment and he would love to make it as a Python film, because all the parts are perfect for it, but it's not going to hap-

pen that way. John's got Mike in *A Fish Called Wanda 2: Death Fish*, or whatever it's called. To get the group together now, I just don't think we'd work
well together.

WARDLE: *I guess it's similar to the Beatles. They spent all that time together,
and then they didn't want to reunite.*
GILLIAM: Except the Beatles have just done two new songs. I've got to go
over there this afternoon to see about doing a video for it. [laughs] I don't
know if I'm going to do it. It's so funny because they won't let the song out.
I've got to go over to the office to listen to it.

WARDLE: *I don't know how I feel about that. They did the same thing with Nat
King Cole, where Natalie Cole did a duet with her dead father. Drew Friedman did
a scathing panel cartoon showing her in the studio sitting next to the skeleton of
her father, and people were outraged. They thought it was in such bad taste, but I
think what she did is in bad taste! I think the comic is bang-on!*
GILLIAM: That's why I've got to go and talk to them, because I don't see
the point in doing this unless we can do something like that. If they're going
to be too sanctimonious about the whole thing, that's not good, but if we
can have some fun with it. . . . It's like when we did this Python twenty-fifth-
anniversary festival last October out in L.A. One evening was dedicated to
Graham [Chapman]. Then at the end of all the film clips and things, we were
doing a question-and-answer period with the audience, and the moderator
said, "It's a great pity that Graham can't be here with us," and his former
boyfriend David Sherlock said, "But he *is* here," and he pulled out an enve-
lope full of ashes and sprinkled them all over the audience. [laughter]

WARDLE: *Oh my God!*
GILLIAM: People freaked. I don't think most people believed it was really
Graham, but it *was* really Graham! [laughter]

WARDLE: *It's like when Cleese, at the funeral, said, "Graham Chapman, the cowriter of the Dead Parrot Sketch, is no more. He has ceased to be. He's expired and
gone to meet his maker," and did the whole speech. If it was anybody else, you'd
say it was tasteless, but you know if Graham was watching from wherever he is, he
was laughing his head off.*

GILLIAM: Yeah. Mike was very funny at that too. He said, "It's hard to believe that Graham isn't here. He's just late, as usual."

WARDLE: *Have you ever thought of doing a children's book?*
GILLIAM: Yeah, I have a couple that are written in my head. I never get around to doing it.

WARDLE: *Maybe in your retirement.*
GILLIAM: This is it. You've got to stretch things out. That's always been my theory. You don't want to do everything all at once.

I've got a couple of good stories. It's getting very weird at the moment, because I've got too many choices. I've reached a point where I don't know which story I want to tell anymore. After *Fisher King,* I went a bit crazy. I was desperate 'cause suddenly I was fifty years old and I could count the number of films on one hand that I'm going to do in the rest of my life. I went manic trying to get the next film going very quickly, and it turned out to be the longest gap between films that I've ever had.

WARDLE: *Why don't you do more performing?*
GILLIAM: Because I'm too busy trying to direct films.

WARDLE: *Do you ever get asked to appear in other people's films?*
GILLIAM: Yes, I always turn them down. Actually, I'm in *Spies Like Us.* Remember the John Landis film with Chevy Chase and Dan Aykroyd? It was a really over-the-top performance. I was a Swiss doctor in Afghanistan. I just did a series for the BBC that went out at the beginning of this year, a five-part series on the beginning of cinema. So, I'm actually doing different characters in it, but it's not that great. I don't really enjoy performing that much now.

WARDLE: *When you were talking about the characters you played in the Python films, it sounded like you had a lot of fun with it.*
GILLIAM: I did, but they were short and to the point. Anything like a serious bit of performing, I don't think so. There were some French people who wanted me to be an actor in this film they were doing, and I talked my way out of it. I just didn't feel comfortable. With the makeup and all, I can disguise myself. I don't want to go up there looking like me.

WARDLE: *What do you think is the biggest misconception about you as a film-maker?*

GILLIAM: I've always had a hard time knowing how I'm perceived, to be honest. You tell me some of the preconceptions. [laughs]

WARDLE: *I guess that you're irresponsible with money, that you just hate author-ity figures, you hate working within the studio system.*

GILLIAM: The one misconception is that I'm irresponsible with money, and that's totally wrong. All you have to do is look at what I've done, and most of the films were done for a fraction of what anybody else would've made them for. The resistance to authority, yeah, totally, and I don't think that's a misconception. I think it's absolutely right, because the people in authority are people I don't respect. If they were people I respected, it might be dif-ferent.

WARDLE: *It's like people who cheat on their taxes. If they felt that the govern-ment was doing good things with their money, they wouldn't feel it was necessary to rip off the government.*

GILLIAM: We're living in a very funny time. Historically the taxman has always been the enemy. Jesus and Mary, they ran from them.

WARDLE: *Even in the parables: "Why does he eat with tax collectors?"*

GILLIAM: There you go. The odd element of democracy is that somehow, we're all supposed to pay our taxes. Then we're good citizens. Bullshit! [gig-gles]

WARDLE: *Meanwhile, they take that money, line their pockets, and* then *get around to fixing the streets and so on.*

GILLIAM: Yeah. Belief in democracy was that it was going to cut through all that crap, all the cheating, the corruption. That's what *Brazil* is about. No matter what the system is, it always goes corrupt. The Maoist theory of con-stant revolution is probably closer to my feeling about things. You've got to constantly throw them out, because they're all corrupt, then you start all over and throw *them* out too. Democracy wasn't set up like that. The idea was that elections would do that, but what it didn't take into account was the civil service, the bureaucracy is in there, but all systems are kind of fucked, so you have to keep breaking them down and starting again. But most people don't want that.

WARDLE: *During the Eisenhower years, there was a feeling that you weren't supposed to question the government. You were just supposed to accept it.*
GILLIAM: You can actually live very nicely without it. I mean, I stopped taking the newspapers for a couple of years. It didn't make any difference. You just get on with what you want to do. It's particularly difficult if you've been raised to be concerned about what goes on, educated to be the people who are trying to make a better world. We're supposed to care about what happens in Rwanda and Bosnia. The fact is, you become totally overwhelmed by the whole thing. I used to get completely depressed because I'd been trained to take this information and try to do something about it, and all I was feeling day after day was more impotent because I couldn't do anything about it and it was driving me fucking bananas! I was supposed to be caring about that little kid starving to death, and I couldn't do it anymore. I just said, "Fuck it! I can't care anymore." I care about what's immediate and plow on. I think that's one of the negative effects of having television thrust in your face day in and day out. People then just start backing away from it.

WARDLE: *Before television, you only knew the news in your area. If you saw a homeless person, you could help him. But when you see the global problem of homeless people . . .*
GILLIAM: That's the problem with the global community. It exists on many levels, but you can't deal with it. That's why there's so many separatist movements everywhere, because people are trying to get back a community that means something. The communist thing about getting rid of the family and having the state educate the children, it doesn't work! Families are still the best unit. The problem with families is we can't afford them anymore. The biggest problem is the number of people on the planet, so why's everybody worrying about diseases and wars? I would encourage diseases and wars. It's nature trying to cut it down. I'm fighting for more wars and more disease! [laughter]

WARDLE: *You can't say that to people. They think you're being callous.*
GILLIAM: That's why the right-to-lifers are just so far wrong. The one problem is there's too *much* life on the planet. The sanctity of human life is being

destroyed by the quantity of human life. I love when the right-to-lifers bomb abortion clinics. I love it! This is why, as you get older, you become more and more . . . not cynical, but I do like the irony of life. [laughter]

WARDLE: *One final question: Do you think there'll ever be a time in your life when you'll either be too old or too successful to still be silly?*
GILLIAM: [giggles] I hope not. That's why my company letterhead is Poo Poo Pictures. I keep thinking that one day I'll grow up, but it hasn't happened. I haven't worked life out at all. I keep hoping I'll get some answers by the time I die. I'm fifty-five this year. I think my silliness keeps me young. Mike Palin and I used to always say that there were people who sat at the back of the class and giggled. We were those people. I was on a radio show in Dallas after the release of *Munchausen* and somebody called who had seen it, and in this southern drawl he said [imitating southern U.S. drawl], "That was just great, Terry. I giggled in awe." That perfectly describes my feelings about things. It's so fucking wonderful you can't bow down and develop solemn tones about it, all you can do is giggle. I want that on my tombstone: "Terry Gilliam . . . He giggled in awe."

Notes

1. *Beyond the Fringe* was a British satirical revue which for years ran very successfully on the stage. It starred Peter Cook, Dudley Moore, Jonathan Miller, and Alan Bennett and was a huge influence on the direction of British comedy in the 1960s and 1970s, especially on the careers of Marty Feldman and the future members of Monty Python. *Cambridge Circus* was a separate show which grew out of England's Cambridge University Footlights revues which became training grounds for many future British comedy legends such as John Cleese, Peter Cook, David Frost, Graham Chapman, and Eric Idle.

2. *The Goon Show* was England's most groundbreaking radio show of all time, elevating silliness to an artform. Beginning on BBC radio in 1951, it launched the careers of Peter Sellers, Spike Milligan, and Harry Secombe, and influenced generations of British comedians. One of the main producers of the show was future Beatles record producer George Martin.

3. The undertaker sketch appeared on the last show of the second season of *Monty Python's Flying Circus,* and signaled the beginning of BBC censorial interference on the show. Many found it offensive when John Cleese, playing a grieving son, enters the undertaker parlor carrying his dead mother in a sack, leading to the undertaker (played by Graham Chapman) describing in nauseatingly funny detail what will happen to her. When he sees that she was "quite young," Chap-

man suggests they cannibalize the body. When Cleese's character registers shock at this suggestion, Chapman reassures him with: "Look, we'll eat your mum, then if you feel a bit guilty afterwards, we can dig a grave and you can throw up into it." Several other sketches and Gilliam cartoons about cannibalism preceded this one on the episode.

Monkey Business

NIGEL FOUNTAIN/1996

BRIEFLY JOIN Terry Gilliam's lope through Soho; Bushwacker hat, dusty black coat, splendidly amiable, piratical demeanour. After his last movie, *The Fisher King*, made money he went back to the same studio with the same screenwriter, Richard LaGravenese, to propose another deal and got nowhere.

"I can't believe it," he said to them. "I just made you guys all this money. Come on! I've now done what I am supposed to do, produce a success. Where's the payback?"

He says he gets excited about everything, which, on the evidence of our meeting, is true. "But," he adds, "nothing to do with Hollywood. Not until it happens." What happens in mid-April is the British release of his new apocalyptic film *Twelve Monkeys*, with Bruce Willis, Madeleine Stowe, and Brad Pitt, largely shot in Philadelphia and Baltimore.

A couple of weeks ago I watched again another apocalyptic film, one from my late adolescence—*La Jetée*, directed by Chris Marker. The credits open to the sound of jet airliners, very sixties modern. "This," intones the narrator, "is the story of a man marked by an image of his childhood." It starts at Paris Orly Airport, "sometime before the outbreak of World War III." The scene deals with a boy witnessing the murder of an unknown man; the persisting image is that of a young woman.

Marker's movie for me, then, was my primary access to a world beyond

Hollywood. Marker, now seventy-five, predated and postdated France's New Wave. He is a man who eschews publicity, a student of Jean-Paul Sartre in the thirties, friend of Simone Signoret, resistance fighter, editor on Alain Resnais's stunning Auschwitz short, *Night and Fog,* and a socialist. He made *La Jetée,* a twenty-nine-minute masterpiece, in 1962. A movie almost devoid of moving images—only for a second does a character, magically, open her eyes—it is a narrative collage of stills about a post-nuked world and an "emissary thrown into time" to restart history.

The emissary, with haunted eyes, somber expression, survived amidst his German-whispering scientist/guards because he had the secret of survival in another time, an image from the past. And "he wanted the world of his childhood."

Back in 1996, Terry Gilliam gets to be the eternal kid, living in worlds inside his head. "And doing silly things like making movies." We are in a Soho office discussing his contribution to the Hayward Gallery's *Spellbound: Art and Film* exhibition—a wall of 100 grey filing-cabinet drawers—and *Twelve Monkeys.*

The film's sound track begins with swirling wind, yielding to Argentinian accordion music—the sound of an industrial society that never quite made it—and a child's eyes stare out of the screen; another airport is in the offing. The credits acknowledge *Twelve Monkeys'* inspiration—*La Jetée.*

Hollywood's visions of the future were shaped in the eighties by an English director with American stars, Ridley Scott with *Blade Runner,* and by an American Londoner with mainly English actors, Gilliam with *Brazil. Blade Runner* was coscripted by David Peoples. *Twelve Monkeys* is coscripted by Peoples—who moved on to write Clint Eastwood's *Unforgiven*—and his wife Jan.

Twelve Monkeys' inception was a corporate affair. An English executive at Universal passed the script to Gilliam, who thought it was great and the ending extraordinary. Much earlier, says the director, an executive producer had shown the Peopleses *La Jetée,* with the idea that they might do a remake. The Peopleses said they didn't do remakes but there were some interesting ideas there.

You must have seen *La Jetée,* I say to Gilliam. He did, but just four weeks ago. He says: "I didn't want to be influenced by *La Jetée.* I was making this script which was influenced by it. I finally talked to Marker two and a half weeks ago. He's in Paris working on a film—him, a computer, and a girl. He can do it all there."

Gilliam can't, but, at $30 million, *Twelve Monkeys* is cheap for Hollywood. When I talked to Keith Fulton and Lou Pepe, two film school graduates making *The Hamster Project*, a movie about *Twelve Monkeys*, they observed that the director almost posed it as Los Angeles versus London. American hierarchy versus English group effort. "It's the British television tradition maybe," said Pepe, "that way of working."

It hasn't always worked for Gilliam. After *Brazil* came *The Adventures of Baron Munchausen*—hailed, denounced, and a financial war zone which unjustly earned him notoriety as an overspender.

"That battle didn't bother me particularly . . ." then Gilliam thinks, collapses into laughter, dances with the absurdity of it all. "Didn't bother me? I hated it! A nightmare! The worst time of my life!" The money was gone, his assets threatened, and his wife was pregnant. Then he made *Fisher King*.

"I go galloping out to Hollywood every few years with a big bag," he says. "I want to get it filled with money, without any strings attached and have control of what I'm doing. For better or worse I pulled it off time and time again. That's all I really fight for. Let me fuck it up, not you guys. The only one I have any problem with is *Munchausen*."

Twelve Monkeys has none of *La Jetée*'s vision of a lost world of modernity. Gilliam's locations are the gutted industrial landscapes of the United States' eastern seaboard, alternating between the lower depths and that brightly lit, blinding Gilliam color. The future is filmed in our present past, in derelict power stations, where burrowing scientists construct cocoon-like time machines. The present is contemporary Baltimore and Philadelphia.

The Eastern State Penitentiary built by Quakers—"with the best of intentions," says Gilliam—in the 1820s, denounced by Dickens (*American Notes*) in the 1840s and finally vacated in 1971, houses *Twelve Monkeys*' lunatics.

Gilliam, born in Minnesota and raised in the new California of the end-of-ideology fifties, had never visited Baltimore or Philadelphia. But to anyone watching his films over the years, Philly, great city of the Enlightenment, seems almost a theme park of his obsessions, an eighteenth-century street-grid system, boulevards, beaux arts, rococo theaters; in the twenties a Tudor skyscraper went up; in the eighties glass highrises reflected revitalization amid factories devastated as industrialism yielded to disinformation technology. In Gilliam's *Munchausen* the credits announce "the Age Of Reason"—

which is promptly followed by a brisk cannonade. In *Twelve Monkeys* science's steel claws scoop Willis from incarceration in the lower depths.

"Philly is a bull's eye," says Gilliam. "Rich suburbs, they're white; then you go into the inner city, a black ring; then 'center city' where the business is and it goes white again. You get into the city hall and all the civil servants are black. Then you meet the mayor—and he's white. The film," he goes on, "is decay, nostalgia, loss, death, and resurrection. Here was this great, lovely city, that wonderful city hall."

It is by the city hall, into a snow-covered landscape patrolled by a prowling bear, that Gilliam's hero first emerges. Sixties nightmares were nuclear physics and superpowers; the nineties dish out biological disaster and terrorism. *Twelve Monkeys* was made through the Oklahoma bombing and released into British BSE. And while *La Jetée* offered its anonymous emissary, *Twelve Monkeys* provides, sheathed in plastic, a Durexed projectile spurted from the future into the unsafe fucked-up nineties. He's bald, bullet-headed and Bruce Willis.

According to Gilliam, people are confused by superstars, resenting them and creeping around them. "It's a very weird relationship." So I ask if it was difficult with Willis. Gilliam says he wouldn't say it was easy. Willis was trying to give the director what he wanted but he is a guy who has always been in control. So Willis would say well, whatever Terry wanted, just tell him, and Gilliam would say, "That's not exactly what I want. It's not for me to tell you what to do. I want you to find within yourself this stuff." Gilliam decided never to confront him, because Bruce felt better when he could shove and push and that was exactly what this tortured character was not supposed to do.

They would talk for hours sometimes, the director trying to wear down his defensive pushing attitude, never arguing, until they got to moments on film when there was total vulnerability, exposure, no cleverness, moments when he lost control. Willis turned into a very good tragic figure, says Gilliam.

The audience's route into the movie is via the shrink straining to sort out Willis, played by Madeleine Stowe. She provides what there is of stability amidst the time warps and Brad Pitt–induced madness. In Gilliam films, women—Kim Greist, the mocking dream girl in *Brazil*; Sarah Polley, the twelve-year-old sceptic in *Munchausen*—tend to be the balance, core, notes of realism, while the hero flies to the moon and the director slams his foot down on the narrative gas and steers into fiery horsemen, demons, scientists, and satanic repair men. There is a slice of the old—but decent—hippy in Gilliam.

"She [Madeleine] was the anchor," he says, "the source of reason, such a critical character, but what I liked was the way her feet seemed to be firmly on the ground but then the ground starts sliding away. Look, the film tightropes so much, it could slide over into bathos, or some cheap sci-fi movie, and I was trying to walk that line. We were all very nervous most of the time, and Madeleine and I spent ages talking. Working with her didn't demand the kind of relationships I had to have with Bruce and Brad. She was someone I could talk to all the time. She was like my psychiatrist."

He shrugs. Women are the muse, he goes on, leading him into dangerous areas when he falls in love, and the women with whom he has had long-term relationships are the solid people in a life where baroque and enlightenment fight it out. The baroque side is still expanding. "It's like you're a kid and you play and imagine everything—and that's baroque." (I remember Munchausen's gondola, sheered from its hot air balloon, sewn from women's bloomers, hurtling through space.)

And then, for kids, comes school, he continues, analysis, categories. "The minute that Adam started naming animals, that was the end of it. For me if you gotta name for a thing, you can control it."

Gilliam's wall at *Spellbound* is a monument to categories and chaos. There is that English surrealism which, forced into acceptance of an immutable social order, the absence of revolutions, invasions, decapitation of monarchs, floats off into fantasy, draws on the wall. Gilliam is in England because he likes a humor that deals with the system's madness, but the American in him strains beyond it. Gilliam, the boot in Python, observes a decade when everybody has given up. "I don't know what we talk about in this country. There is just this awful acceptance."

All 100 drawers at the Hayward are labeled. Ships in the Night, Vox Populying Bastards, Birth of a Notion, Communications with the Outside World . . . *Brazil's* 1948/84 technologies interbred with microchips and extinguished Jonathan Pryce while crystallizing Gilliam's affair with the filing cabinet.

Onto the rear of the wall excerpts of *Twelve Monkeys* are projected—stuff art, we're talking great promo here—and distorted images spill out past the onlookers. Stowe murmurs, Willis pleads, Pitt cackles.

I stuck around when the lights came up and they rewound the film, so then I watched the new crowd watching the wall. They were tentative. Did the drawers open? Was it allowed? Did you touch? A brave woman stepped forward, opened a drawer, light cascaded out. She turned out to be a Swedish-based Romanian. The crowd surged forward, emboldened explorers, sifters. I checked out a drawer labeled The Public Speaks . . . and Speaks . . . and Speaks. It was stuffed with copies of a questionnaire from a Washington, D.C. *Twelve Monkeys* preview screening.

"*Why did you rate the ending that way?*" it said. A Washingtonian had retorted: "I liked the fact that everything didn't turn out great."

"*What parts of the movie did you find confusing?*" "When he appeared in 1991 all of a sudden," came the reply.

And then, as an afterthought, "the scientists."

I went back to the Birth of a Notion drawer, which contained Gilliam's notebooks, and a small stuffed bear. The damn bear had moved since I had last looked, and the rubber gloves protruding into the side of the cabinet had been screwed up. I was irritated, people are so *thoughtless*. I stood on a ladder and observed my fellow researchers. We looked like time-traveling quality controllers. Gilliam had turned the present into a past, and we were implicated. I thumbed obsessively through the notebooks. "Never forget the Tunisian charcoal makers!" he had observed.

Why not? I asked him later.

"You're in these scrubby desert flatlands and these mounds would rise up and smoke steamed out of them and these dark figures were moving around and it was so medieval. I've got to put them in a film!"

We talk about the Washington screening. "There was a discussion afterwards. I said one of the things that intrigued me about the film was that it was very anti-American in that there is a sense of fatalism in it, an idea that you can't fix everything. Certain things are beyond one's control. This guy got up and he's really pissed off and he referred to my attitude as 'the pornography of fatalism.' I said great, there's a book there, because he was an American and he couldn't accept it. Americans do believe you can fix it all."

After a while at the Hayward a man had come up and stared at me. "Are you part of the exhibit?" he asked.

Time and the Machine

NICK JAMES/1996

T ERRY G ILLIAM OUGHT to be experiencing *déjà vu*. What should have happened after *The Fisher King* is happening now. He has a hit movie in *Twelve Monkeys,* with major stars Bruce Willis, Brad Pitt, and Madeleine Stowe, which he brought in for a modest (by Hollywood standards) $30 million and is now "a very popular boy" in Hollywood. His turning *The Fisher King* into a successful vehicle for Robin Williams and Jeff Bridges was much the same thing, and it also proved he could work with other people's ideas and material. But its success was somehow forgotten, and a three-year hiatus of unresolved projects followed, right up until he was presented with David and Janet Peoples' script for *Twelve Monkeys.*

Twelve Monkeys is a complex time-travel thriller about a convict, James Cole (Willis), from a desolated 2035, when a killer virus has wiped out most of mankind. He is coerced into traveling back in time to 1996—just before the epidemic broke out—to discover the source of the virus, not to prevent the cataclysm but for the future's research. Arriving by mistake in 1990, he is diagnosed as a dangerous lunatic. Sent to an institution where he befriends another patient, Jeffrey Goines (Pitt), he is put in the care of Dr. Kathryn Railly (Stowe). Yanked back and forth through time again, he once more meets up in 1996 with Railly and Goines, who both prove to be crucial players in the events unleashing the virus.

The script is based on Chris Marker's twenty-nine-minute 1962 film/*photo*

From *Sight and Sound,* vol. 6, no. 4 (April 1996): 14–16. Reprinted by permission of *Sight and Sound.*

roman, La Jetée. Like Marker's protagonist, Cole is haunted by a single image from childhood—an airport shooting—and *La Jetée*'s existential melancholy finds its way into Gilliam's film. But the Peoples scriptwriting team have spun Marker's narrative into a fable of interleaving worlds, each connected to the other and all located in Baltimore and Philadelphia.

NICK JAMES: *There are several worlds within* Monkeys—*the Philadelphia of today, the virus-ridden desolate above-ground world of 2035, the underground future world where the surviving humans have rebuilt society using ad-hoc mixtures of technologies. Where did all those images come from?*

TERRY GILLIAM: This film was less about design than "found art." We didn't storyboard it. I've got this little Hi-8 camera which I'm taking everywhere because I trust it more than my eyes. We went to Philadelphia and Baltimore because the script named them. Philadelphia has an amazing mixture of architecture, nice nineteenth-century stuff and '20s power stations which are now disused. A series of civilizations lived and died there. The City Hall is this wonderful Beaux Arts building which we used as a centerpiece for the above-ground future, which we got because the mayor controlled it. He said: "It's yours, you can use it." So I didn't really have any specific images when we started.

NJ: *Throughout the film there's the idea that time travel may be a figment of Cole's delusional imagination. But you then go out and find already existing places to transform into what he imagines.*

TG: I made choices based on keeping the audience uncertain about what is real and what isn't. For example, the present-day mental hospital dayroom, where Cole is locked up, is built like a wheel with spokes and a hub, and we used just one section where three of these seemingly endless quarters headed off. I've always used architecture as if it was a character, so it seemed to me this trifurcated room was right for multiple personalities. In three ways it extended to infinity—or escape or the future—and which one do you choose? If I want to use that room, I find a way of justifying it, that's the way I make movies.

NJ: *Bruce Willis brings a certain known persona with him. How do you deal with that when making something so different from his usual vehicles?*

TG: Bruce wanted to do it and I was certain he could be right. We talked and he asked me, "Do you think I bring the wrong kind of baggage to this show, do you think that who I am could hurt the film?" It's swings and roundabouts. People may not go see it because they don't like Bruce Willis films. But what they really mean by that is that they don't like *Die Hard* and *The Last Boy Scout*. I'd heard all sorts of stories about entourages, and I told him, "I don't want Bruce Willis the superstar around this film, but Bruce Willis the actor. You've got to come here like a monk. You've got to be naked in every sense and you've got to make yourself vulnerable. You've got to trust me—and you can't direct the film." There are trappings you'll never get rid of because he's become accustomed to them, but they didn't get in the way.

N J : *Why do you think you identify so much with objects from the redundant past?*
T G : I love things from the industrial revolution because I can understand gears and pulleys, cars and wheels. I don't get the electronic revolution because I can't get my hands on it. I'm impotent. I think that's growing up in the country—if something broke you had to fix it, and so without that ability I get very frustrated. So a lot of the gear you see in my films is harking back to some kind of Victoriana.

N J : *If you think of where your ideas come from, what was the key original influence?*
T G : It was listening to radio. I lived out in the country so it was a Tom Sawyer world of dirt roads, trees, forests, and lakes. There was *The Shadow* and *Let's Pretend* and *The Fat Man*: a whole world in sound and you had to invent the faces, the costumes, and the sets. Even the films I grew up watching were the big epics and all the escapist films—I loved that. All these different worlds out there to be seen and experienced. It didn't matter if they were a thousand years old or in the future or from the present.

N J : *Do you think you'll follow the "found art" process again?*
T G : Everything is now designed to avoid me getting depressed, because if I have a very clear image in my head, and we can't do it, I just go into a spin, and I keep fighting that. There's a shot in the opening of the film when we first see the decaying city. We shot it and I just didn't think it worked. It took weeks before I said, all right, we will just have to use it because we don't have time and money to do it the way I want it. Things always cost that extra bit

because I've got this eye that demands feeding. So you make this leap into commercial filmmaking. It was interesting watching the distribution of this one because they were very clever. It was released just after Christmas and a lot of the big guys, *Nixon, Casino,* were stumbling. The exhibitors wanted them desperately until they started failing, and then ours took off. Out goes *Nixon,* out goes *Casino,* in comes ours—ruthless! So the question is, can you make films in that system that are intelligent and demanding? That's what intrigued me about this one, because I think we've done it. We've pulled off an art film.

Dreams

PHIL STUBBS / 1997

'' IT'S COMING TOGETHER. When you first put it together, you've chosen the block of marble, and somewhere in there is the film, is the statue. It's like chipping away. . . . You chip away and it comes closer to the thing you've imagined.''

It's early December 1997, and Terry Gilliam is in his office in the West End of London—working on the post-production of his latest project, *Fear and Loathing in Las Vegas,* based on the '70s writings of Hunter S. Thompson.

Gilliam wrote the script with assistance from Tony Grisoni, at a frenzied pace. It was put together in eight days. He rejected it, and a further script took two days to prepare. Filming took place in Las Vegas during the summer, and the project has attracted many famous faces. Johnny Depp is the hero, with Benicio Del Toro as his attorney. Also cropping up during the movie will be Christina Ricci, Gary Busey, Cameron Diaz, Lyle Lovett, Harry Dean Stanton, and Ellen Barkin, among others.

Here, he talks to *Dreams* about *Fear and Loathing,* and his possible next project, *The Defective Detective,* about a burnt-out cop who ends up in a child's fantasy world.

Q : *What have you been doing this morning, Terry?*
A : We've been trying to put some music on the film. We're at that stage—fiddling with music. One room is busy trimming the film shorter. And I'm in the other room where we're slamming sounds on.

Q: *Music will be crucial to a project like this.*

A: Yes, there's a lot of different kinds of music on this thing. It keeps shifting gears and we can use the music to tell the audience where they are. In a lot of cases we're using stuff that's obvious, it's obvious music. The film itself needs signposts along the trail and the music is one way of doing this.

Q: *How do you feel about the movie at the moment?*

A: You've got a book and you write a script that hopefully captures the book which still works as a script and then you go and shoot the movie and you deal with all the realities of shooting. Some things go the way you want and some things don't, but then you put together ways that you intended when you wrote it and shot it and you realize that half the stuff doesn't work that way. So then you start shifting it around. What's so interesting about this stage is trying to find the best film from all of the stuff we've done as opposed to the best version of the script or the best version of the book.

Q: *I read a couple of days ago that Katherine Helmond was in the movie. She's given you two of your best performances—Mrs. Ogre and Mrs. Lowry. What role have you given her in this one?*

A: Unfortunately, she has a very small one. She turns into a moray eel. She's a reception clerk in a hotel. She becomes a moray eel. Due to the effects of LSD on the hero.

Q: *Do you think there'll be a controversy when the movie is released?*

A: Probably. I hope the movie becomes fairly controversial. I hope it makes a noise—I don't want it to go unnoticed. A lot of people will get angry but they'll probably get angry for the wrong reasons, though. I actually don't think it's a drug movie, strangely enough.

Q: *Why is that?*

A: If you make a film where people are at a bar drinking and smoking a lot, you don't say it's an alcoholics' movie, or a smokers' movie. It's not about that. The fuel may be drugs, just like in other movies, with Sam Spade the fuel may be alcohol and cigarettes. What we do is allow our characters to get caught in a distorted world, which is already distorted by reality. We make it an altered reality, which may be for the better and sometimes for the worse, depending on how much you have just imbibed.

Q : *Do we get to see the bats?*

A : Oh, I'm not gonna tell you that . . . you gotta pay your money!!!

Q : *What assistance did you get from Hunter S. Thompson?*

A : Hunter was on the end of the phone quite a bit. What was the most useful thing was that Johnny spent a lot of time with him. And basically stole a lot of his clothing and his car, which were then used in the movie!!!

Q : *Are there any filing cabinets in the movie?*

A : Let me see, I don't think so, I think this may be free . . . there is a cage in the movie. There's always been cages in my movies.

Q : *And in* The Defective Detective *there's Nicolas Cage . . . ?*

A : There you go, see.

Q : *Has* The Defective Detective *been green-lighted yet?*

A : No. This is one of the long unclotting open wounds that I carry with me. You're pushing a project up the hill and then it rolls back on top of you. You push it up and it rolls back again. I'm not sure if we're pushing it up or if it's rolling back at the moment.

Q : *I understand that in* The Defective Detective, *you intend to film some of the fantasy sequences that you were unable to do in* Brazil. *Is this true?*

A : Not really. The script started from me going into my files and my drawers and digging out all the bits I'd cut out of *Brazil* and *Munchausen* and everything else I'd ever done. These are all good bits, let's knit them together. And some of them have found their way in and some haven't. It was a starting point, really.

Q : *Would it share more with* Brazil, Time Bandits, *and* Munchausen *than your other movies . . . ?*

A : It's all of 'em—it combines all of those elements. It's all of those things— like *Fanny and Alexander* was kind of a compendium of all the best of Bergman. That's the idea on this one.

Q : *Do you intend to shoot in the U.K. or in the U.S.?*

A : Well, the idea was that I'd do it here. I mean, it's proving to be a very frustrating project. It's the one I want to do and it's the one that keeps eluding me and, because of different glitches that come along, I end up doing other films like *Twelve Monkeys* and *Fear and Loathing.* I've had this ever since I finished *Fisher King* a few years ago.

Q: *Is* Don Quixote *still a possible future project?*

A: Well, again, it's another one that floats around. I've never felt we'd got the script right; it's a very complex project to get it right. It's a bit like a painter who's got several canvasses going at once. You walk away from it for a bit and don't look at it. And you look back at it and you begin to see what's right and what's wrong. And this is one we haven't got right yet. That's all I can say.

Q: *I understand that during the filming of* Munchausen *you met Fellini—what happened?*

A: Actually, the first time I met him was when Jonathan Pryce and I were in Rome promoting *Brazil.* He was shooting *Ginger and Fred.* We went down to the set—he was a big hero. What was interesting about being in Rome [making *Munchausen*] was that there I was in Cinecittà with Dante Ferretti, who had designed several of his films. I was on Fellini's home turf with his people—an interloper clearly. Federico would pop into the art department—my office was in the middle of the art department. He would pop in occasionally and he would bless the whole thing and walk out.

One of the funniest things was when he was shooting *Intervista,* he actually put Mastroianni up in this Mandrake the Magician costume in a tree right outside the door of my office in the art department so we couldn't get in and out while he was shooting. He was saying, "This is mine; this is my place. You work when I let you." He was great; I just loved him. And then during the course of the film, there were several dinners arranged which never quite happened, and then finally on the very last night before I left Rome after we'd finished shooting, finally I had dinner with him and Giulietta Masina and Dante Ferretti, and it was great. One of the great memories was wandering around after dinner around the Trevi fountain arm in arm with Fellini—that was worth all the pain of *Munchausen.*

Q: *How do you feel about the pain of* Munchausen, *now? Do you feel you have learned from it, adding to your experiences, or do you box it away at the back of your mind?*

A: It all goes into the computer. Certain things you don't do again. And there's certain things you do. It's because it was so painful that I'm not really the best judge of the whole thing. The pity is . . . the thing that bothers me the most was not the making of the film, or any of that. It was the final hurdle in dealing with the studio, trying to get them to show an interest in the movie.

I agreed to cut it down to under two hours. I think it probably would have been a better film at two hours and five minutes. It just needed a bit more space and air around it. And I did, and I mean it was my cut, but they made all the noises that if I cooperated with them they would then get behind the thing, and that was then what they didn't do. That was a big betrayal and that's what hurts the most, not anything else. It's the only time I made a trim for political reasons and it didn't pay off. That's what really is painful, because the film would benefit from a few more minutes in there. It's a pacing thing. It's not about scenes; it's about pacing.

Q: *In* The Fisher King, *Tom Waits puts in a really memorable performance. I've been a fan of Tom for ages. It was a real shock to see him since he wasn't credited. How did Tom get involved?*
A: He was a friend of Jeff Bridges, basically. He said, "You ought to meet Tom." It's funny, because when I met him and even in the course of making the film, I'd never heard a Tom Waits record. I'd never listened to them at all. I just met him and liked him immediately. So into the film he went, and he was great. The studio was trying to cut him out. They felt it wasn't advancing the narrative in any significant way, so they thought that was things that could go. They were totally wrong.

Q: *There's been a lot of discussion regarding* Twelve Monkeys *about the insurance woman at the end. Was the intention of that scene to close any ambiguities in the movie? Or should the ambiguities remain open?*
A: I think there are several ambiguities, but the intention was in our minds, there was no question that she was the scientist from the future. My reading of the whole thing is that she gets the virus with which she is able to go back to the future and eventually save the future. Five billion people still die—all that's necessary. So it was a very long-term solution!!!

Quite honestly, I like the fact there's all of this discussion. I just read something on PythOnline—the whole thing about the kid—is it all in the kid's head. I think that's wonderful, so I don't want to limit the possibilities. Certainly our intention was that she is the scientist. She does get the virus and she goes back to the future and somehow allows the future generations of her generation to eventually reclaim the earth. A lot of people can't accept the idea that five billion people have to die in the course of all this.

Q : *Quentin Tarantino has said that you taught him the importance of delegation in moviemaking, but I understand you have very specific demands about what goes on screen. How do your relationships with other artists on the movie actually work?*
A : You gather hopefully a really good group of people and then spend a lot of time talking about what you're trying to do. I don't spend a great deal of time saying, "Roger [Pratt], you've got to light it like this." We'll talk about it. It's a very collaborative thing. You discuss it—they've got ideas and I've got ideas and we tend to leapfrog. I start with a specific idea and they come up with a better one and I come up with a better one and they come up with a better one. It works that way, so if everything is rolling right, my function is just to be the filter, to say, "Yes, that goes in, and that doesn't go in."

I end up getting what I want, but I can't say that I did it. Some directors I hear about are just so specific. They leave no room for creative partners to do anything and I don't want that. I want everybody to bring their own skills to the film and then I take full credit for the whole thing in the end. That's where the unfairness comes in. It's a lie. You can print that!

Q : *I understand that in March '98, you're going to meet up in Aspen with your Python colleagues.*
A : There's this comedy festival there and we all seem to have agreed to turn up there for an evening of I don't know what. It's really I think just a Q&A.

Q : *Do you expect to put any firm plans together at that meeting?*
A : Well, when we got together in May we decided we were seriously going to talk about doing another film. And in October, Mike, Terry, and Eric were supposed to be getting together to get started. They didn't, so nothing's happened so far, so we'll get together in March in Aspen. We'll talk again and see what happens. I think it's less likely than we thought it was going to be in May. We all seem to be so stuck in doing our own things now.

Q: *You said before that you go to Hollywood to get a bag of money and you go away and make your movies. If you didn't get any money from Hollywood in the future for whatever reason, what would you do with the rest of your life?*

A: Go to France and get money. Go to Germany and get money. Go everywhere else and get money!!! What's interesting about *Twelve Monkeys* was that 52 percent of the budget was from England, Germany, France, and Japan. So it was really a coproduction, and on this one even though Universal has come in, there's been a lot of presales before Universal got in, to Germany and France. It's kind of a hybrid—there's a lot of money floating around in Europe at the moment. The trick is that if I can't get it in the States then I'll go elsewhere, and ultimately I'll have to reduce the scale of what I'm trying to do to whatever I can get. It's as simple as that.

Q: *What future work remains on* Fear and Loathing?

A: In the next few weeks we'll get a fine cut of the thing and then the soundtrack becomes the biggest thing, plus a lot of the opticals and the special effects that're still in the works. The idea hopefully is that we'll be done in time for Cannes.

Q: *So it'll be ready for May.*

A: Yeah. And I think they're talking about releasing it in the States in May as well.

Q: *Are you hoping it's going in competition?*

A: I don't care if it goes in competition or not. It doesn't really matter to me. I just wanna make sure we've got the best film we can get out of it. So far the thing seems to be forming itself nicely.

On Being an Impish God

PAUL WELLS/1997

B LOWN UP TO billboard dimensions, the marble busts, cardboard dummies, and Victorian nannies have a fie-fo-fum menace, more threateningly funny than ever . . .

Terry Gilliam's now celebrated animated links in *Monty Python's Flying Circus* were the first animated films that I recognized as specifically distinctive from American "cartoons" in the Disney, Warner Brothers, MGM style. They seemed to share the same language as the cartoon but possessed an altogether more subversive edge. As a teenager I could not fully determine what made these links challenging and somehow "taboo"; now it becomes clear that Gilliam's imagery speaks to adult audiences through the "naïveté" of the animated form. Gilliam's simple yet iconoclastic pictorial juxtapositions make direct comic statements but also suggest alternative meanings by exploiting the assumed innocence of both cartoonal imagery itself and, more importantly, its reception. Only in recent times have scholars sought to interrogate animated films for their textual and subtextual agendas, fearlessly crossing the divide between the prevailing view that animated forms are merely marginal kinds of cinematic practice and critically dismissible, and the more enlightened suggestion that animation is one of the most significant art forms of the twentieth century, because it inherently accommodates a hybridity of artistic and cultural practices that accurately reflect the tensions between modernity and the postmodern condition. Gilliam's animations engage with the logic of cartoon, and its predominately over-deter-

From *Art and Design Profile*, no. 53 (1997): 61–65. Reprinted by permission of Paul Wells.

mined style, only to "smuggle" in more complex issues concerning the status, execution, and achievement of creative expression, and the ambivalence of "art." Gilliam freely collapses the distinction between notions of "the real" and "the surreal"; between the organic and the mechanistic; between control and chaos, using the animated form to ultimately delineate the absurdity of humankind in submitting to the illusory notion that existence may be ordered and subjected to human will. Further, his work resists the idea that the rational is preferable, debunking the very existence of reason in literally illustrating the collapse of the boundaries between what is assumed to be real and what is assumed to be fantasy.

Born in Minneapolis, Minnesota, Gilliam has suggested that much of his outlook is informed by a response to his "Huckleberry Finn/Tom Sawyer" childhood, and his subsequent successes as a "straight A" student. Arguably, Gilliam's career is a reaction to the ease with which he worked within "orthodox" contexts. Literally creating or discovering "other" worlds has proven more challenging and demanding, ultimately determining Gilliam's originality. What follows is an interview/analysis of some of Terry Gilliam's animations, perhaps the touchstone to his vision, and a valuable contribution to the art form.

PAUL WELLS: *Though you have now achieved great success with films like* Brazil *and* The Adventures of Baron Munchausen, *and latterly with* Twelve Monkeys, *I'd like to take you back to your work in animation. For me, it still seems part of what you have achieved in live-action filmmaking. How did you first get into cartooning?*
TERRY GILLIAM: I started as a kid, at eight or nine years old. I was always drawing. I drew cartoons because I was drawn to the grotesque. I liked distorting things and reinventing reality. I wasn't interested in recording it accurately. The thing with cartoons is that people respond really quickly. They laugh! I enjoyed that immediate feedback. It was nothing more than that: impressing people quickly and getting them to say, "Aren't you clever, Terry!" And also, of course, to make myself laugh.

John O. Thompson has contextualized the whole of the *Monty Python* canon within a discussion of the grotesque, citing theorists as diverse as Michael Steig, Susan Stewert, and Mikhail Bakhtin in order to play out some of the themes informing the seemingly arbitrary distortions and manipulations involved in surreal imagery.[1] Bakhtin's notion of the *carnivalesque* is persuasive in that it recognizes a world turned upside-down, temporarily liberated from its routines and repressions. This clearly informs Gilliam's work, but most crucially, Bakhtin's view of the "grotesque body" as "a body in the act of becoming"[2] is especially appropriate in the way that it chimes with the metamorphosis and graphic montage available in animation which either extends the parameters of the body or reconstructs it in a spirit of new unrealized forms. Further, this sense of improvisation provides an uninhibited continuity for the animator as he or she reconciles the act of animating with the moment of expressing the idea. Gilliam, like all animators, simultaneously invokes the new logic of the image at the moment that he changes the previous assumptions of its material condition. The "body," for example, merely becomes a vehicle to be acted upon as a form, but this clearly changes the possible meaning of its functions, identity, and limits. The incongruous collapse of the viewer's previous conception of the subject in animation, and the way in which animation redefines the object viewed, clearly provokes laughter, but something potentially threatening and unsettling too.

P W :   *How did you get into animation as a career?*

T G :   I was the assistant editor of a magazine in New York. The editor was Harvey Kurtzman, who was really the "Pied Piper" of my generation in terms of comic-book people. He began *Mad* comics. Everybody in the comic-book world during the '60s was essentially his product. One of the things we did in the magazine were photostories called *fumetti*—these are like a comic strip of movie stills where people spoke in "balloons." I was looking for actors for these strips who would work for the princely sum of $15 a day and met John Cleese, who featured in one of these stories. We went our separate ways—I went to Europe, returned to the States, then came back to London—and ended up as an art director at a magazine called *The Londoner,* which I wanted to get out of. John Cleese was established in television and introduced me to a producer called Humphrey Barclay, who was doing a program called *Do Not Adjust Your Set,* and just happened to be an amateur cartoonist. When I met him I had my drawings with me as well as written sketches, but he liked me better as a cartoonist. He gave me a chance. When LWT (London Weekend Television) started, there was a show called *We Have Ways of Making You Laugh,* hosted by Frank Muir, and I ended up doing cartoon caricatures of the guests on the shows. I would do a drawing and the camera would come over my shoulder as I finished it, and they would mix through into the guest. After that, another opportunity arose. Writer and producer Dick Vosburgh had collected a lot of material together which he didn't know what to do with; I suggested I would make an animated film out of it. I had £400 and two weeks to do this in. Dick had collected all the "punning" links from the *Jimmy Young Show* on the radio, and they were very funny but shapeless. Because I didn't have much money or time, I decided the only way I could do this was with cut-outs, so I cut out pictures of Jimmy Young and started doing silly things like putting his foot in his mouth. This was crude animation. It appeared on television and overnight I was this famous TV animator! I later did animation on another series of *Do Not Adjust Your Set,* met up in spurious ways with the other members of *Monty Python* who were also working on these comedy programs, and, of course, started doing animations for *Monty Python's Flying Circus.*

One of Gilliam's sequences for *Do Not Adjust Your Set* was entitled *Elephants in War* and demonstrates his particular skill in recognizing the associational aspects of shapes and forms, aligning the bulbousness of an elephant with the ascendent bulge of a hot-air balloon, having one double as the other in a contradiction of physical space and the laws of gravity. Gilliam is especially adept in "emptying out" physical forms of their properties, qualities, and meanings, redetermining them only in a spirit of what is required to alter graphic orthodoxies and create comic scenarios. In the same sequence, for example, he creates a sight gag in which, by pulling an elephant's tail, the body reverses as if its head had been pulled through its torso and reemerges where its tail used to be. This humor self-evidently emerges from Gilliam's audaciousness in redefining the sheer weight and slowness of a elephant as if it were something that *could* be imposed upon and treated as if it were something weightless with the ability to easily change its form. This is one of the key qualities of animation: forms which are previously seen as stable, coherent, and immutable are subject to change and redefinition. This kind of visual joke follows in the tradition of the Fleischer Brothers in *Betty Boop's Snow White* (1933), in which a dragon is pulled inside out, its skeleton constituting its new form, and Tex Avery in *Slap Happy Lion* (1943), in which a lion swallows itself—its head, with a tail hanging from its mouth, suspended in midair. The arbitrariness of the body and its interior and exterior composition is the subject of much cartoonal address, significantly operating as the most explicit expression of "the taboo" and the assumed notions of personal and social stability.

PW: *What do you think is the special quality of animation?*
TG: You get to be an impish God. You get to reform the world. You get to take the piss out of it. You turn it inside out, upside down. You bug out eyes. You put moustaches on Mona Lisas. You change the world, and for a brief moment have control over it. You get to humiliate it for a while, and that's what all cartoonists really get their kicks out of!

PW: *When you first drew comic strips, did you caption material, or did you purely draw?*
TG: They tended to be mainly drawn. Some stuff I would caption but really I was always making silent movies. I was never as good at words as I was at images.

PW: *What would you say is the difference between being a cartoonist and making animated films?*
TG: I was pushing towards that for a long time because cartooning and illustration was getting frustrating. It was two-dimensional; it didn't move, it didn't make noise. I had always wanted to be a filmmaker. I never wanted to be a cartoonist or an animator. I just wanted to make movies. To do that I had to find an outlet, so I started to make animated films. I could put movement in things and put on silly sound effects, so everything was happening but I had a problem—I was a dilettante animator! I wasn't a serious animator as I hadn't the patience to draw frame after frame of meticulous, fluid drawings. I just wanted to grab things and do them quickly. The advantage of working on the *Monty Python* series was that I always had the excuse of not having enough time to do things properly!

PW: *So, how did you approach your work for* Python?
TG: I would run to a book and find an image, then I would have it photocopied. I would cut it out, color it in and play around with it. I didn't think much about technique, other than going the quickest, cheapest way towards the finish!

Gilliam's wholesale plundering of the color supplements and prints of the world's great paintings resulted in collage animation in which familiar images became strange through their juxtaposition or reformation in new pictorial contexts. Significantly, though some (comic) purchase is sometimes gained by the overt reworking of a major art work—for example, Botticelli's *The Birth of Venus* with Venus as a dancing dervish with an on/off nipple switch, or Da Vinci's *Last Supper* as a situation in which one of the Python cast represented as a cutout falls onto the table and knocks over a bottle of wine—much of Gilliam's achievement is in decontextualizing imagery and reinvesting it with iconic status. The most famous example of this is his use of Cupid's foot from Bronzino's *Venus, Cupid, Folly and Time* in the *Monty Python* title sequence where it appears as a God-like trope, stamping on objects, accompanied by a whoopee-cushion squelch. Not merely is the foot decontextualized from its original painting, but it becomes unrecognizable as part of a Mannerist masterpiece because it constitutes one of its most insignificant and unnoticed aspects. Gilliam simultaneously reduces the status of the original painting and heightens the functional nature of his one chosen aspect of it. The foot, ironically, only becomes meaningful in its own right divorced from its source and invested with iconic largesse. Few would even know of its proper context, and most importantly, nor would they be required to know, given the way the image has been deployed. Gilliam thus has it both ways. He creates a joke at the expense of high culture, mocking the supposed coherence and durability of classical art, while at the same time servicing the base comic appetites of popular culture in emphasizing the utilitarian aspect of an unappealing aspect of the body. The joke would not work so successfully if Gilliam had used a face or a breast or a hand because these parts of the painting carry erotic and aesthetic weight in a way a foot does not. Gilliam essentially reanimates an image which is denied any pictorial dynamism both in the original painting and as a representational cultural form. Gilliam's "juxtapositions," therefore, are not merely comparisons between forms, nor syntheses of the conflict between images in the spirit of Eisensteinian montage, but narrational continuities that are invested with fresh effects and alternative meanings.

P W : *But what about the gags, though? Did you instinctively know if something was funny, or was there a more conscious target for your humor?*
T G : I didn't realize that my viewpoint was particularly funny most of the time. I just thought that's the way the world is. I only discovered later that people didn't see the world like I saw it. There was so much in the *Python*

cartoons—the more I could make something beautiful then humiliate or destroy it, the more it would please me. A lot of it was destructive—cheap, violent, and infantile—all those things which I think made people respond because they were so direct and simple.

P W : *In my view, though, your animation demonstrates a particular lack of inhibition in its approach to humor. There don't seem to be any "withholds," as it were, whether in trashing "high art" or in depicting women with exploding breasts!*
T G : I have always tried to find the humor in a thing because it is a way of understanding it, and even admiring it, in a strange way. I was raised a Presbyterian and at one point I was going to be a missionary. I was a right little zealot in my youth! But it all came to an end because I used to make jokes about God or Jesus and people would take offense. And I said, "Hey, wait a minute, what kind of a God is this that can't take a joke?" In some senses, making fun of something is a way of finding out how important it is to you—how great it is. Because, if it's really great, no matter what you do to it, it's still going to remain great! I think I often use humor in that sense because I want to believe in things of importance; I want things to be wonderful and wise, so I use humor as a way of testing them.

P W : *Such an attitude evidently found empathy with the other members of* Python.
T G : With *Python* I always felt totally at ease. I think we shared the same point of view but we expressed it in totally different ways. Theirs was verbal and much dryer; mine was visual and crude. But then, I could be "the American" in the group. What was strange was that we really influenced each other. Some of the sketches were like the cartoons and the cartoons were pulling things from the sketches, and it was such a mutually fertilizing, cross-pollinating kind of world. I shared their desire to pinprick any sort of pomposity and to attack authority figures—we tried to show people with their dirty knickers round their ankles if we could—but in many ways, that kind of thing has universal appeal because it's a universal theme.

One episode of *Monty Python* shows a man wearing a bowler hat, wearing a nappy and sporting antlers, undergoing therapy. Unfortunately, he fails to respond to the Pavlovian rewards of therapy—in this case, a naked woman—and is crushed by a huge hammer, all because he cannot deny that he is a

Mason. This animated sequence is unambivalent in its use of class caricature. Further, it clearly attacks the fetishized model of the privilege, authoritarianism, and secrecy embodied in Freemasonry. This obviously underpins the broad anti-establishment "feel" of much of *Python*'s output but operates in a less sophisticated fashion than when Gilliam's animation, with its surreal inner logic, finds a specific way of linking into live-action sketches. For example, adopting a model which he uses often, Gilliam creates a sequence in which the lyrical descends into the absurd, and one graphic—in this case, a hand and a piece of string—extends its own narrative by changing its associated function. "Trees" (actually hands) grow out of the ground; "birds" (also hands) fly past; a cowboy riding a hand as if it was a horse then rides through, spinning a lasso. The "rope" of the lasso loops into the next image and becomes an extending necklace around two nubile 1920s vamps with butterflies on their breasts. As the camera passes, one of the girls extends a chameleon-like tongue to eat a butterfly and expose the other girl's nipple. The "necklace" becomes a strand of knitting wool in the next live-action sequence. Smuggled into this surreal, free-associational narrative is a subversive image of lesbian sexual intimacy. Interestingly, the very stillness of the photographic images coupled with the minimalism of the *actual* animation within the sequence directs the viewer to the intensity of the action, and its instant comic appeal, yet filters the extent of its daring. Another sequence which operates in a similar way features a Scotsman wearing a sporran sitting next to two other men. He claims, "I've a nasty feeling I am somebody's lunch hour," as the viewer hears the sound of eating. Suddenly, a pair of legs descend from his sporran, which proves to be the back of a child's head. The child, an "Alice"-like little girl, steps away and is kicked along by a row of Gilliam's archetypal Victorian cut-out figures, whose legs ultimately fall off. The shock of these comic amputations obscures the daring of implied child fellatio. Whether this was intended or not is uncertain but merely confirms that the supposedly innocent conditions of animation can filter out the intensities and implications of imagery that would be taboo or transgressive within the live-action context. It remains, however, that by interrogating such imagery more closely, the animated context actually amplifies its effect.

P W : *Though you claim that your initial approach was crude and instinctive, how did you develop as an animator? Did you come to understand the language of animation as being particular and special?*

TG: No, I don't think I developed at all! I think I was born fully formed and died less fully formed. I don't think I got any better, frankly. I think I picked it up quickly; it was such fun, but as the *Python* series went on, it got harder for me because I was less interested in it in that form. In some ways I began to think I wanted to do real Disney-style animation. I wanted to be fluid, beautiful, and graceful. In a sense that's why I stopped doing animation, because I couldn't express myself as well; I didn't have the patience or desire to do it properly.

PW: *Arguably, though, your work remains distinctive because it retains its "energy." Ultimately, that's what I like about cartoons by Tex Avery or Chuck Jones. Over and beyond being "funny," there is an intrinsic "life" in the films which distinguishes them from some of the now-dated lyricism and sentiment of the Disney canon. Were you influenced by Avery and Jones?*
TG: I was and I wasn't. Tex Avery and Chuck Jones were names I only discovered much later in life. I knew their cartoons. These were an inescapable part of childhood and they made me laugh, but I've always done my education in art, film, or animation in reverse. Basically, I've done the work first, based on things I've seen growing up, just knowing "that's funny," "I like that," going to the movies and not knowing who made them, sometimes knowing who was in them but just going as your average punter. Only later did the world know of Tex Avery and Chuck Jones. You knew Walt Disney but then everyone knew Walt Disney. I've always been really naive in my approach to things. Later in my career, I read a review of *Python* by George Melly, and he referred to my cartoons as Max Ernst-like, and I had never seen Max Ernst, so I looked him up and I knew what he was talking about.

PW: *That's interesting because it demonstrates that there still can be original work that is the sum of its cultural influences rather than self-conscious, postmodern rehashes of overacknowledged ideas.*
TG: It gets more difficult as you go on. I think the more you know, the more you're inhibited. Now I keep thinking, "I'm copying *him*," but in the past I carried on naively. I didn't know all these people had been doing these things far better for far longer! I remember when I was doing *Baron Munchausen* seeing a picture in a [British Film Institute] catalogue from Karel Zemen's *Baron Munchausen* and saying, "Wow, what is this?" and eventually seeing the film, and saying, "Wow, that's great," because he did what I'm

still trying to do, which is to try and combine live action with animation. His Doré-esque backgrounds were wonderful. The film captured the real spirit of the character.

Gilliam's engagement with other art forms serves to redefine the nature of their artifice. By accommodating classical imagery, for example, within the highly self-conscious parameters of the animated form, the condition of art as artifice is exposed and interrogated. Gilliam's contentious gag at the expense of Da Vinci's *Last Supper,* for example, is more than just the crass incongruity of a Python character knocking over a bottle of wine at what has now become a functional meal rather than a sacred or mythic event. It is a formal disruption of Da Vinci's intricate composition of twelve disciples con-joined in groups of three linked by a number of determining gestures. Sud-denly, this "individual" figure, propped on the table, distracts and distances himself from the coherence of the former image and its meaning. Michelan-gelo's *David* suffers similarly in that the compositional perfection of a classi-cal nude, and ironically the sense of de-eroticized or defunctionalized "neutrality" that accompanies it, is reformed by making the genital area taboo with the addition of an animated fig-leaf and an ever-extending hand trying to remove it. Gilliam uses Botticelli's *The Birth of Venus* as a vehicle to critique overelaboration and the illusory grandeur of illustration. As a figure divorced from her context, Venus appears embarrassed and self-conscious, her nudity crudely exploited by yet another extending hand tweaking her nipple. In many ways Gilliam uses the free vocabulary of animation to make what may be termed "exploitation" films because he constantly underlines the aesthetic intention of images to re-engage their literal and subtextual alternatives as pictorial forms. He essentially uses animation to progress or regress the narrational *stasis* of images, bringing to them "movement" and an alternative "illusion of life."

P W : *Did you find that when you started to make live-action films in your own right, you were essentially working in the same way, or did you find a more sophisti-cated comic voice?*
T G : *Jabberwocky,* the first film on my own, is very Pythonic because it's still concerned with gags and sketches, but the best way to see it is without the soundtrack! We showed it to some Dutch distributors in silence, and it's a beautiful film! Take the jokes out and it's a much better film! I was still in the

stage of making jokes, and many of them are cartoon jokes, but they're done live. I designed it like a cartoon. I was trying to force normal-shaped actors into frames which were drawn in a cartoon fashion, which, of course, normal people can't fit into. In *Time Bandits*, I move away from Python a little bit more, but cast small, cartoon-like people to fit my storyboards!

P W : *Your work, both in animation and in live action, constantly mixes fantasy and comedy and consequently extends the boundaries of both forms.*
T G : I entwine humor with the fantastical because it makes it a little more palatable, it avoids it becoming pretentious. Much fantasy becomes airy-fairy, pretentious crap, it seems to me. It's got no life in it and comedy always brings life to things. Everything I do is ultimately about the conflict of fantasy and reality, between beauty and grotesqueness, between serious issues and the comic. I don't know which is winning at any one point in my work. There's one side of me that's totally cynical, that wants to pack it in; then there's this irrepressible kid in there, who wants to believe that things are better, who is always looking for surprises. Surprise is the key to me. It seems to me that for most people growing up is about trying to eliminate surprise. For me, that's the very thing that keeps me going. It is the very thing that's important about animation.

Notes

1. Alexander Walker, writing in the *Evening Standard* (30.9.71), cited in John O. Thompson, *Monty Python: A Complete and Utter Theory of the Grotesque*, BFI, London, 1982, p. v.

2. Ibid, p. 42.

Chemical Warfare

BOB McCABE/1998

IN 1967—AMID THE TURBULENCE generated by the escalation of the war in Vietnam, the build-up to the San Francisco summer of love and the explosive Los Angeles race riots—Terry Gilliam left his home country of America for England. Thirty years later he went back to take "a savage journey to the heart of the American Dream" by bringing Hunter S. Thompson's *Fear and Loathing in Las Vegas* to the screen. Thompson's 1971 book began as a magazine article for *Rolling Stone,* which itself sprang from an assignment to cover the Mint 400 motor race on the outskirts of America's gambling capital. Armed with enough drugs to kill a weighty bovine, Thompson went to the edge, peered into the abyss and came back with a news report that the American Dream was well and truly spent. His writing hijacked Tom Wolfe's groundbreaking "new journalism" and forever made it "Gonzo." Alongside *Easy Rider, Fear and Loathing in Las Vegas* introduced a level of realism and pessimism to youth culture that helped define the '70s. "Thompson didn't go to Vietnam," says Gilliam. "He's a journalist who didn't cover the war. So by taking drugs he's creating a war zone in his head, bombarding his psyche, and then he goes to Vegas and reports as if he were a war correspondent. He created a chemical war in his head to deal with the world there rather than going out into the real war and getting shot at with real bullets."

To avoid real bullets himself Gilliam joined the National Guard in the

From *Sight and Sound,* vol. 8, no. 6 (June 1998): 6, 8. Reprinted by permission of *Sight and Sound.*

mid-'60s while working as associate editor on the New York–based humor magazine *Help!* As a result he spent most of the hippie-birthing period sporting a military crewcut—his current ponytail seems a gesture of constant defiance. During the Watts riots he was working for an ad agency and drawing and distributing antiwar posters in his spare time. Once in London he sought out all the locations he recognized from *Blow-Up* and scaled the fence at Shepperton Studios, calling it his own for the day as he wandered around the sets of *Oliver!* Ten years later he would make his first film as sole director, *Jabberwocky,* there.

In between, of course, he became an animator and member of *Monty Python's Flying Circus.* Gilliam remained in England to make a trio of films— *Time Bandits* (1981), *Brazil* (1985), *The Adventures of Baron Munchausen* (1988)— that brought the studios to tears in their arch defense of fantasy. *Brazil's* Sam Lowry chooses fantasy over sanity, while Munchausen railed against the rational world as the film's budget soared into notoriety.

Fear and Loathing could be seen as completing Gilliam's U.S. trilogy. Unlike his British-made movies, he did not generate the source material for these, though the films are equally personal. *The Fisher King* (1991) again had one of its central characters escape into madness and myth, while *Twelve Monkeys* (1995) took Gilliam to Philadelphia, the birthplace of the U.S., where an unwitting hero from the near future tries in vain to find out how the country has gone so wrong. With *Fear and Loathing* Gilliam goes back to the America he left. Vietnam is a constant on the news, racial tensions are high, and the length of your hair is a statement of intent.

The words are Thompson's, but the film is very clearly Gilliam's. Alex Cox was originally slated to direct, with Johnny Depp starring as Thompson's alter ego Raoul Duke and Benicio Del Toro as Duke's Samoan attorney known only as Dr. Gonzo. When Cox left the project Gilliam signed up, cowriting a new script with Tony Grisoni, writer of Jon Amiel's *Queen of Hearts,* with whom he has been working for some time on a project about the Minotaur.

BOB McCABE: *Your adaptation of* Fear and Loathing *is extremely faithful to the book, with most of the dialogue coming straight from Thompson.*
TERRY GILLIAM: If you're going to do a book, you've got to try to do the book. It's a collaboration: it's as if the writer wrote the symphony and I'm the conductor, though I also change the arrangement, add some saxes and a few other bits and pieces. What we did was to shape the book in a new way,

because the second half falls apart. There's no point in rewriting the dialogue—it's great—but what you can do is reorder it: some of the scenes didn't
play as funnily as they do now. Other bits we've cannibalized or moved, but
I think there are hardly any words spoken that aren't Thompson's.

BM: *By rooting your film firmly back in 1971 you get away from the image of*
Thompson as a cool outlaw figure and show that this is basically about two junkies
in a room, and it can be unpleasant and bleak at times.

TG: A lot of people said, "You've got to update it to make it relevant to the
'90s." I don't think you have to make it relevant, it's relevant whenever. It's
basically about two people going to excess, and what we were trying to get
across is that the excuse for this behavior is the loss of the dream of the '60s
and the continuing war in Vietnam. The book's very reflective—you read it
as funny and outrageous, but then it goes into something else. In the Alex
Cox script that stuff was incidental, but I thought I had to keep playing this
other side; otherwise it becomes boorish and tiresome, just two guys rampag-
ing around the place.

The characters are products of the '60s—'60s guys with all that passion, all
that energy and belief that they could change the world. And for all its besti-
ality and madness, their behavior is intelligent. It was really intelligent people having the last hurrah, one last chance to say, "Fuck it."

We were very clear in our thinking. We decided to see it like Dante's
Inferno, with Gonzo as a kind of Virgil, a pagan, primal thing that is out of
control half the time. Then you have Duke/Dante watching and being
guided. Duke is sent to Hell to suffer for the sins of America is the way we've
approached it, though whether any of this comes through I don't know. But
it helped when we were writing.

BM: *That seems to be Thompson's intent too: he certainly sets himself up as a*
conscience figure.

TG: He's from Kentucky and his references are almost biblical at times, or at
least coming from Christian morality. But he hides them, he ducks and dives.
What's interesting in the writing is that he equivocates all the time; he never
takes a real stance. We found out talking to him that there's a lot of fabrica-
tion in the book—for instance, he was married at the time, but he disguised
all this. Perhaps it was the two sides of his personality, I don't know.

B M : *The soundtrack mixes Bob Dylan and Janis Joplin with Perry Como and Julie Andrews. The Stones are in there—but "Sympathy for the Devil," which Thompson recently described as "as much a part of the writing of that book as my own rhythms in the prose," isn't.*

T G : There's a lot of pressure to have it in the film, but it doesn't work. The rhythm isn't right for the way we're cutting the front of the movie and the lyrics, which are great, can't be played with Johnny Depp talking as well. I wanted to start with a bang so what I used is a song by Big Brother and the Holding Company. There's a raw San Francisco guitar shit that band has. And the title of the song—"Combination of the Two"—is strangely appropriate.

B M : *Initially it was a low-budget project with Alex Cox attached, then Cox was out and you were called in at what seemed like the eleventh hour.*

T G : Somehow Alex managed to alienate everybody, I don't know the details but they all wanted him gone and so he was gone. He went up to Hunter's house and completely alienated him in one fell swoop—I mean Hunter's an easily alienated person, but you have to show some respect, some deference, some intelligence in dealing with somebody like that. When Alex was first involved it was a $5 million film and then Johnny Depp and Benicio Del Toro's presence raised it to $7 million. I discovered in retrospect that these budgets were just inventions. When I got out there I said, "OK, I'll do it but I want to write a new script and I think I'll just double the budget to start with and see how we go." So we wrote the whole thing in eight days—we just went through the book, underlined all the bits we liked and then said, "OK, we've got that, that, that." It was building blocks. And at the end of this we took it home, read it, hated it, came back and spent two more days writing like mad.

B M : *It seems a remarkably tight time frame.*

T G : We've done this whole thing in less than a year from writing it to finishing it, and that was part of the exercise. I did it partly to try and break out of the responsibility of making good films, making them well. I just wanted to do something fast and Gonzo, Gonzo filmmaking. That's why the low budget and short schedule were important. I knew that once we got into it, I'd start screaming and shouting very much like Duke in the book, but that's the spirit of the piece, so why not go for it? The worst thing was when I realized I wasn't as young as I used to be, I don't have the energy I used to have. But we still got through it.

Then it got very messy because the production company Rhino reneged on everything. In other circumstances I would have walked away, but I'd set my mind on doing it. I made less money on this than on *Life of Brian* way back—but I always said I wouldn't work just for money and I'd been getting paid more and more as the films had gone on. It got very funny—Johnny was so incensed he said that if the guy who ran the production company came on the set he was going to put in his contract that this guy has to drop his trousers and Johnny gets to whip him with a wire coat hanger.

B M : *It seems on the surface to be the least Gilliam-like of all your films.*
T G : Good. In this one I'm not sure which character I am. In earlier films it was easy to see who I was identifying with: Baron Munchausen, Sam in *Brazil*, the kid in *Time Bandits*. But the last three films have had split protagonists: in *The Fisher King* you've got Jeff Bridges doing the bulk of the work and Robin Williams doing the fireworks; in *Twelve Monkeys* there's Bruce Willis and Brad Pitt; in this one Johnny's doing the work and Benicio the fireworks. I find it very odd that these three films that I didn't write have a similar relationship between the two characters, and I can identify with both of them.

With every movie I've made, there's a connection between the making of it and what it's about. And this one was just go for it, leap off the edge of the precipice and see what happens. And it's hellish—it's all the things the book says it is. It was the most uncertain experience I've had for a long time. Usually I know my films so deeply before I start shooting I feel I could shoot blindfolded. But this one we were doing as we were going along, making really fast choices, and my stomach was always in a knot. I didn't want to like the film; I didn't want to love it; I wanted to maintain an objectivity because I didn't know what we were going to make. It's only been in the editing that we've slowly honed it down.

B M : *If* Fear and Loathing *could be read as your own search for the American Dream, what did you find?*
T G : I think America is still a very confused place. What I can see now is that it's got wonderful things that I rejected before, yet there's an inherent dumbness that floats through the whole thing. Vegas is a wonderful display of

America now because it's about the infantilization of America, which we've all been making cartoons about for a long time. But I found Americans have all changed shape: there are huge fat people, who didn't exist before, and the guys who used to be geeks and nerds have all body-built so now they've got huge bodies and necks with a little head that sits on top. And they all go to Vegas with their kids and wander around gawking. Vegas brings out the best and the worst, there's some kind of truth in it. For me it was just like Thompson going there.

A Dialogue with Terry Gilliam

STUART KLAWANS/1998

MODERATOR: *Let me welcome you to our Regis Dialogue, which closes an extraordinary retrospective of the work of the writer, director, performer, animator, and Minnesota native Terry Gilliam. Terry was two days ago on the Grand Canal in Venice, celebrating his silver anniversary with his wife and family, and is here tonight with a little bit of help from our friends: the Regis Foundation and North-west Airlines. And also his personal generosity to come and make a really remarkable visit, to be here and in New York and then back in London for the opening of* Fear and Loathing *on Saturday night. This is not Terry Gilliam's first visit to the Walker. He reminded me that when he was eleven or twelve years old he came for a Saturday drawing class here and was mightily impressed with the level of instructions. It was about twenty-two years ago that he had his next visit on this stage, when he was invited after directing his first feature,* Jabberwocky, *his first solo feature, and he said that he came on to do a presentation with a very famous British photographer. There were just the two of them that night, a podium was here, and he said he had come in before the show began and hidden inside the podium, so that when he was introduced, his hand went up and grabbed the mike, and the first fifteen minutes he delivered his talk inside the podium. You notice there's no podium here tonight. Terry's going to be here in full view and we'll have a chance to hear not only about the early career, when he ran away to the circus, or the* Flying Circus, *but also the extraordinary films he's done in the '80s and now into*

From *The Films of Terry Gilliam,* a Regis Dialogue and Retrospective, Walker Art Center, Minneapolis, October 14–November 5, 1998. Transcribed and published by permission of the Walker Art Center.

the late '90s. Films like Time Bandits, Brazil, Twelve Monkeys, Fear and Loathing in Las Vegas. *He's made some of the most impressive, visually arresting, powerful work in contemporary cinema. And he's very kindly come here to discuss that
career with us. To lead that discussion, one of my favorite critics, but I think one of
also the most serious thorough-going critics in North America. He started out as a
book reviewer in his twenties, graduated to film in his forties, and for the last decade
has been the main film reviewer, the only film critic, for the* Nation. *Stuart Klawans is an extraordinary writer, with very insightful and very deeply felt views
about the cinema, and he has agreed to join us in looking at the career of Terry
Gilliam. So I'd like to ask you to join us in welcoming him back here, his first visit
in twenty-two years, and I hope we don't let that much time go away before he's
here with us again. Mr. Terry Gilliam, Mr. Stuart Klawans. (loud applause)*

TERRY GILLIAM: That's enough. (laughs)

STUART KLAWANS: *This is a homecoming for you, and I know that today you
actually located the house you grew up in in Medicine Lake.*
TG: Yeah, it's a tiny, tiny little place, out Medicine Lake, and strangely
enough it's the one little area out there that hasn't seemed to have been
touched by development. We ended up on the wrong road to begin with and
there was no shape of this memory of mine, and finally we had to call a
friend of my parents who had called the newspaper to say she would tell me
where I used to live if we gave her a call, and they took us to this place and
this tiny, tiny place, it was this wee little place, and you could barely squeeze,
you know, a couple of people in, and there were five of us who grew up in
this and it was actually . . . it's kind of moving in a weird way because I have
such a strong memory of the place and the roads and the houses and they're
all basically there and it's, somehow it's the only area around Medicine Lake
that hasn't been touched, and I don't know if it's because my memory kept
it intact or not. I mean, I want to believe these things. (laughs) They're probably not true.

SK: *In a sense though, Mr. Gilliam is here under false pretenses, because he did
leave for Los Angeles. I'm very curious, when at age eleven, twelve you went to Los
Angeles from this area, what were your impressions of the architecture out there, of
the physical landscape of L.A.? It must have been enormously different.*
TG: Yeah, well, we went out there and I really did think I was going out to
the land of cowboys and Indians. I thought that's what L.A. was going to be.

Great spaces and men riding on horses, you know, and it ended up we moved into a tract house in the middle of the San Fernando Valley that two years earlier had been orange groves. Like, you know in *Chinatown,* when Jack Nicholson drives out into those orange groves? That's what the San Fernando Valley used to be like. And two years earlier they took it all down, Kaiser Aluminum built these tract houses and they looked just like the houses in Tim Burton's *Edward Scissorhands,* each one a sweet little pastel shade, and it wasn't anything of what I hoped it would be except, except there were the movie studios and there were, the old movie ranches were still out there. There's a place called Stony Point out in North Ridge where the old serials—television cowboy serials—used to be shot there. They constantly rode past the same trees, the same rocks, and that was there, so there was a bit of that magic still there, to climb around and to imagine that I was in the movies.

s k : *But you didn't find the romance that you'd been hoping for yet.*
T G : No, and I still haven't. (laughs) It's a life, the life of a failed romantic.
. . . I mean, the dreams keep appearing, the movies keep telling me life is going to be a certain way that's all wonderful, and it's not, it's this other thing. Which I'm actually getting better at coming to terms with.

s k : *I'm also curious . . . when you first saw . . . your first art-historical naked lady.*
T G : Are you asking me about the Encyclopedia Britannica? I think you are.

s k : *Is that it?*
T G : Yes, porno for the thinking child. (laughs) I mean, that was actually my first brush with eroticism and it was in the *Encyclopedia Britannica,* and it was in the Greek sculpture section. And there they were, Venus de Milo and all these luscious porcelain, marbleized women with, you know, no pores and hair or anything . . . they were wonderful. And I was obsessed with these things for a long time. I think I moved on from the Greeks to *Mad* comics somewhat later because . . . *Mad* comics, when they began, there were a couple wonderful cartoonists, Wally Wood and Jack Davis, who drew these wonderfully zaftig women and I . . . I mean *Mad* magazine or *Mad* comics was not known as a porno magazine, but I felt guilty about it and used to hide it in

the garage, you know, in fear that I would be found out that I wasn't reading it for the comics, I was reading it for those girls.

s κ : *And [Harvey] Kurtzman too eventually. But you became a cartoonist, also switched from an interest, when you went to college, from physics to art and architecture.*

T G : Yeah.

s κ : *What movies were you watching at the time?*

T G : I mean, I was watching everything and I've always been totally eclectic. I didn't think of movies as other than what most people think of movies. They're just entertainment, things you go to do on a Saturday or a Friday. I was a huge fan of Jerry Lewis and Dean Martin. I loved . . . actually, I loved epics, epics, *Ben Hur*, you know, *The Fall of the Roman Empire, Silver Chalice.* Those were incredible because they were the first chance of real escape I felt from the world I lived in, this rather mundane suburban tract life with things very much as what you saw . . . what was there. There was no mystery to it. And suddenly to go back into ancient Rome or Greece or . . . that was fantastic for me. That was exciting and those were the things that I held onto as a kid mainly. I've actually . . . it's taken a long time to discover what I watched when I was a kid. A few years ago I was at the Sundance Institute, and Stanley Donen was there, and it was after I made *Fisher King,* and Stanley one night showed a lot of tapes, clips from all the films he had made, from, you know, *Funny Girl* to *Singin' in the Rain,* and all these movies with Cyd Charisse, all these, basically, song-and-dance films. And I suddenly realized how important those had been in my life and I'd never recognized them. And I said, had I seen them before we'd finished *Fisher King* I would have dedicated the film to him because they were wonderful, and they were romantic, and people fell in love, and they danced, and they sang and did all these things, and I said to Stanley, "What you actually did, now that you've reminded me of what you did, was you ruined a great deal of my life," (audience laughs) because I believed in those movies. I believed in that innocent, virginal kind of world. And he said, "You think you've got it bad. I still do." I think he was on his fourth or fifth wife at that point. (laughs) . . . So looking back, I realize that all sorts of movies are having a big effect. Some early movies that I remember from Minnesota were I think *Pinocchio, Snow White,* the early Disney animation films, which to me still are extraordinary creations because the world is so dense and beautiful, the detail in it is just extraordinary. And I think also *Thief of Bagdad,* the Michael Powell/Korda movie . . . and I remember as a child the first real lasting nightmare I used to have was a scene where the character is caught in a spider web and the spider's coming down on him, and I used to wake up in the middle of the night completely wrapped up in all of the bedclothes, the sheets and the blankets, and I have been struggling, trying to get out of that web, and that nightmare stayed with me for years, and I think maybe now I make movies to give nightmares to new generations of kids. (audience laughs) I think it's very healthy, I think nightmares are very good things for you.

S K : *Moving on from childhood, though, when we got into the middle '60s when you were already getting out of college, having your first jobs. . . . You'd done a stint in the National Guard, I think?*

T G : Yeah.

S K : *But what were . . . I read that you were watching Antonioni at that point.*

T G : Yeah.

S K : *How about Richard Lester, Stan Vanderbeek, were you watching any of this stuff?*

T G : There was that point after college, going to New York, when I basically discovered foreign movies, is what it was. Kurosawa, Bergman, Fellini, Antonioni, Buñuel. . . . I completely rejected American filmmaking at that point, I thought it was just crap, rubbish, and the truth was in the foreign filmmakers, and again, they were opening up new worlds to me, different ways of looking at the world, different cultures, and that was really exciting. . . . And of course there was Dick Lester with *Running, Jumping and Standing Still Film* first and then the Beatles films, and Stan Vanderbeek was doing cutout animation, and I always remember one where it was a cutout of Nixon and he had his foot stuck in his mouth all the time and I just thought, you know, it was just very funny stuff, and years later, when I started doing cutout animations, I think that was what was in the back of my mind. But Richard Lester was probably one of the reasons I went to England because, as an American, he went there and met some famous pop stars and he made some really good films, so I'll follow in his footsteps.

s k : *I think this may be a good segue to look at our first clips. So we're going to look at one of Terry Gilliam's early animations. This is from the compilation film* And Now for Something Completely Different. *So let's roll the first clip.* [CLIP]

s k : *Of course, one of the things that I admire most about that is with the dancing teeth, how you wait as long as possible before anything happens . . . (TG laughs) Just keep 'em going.*

T G : That was me stalling, basically. I knew I had to produce X amount of time worth of animation. The longer I could drag it out, the least amount of work was very important.

s k : *I also wanted to begin with this one because it really brings back the smell of the coffee from those years, it's really rich with all the political and social and cultural currents . . .*

T G : It's funny, it's like, having left America because I felt I had to either get involved in politics in a very serious bomb-throwing kind of way or get out, and I got out and went to England, and that was one way of dealing with the Vietnam War.

s k : *Right. There was an incident with a man in a wheelchair at a protest in Los Angeles, if I remember that . . .*

T G : Yeah, it was the first political poster I did 'cause there was a police riot, it was the first police riot in L.A. Lyndon Johnson had come to Century City, which at that point was basically the Century Plaza Hotel in this great vast wasteland waiting for this huge development, and there was a protest against the war and I was with my girlfriend, who was a reporter for the *London Evening Standard.* We were on our way to a party and she said we better just stop by and check this thing out. And we got there and I mean, it was terrifying. These huge crowds of people who were very jolly. It was all sorts of people . . . university professors, dentists, lawyers . . . it was a very middle-class crowd, to be quite honest, and the police were lined up, there were helicopters low, there were searchlights, there were snipers on the roofs, it was. . . . The paranoia of the police was absolutely terrifying, and at one point in what was a very peaceful demonstration a group of people sat down and started singing, "We shall not be moved," and the police used that as a signal to suddenly go berserk, and they drove Harley-Davidsons into these people and then people started shouting and there was a second rank of police behind the first group and they charged through . . . batons were being wielded, people were crashing and it was terrifying. People were literally in wheelchairs, trying to get out of there, being smashed by cops going berserk. And we got smashed up a bit. And it was the first, it was one of the moments that I felt, I got to get out, I'm getting angry now. Because this was totally, completely wrong. One of the best things about that was that the *Los Angeles Times* wrote saying it was a bunch of left-wing hippie commies who had gone berserk, and the *L.A. Free Press* actually started putting out free broadsheets, handing them out to people on the streets, cars and everything, with interviews with everybody who'd been there, which completely denied what the *L.A. Times* was saying and painted a completely different picture. And what was extraordinary was, by the end of the week they were so successful at doing this that the *L.A. Times* reporters actually mutinied and demanded that the truth be told, and the *L.A. Times* recanted and told the story truthfully. And I thought that was an amazing moment, but I felt things were getting ugly and I . . . my reaction to that sort of ugliness was to behave even more ugly, and I didn't really want to do that, so I used that as a reason to escape to England and behave in a silly way as opposed to a dangerous way.

S K : *What also interests me about this particular clip is the way you work in this political side with your experiences working in advertising . . . they're all smushed together here.*

T G : Yeah, I mean, in a sense the world has become like that to me, and I mean, what is news? What is advertising? Everything is, and everything splits into the next thing. It's hard to know where the dividing lines are, and I think, in fact, that's the world we're living in and even more so now. It's very hard to know what truth is, what fact is, because everything is sort of blended together. News is entertainment, entertainment is . . . not entertaining, actually. And I think that . . . at times it seemed important to say those things, and now I think it's even more important to say it, strangely enough. But nobody seems to notice now.

S K : *As for the cutout animation which you did for years for the Monty Python show, where did you get all the things you cut out? I'm just curious about the process. I mean what sort of things did you loot to get the cutouts?*

T G : Basically everything I liked I took, and I . . . my house is full of lots of books and so, like in that instance there, *The Boast* is by Peter Bruegel, it's an engraving done by Bruegel, so I just cut it out, painted it, duddum. I used whatever was at hand, things like the little, the Chinamen, all the rows, I just got a rubber stamp made in the shape of little Chinamen and stamped them out, just like they do in Beijing. (laughs) For real. And I was always, because of the nature of doing animation shows, I really didn't have much time. I had kind of two weeks to do each show and I was basically working on my own, and so I had to grab things and cut things out, and so there's a lot of Bruegel, there's Dürer, there's any painter that I liked. I'd go down to the National Gallery in London whenever I'd run out of ideas and start walking around and suddenly things, the paintings, provided me with jokes and ideas. Then I'd buy postcards of the paintings and take them back and cut those out. I mean, now I couldn't do that because every image is owned by, probably Bill Gates by now. This is what's happened, that everything you touch. . . . What I was doing is, I would take magazines, newspapers, I'd see faces, I remember there was a beautiful book of Richard Avedon photographs, using distorting lenses, so I was using those. Now, if I were to do that now I would probably be sued every week for the kind of work I was doing. We, as a culture, as a public, don't own things anymore. I mean it's so bizarre. If you're making a film, if I go down the street and let's say, for instance, in *Fear and Loathing* there's a shot that's taken just off of Hollywood Boulevard and it's a mural, of Dolores Del Rio, that somebody painted on the side of a building. Now, this is a public space, or so you would think, it's out there for the public. Now, we had that in the shot as the car drives past, and the person who did that mural has sued the company and got a lot of money for that. There was that film that (pauses) Al Pacino and Keanu Reeves did, *The Devil's Advocate*. And there's this scene in there where there're these entwining figures above his fireplace that start animating. Now it turned out that was from . . .

S K : *Rodin, the* Gates of Hell.
T G : It wasn't, actually, it was from Washington D.C. above a cathedral or something.

S K : *Oh that's right, that's right, yes. The National Cathedral.*
T G : And they sued. So, we're living in this time where you can't . . . public things don't exist anymore. We can have all these billboards and signs and signage leaning down on us saying, "Look at me, look at me," but if you

want to make a film and use those signs, you can't without their permission. Interesting times. Boy, I'm angry. (audience laughs)

s k : *Well, have some water, cool down. There may be Python fans in the audience who will be disappointed, but I don't want to prolong the Python period tonight because I'd much rather talk about you as a filmmaker, and so I'd like to jump ahead to* Jabberwocky. *A film which, for the record, I saw about three times in its first year of release.*
T G : What a fool. (audience laughs)

s k : *Oh, not at all. Not at all.*
T G : I had great respect for you before we sat down. (audience laughs)

s k : *Were it just for the title sequence! (laughs) No, it was in a way a continuation of Pythonism because, you know, the first thing that happened was a foot came down and smashed something. But tell us a little about how you got to make* Jab-berwocky, *how you made the transition to doing that.*
T G : Well, basically, having made *Holy Grail* and been one of the two direc-tors . . . it's really simple . . .

s k : *Yeah, how did that happen, how did you divide the labor with Terry Jones for* Holy Grail?
T G : Well, Terry and I had always been very close; we seemed to see things eye to eye, and when it came time to make *Holy Grail,* both of us sort of said, all right, anybody named Terry gets to direct this film. (audience laughs) And the others went along with this ridiculous idea, and so Terry and I got to direct the film. And then at the end of the whole process, your name's up there, saying "film directed by," you know, Terry Gilliam and Terry Jones. You're a film director, it's as simple as that. And when we were making it it was odd, because even though in preparation we seemed to agree on every-thing, when we started working it was clear that we had slightly different ideas, and at first it was two voices, sometimes shouting different instruc-tions, which is not a good thing for a crew. And so we decided, to simplify this we'll have a single voice, so we got the assistant director to be that com-mon voice. Well, it turned out he wanted to be a film director as well, so the common voice was a different voice. (audience laughs) And Terry basically concentrated on talking to the others in the group, who by then I hated,

didn't talk to at all, and I spent my time back with the camera, is the way we worked. And it worked quite well, we got through it. And at the end of all that I really wanted to do something on my own, and we were able to get the money in the same way, because at that point in England there was a time when the taxation was really ruthless. If you made a lot of money you could actually have to pay 90 percent of your income in taxes. That's a lot of money. So there were a lot of pop stars—Pink Floyd, Led Zeppelin, Elton John, some record companies—that were looking for ways to alleviate their tax burden, and one way was, you could invest in films, and write it off. And so that's how *Holy Grail* was financed. *Jabberwocky* was done in the same way. And so we were in these positions of having total control over what we were doing, we didn't have to go out and sell our ideas to a studio or anything, we just . . . there it was. And *Jabberwocky* was one of those things that . . . I had this idea of trying to make a film out of Lewis Carroll's poem, for whatever loose connection we have with it, it was there, it was a starting point. And . . . I really wanted to do . . . the things that we hadn't been able to do in *Holy Grail*. In a sense, I wanted to deal more with the atmosphere and really, really get into the filth and the mire of the Middle Ages. And that's how it started. I just at the same time wanted to be free from the limitations of what we had to do in Python, because with Python everything had to be funny, that's what we were in the business of doing. And with *Jabberwocky* I wanted to play more with a bit of suspense, a bit of romance, a stronger narrative, those aspects, and the foolish thing of all of that was that you make a film about the Middle Ages, with a lot of comedy in it, with three Pythons—Terry Jones, myself, and Michael Palin—involved, and you put it out to the world and don't want to be judged like a Monty Python film! (laughs). Really stupid. (audience laughs) And it was treated a bit roughly, because they were still trying to judge it in Python terms rather than its own terms.

S K :   *Right. Well, the only meaningful link I can think of is the "bring out your dead" sequence from* Holy Grail *and all the dragging through the muck in* Jabberwocky, *but for someone who revolts against the blandness and regimentation of modern life, your view of medieval life is awfully anti-romantic at the same time. I mean, you escape to a fantasy that you can't stand.*

T G :   Yeah. What intrigued me was playing with fairy tales, but it was like the hero wins one . . . it ends up in a fairy tale . . . a supposed happy ending, but it's the wrong happy ending. That's what I like about it, he gets half the kingdom and the beautiful princess in marriage. That's not what he wanted, he wanted his little shop, with the fat girl living next door, that's what he wanted, and I thought, the idea of a man with such low aspirations, such pathetic dreams, is forced to become the hero and at the end gets everything you're supposed to want and . . . unhappy seemed to be, you know, something to play with.

S K :   *When did you fall in love/hate with the Middle Ages?*
T G :   I don't know . . .

S K :   *It's certainly a big part of what you've done.*
T G :   Yeah. As a kid, I remember in Panorama City, out in L.A., you used to take five-gallon containers for ice cream, and you'd cut out a slit and make a visor, and use eucalyptus branches for swords and build shields. I was obsessed with the Middle Ages. Even in Minneapolis I was into heraldry, there was something about that imagery that I like. I think, when I started working in films . . . the advantage of the Middle Ages is it's a bit like a Western, it's archetypal. You know who the characters are, there's a clear hierarchy, there's a king, he's up there, there's a peasant down there, there's a knight, there's a priest, a bishop, you kind of know where they all fit within the society, and then you can play with those archetypes. I mean, I've always liked doing that, I've always liked taking objects that are known and then twisting, and that's I think what the Middle Ages were. But I also like the imagery of the Middle Ages, you know, pre-Freudian. Things weren't abstract, you know . . . if you had a brain problem, there was probably some devil here with his teeth in your skull, sucking your brains out! It was much more vital, the imagery, I thought. You know, dealing with dragons, I don't know, I can't grow up, I don't want to, it's so sad. (laughs)

S K :   *(laughs) I think we're almost in time for another clip, then. It's interesting to hear you talk about how clear the archetypes are in the Middle Ages and how that's useful to you. I'd like to jump ahead, we're going to do a clip from Terry's next film,* Time Bandits, *which, as Terry was pointing out today was until very recently the most successful independent film ever made. We're about to look at a sequence from* Time Bandits, *near the end of the film, when little Kevin and the Time Bandits are in Hell, and are finally going to meet Satan. So let us roll the next clip please.*

[CLIP]

SK: *Well, you've got your archetypes, you've just got all of them, all at once.*

TG: Yeah, I think I've been accused of being too greedy, too often. There was a kid, he's got to battle with evil with all those toys you have, your cowboys, your Indians, your knights, that's what it was about. I wanted the messiness of a kid's playroom. And then the architecture is basically these gigantic Lego blocks, piled up. It was a chance to do a film from a kid's point of view, that's what it was all about, basically, the whole world as seen through a kid's eyes. And it grew from that, because I started from that premise and I wanted the camera to be about there, and I didn't think a single kid could maintain it all, so I had to surround him with people the same size as him. So that's where the Time Bandits came from, yeah. And there was a chance for little guys like that to play heroes for once in their lives, they didn't have to be inside of an R2D2 tin can or inside a Womble costume and all those things that they normally have to do, they got to be heroes. Because most of them were almost as tall as Alan Ladd . . . was, so . . . (laughs) it's not a great leap. And if he could do it, why can't they? And I've always liked taking improbable people and making heroes out of them. Later on, in *The Meaning of Life,* we do it with old men, eighty-year-old men, we allow them to be pirates. It's the same thing.

SK: *But . . . there was all this jumble of times . . . well, you'd done it before with your cutout animations, but now you were doing it with live action, and the film was a surprise hit. Wasn't it, I mean . . .*

TG: I mean, it totally surprised me, because we made it, and I remember getting off a plane in L.A. when we were about to bring it for the first screenings there, and I just looked at the Americans that were hanging around that airport, and said, they're gonna hate it, it's not gonna work, and it went out and it was huge. I mean, by today's standards it's well over a hundred million dollars it made in the States. Which surprised everybody, because at the time it was a film that was . . . the result of madmen. Because we went out with that script, tried to sell it, nobody wanted it. So Denis O'Brien and George Harrison, who, along with Python, had formed a company called Animated Films to make *Life of Brian,* came up with the goods. They paid for the making of the film. When the film was finished Dennis took it out to Hollywood, it was turned down by every studio, again, the finished film, and it ended up ultimately being distributed by . . . the mini-est of the majors, and basically

Denis and George guaranteed five million dollars in prints and ads of their own money, and we used this company as a distribution organization. And by all the rules it shouldn't have worked, and it did. Also, I remember at the time we opened, I think it was November 4, and that was apparently a time when you couldn't open films because nobody went to movies then, and it seemed to me absolutely a perfect time because there was no competition and it seemed to be quite reasonable to go, and we did everything the wrong way and succeeded, so that was both a wonderful and actually maybe a damaging thing, because it builds up your hopes that you can always do that, which you, of course, can't.

S K :   *It's occurred to me that you were, with* Time Bandits, *one of the last success stories of what's considered the golden age of the studio breakdown of the seventies. Maybe our audience knows Peter Biskind's book on seventies filmmaking . . . it has this aura of the era when the rebels got to make their movies, before everything clenched down again, and* Time Bandits *was in a sense one of the last to do that.*
T G :   It was interesting because the studio just didn't want to do it, they couldn't understand that you could make a film for all the family. This was before *E.T.* I mean, *E.T.* came out about a year after, I think, less than a year after [*Time Bandits*] . . . and there's a very innocent . . . what I like about the film, it's a growing-up kind of film too, because the character, Kevin, has got all of his heroes and he goes and meets most of them and they all end up being fools, or knaves, or whatever . . .

S K :   *Not Agamemnon . . .*
T G :   He's the only one! What's interesting with Agamemnon, the Connery character, he wants him to teach him how to kill Trojans, to swordfight and do the wonderful stuff that Agamemnon does when we first meet him. And Agamemnon doesn't do that, he teaches him magic tricks.
[CLIP]

S K :   *There are a bunch of reasons why I wanted to put those two* [Brazil] *clips together, but the first of them is because in both of them, obviously, we have these big, rather empty architectural spaces in which we have these little animated clumps of people wandering through, which, you know, seems to be a theme that runs through your work. Even though the agents in* Brazil, *the ones running*

*through, are evil people, I think you rather enjoy them, for the way they scuttle
around.*

T G : I'm not even sure if they're evil, they're just, like most people [doing]
other jobs, they're pathetic. You know, they're doing whatever the boss
demands of them, they're evil in the sense that they're not taking the responsibility for their own actions, they're just desperate to please whoever it is
that. . . . The thing in the *Brazil* corridors, there's only one corridor in that
whole sequence, that's all we could afford; that corridor you see is about fifty
feet long, maybe less. From here to the back. And that's all there is. And . . .
what we're doing is tossing, swinging the camera into, or off the corridor
into a bit of black and then continuing that move starting with another
camera over on this side of the corridor and swinging onto the corridor again
and it's . . . I haven't seen it for a while and it really impresses me because I
know, there's nothing there. (laughs) It's all sleight of hand. It's just this one
card we've been showing you, it looks like a pack of cards.

S K : *Another reason I wanted to show this clip is because I love the cheapness of
the joke with the desk. It's something that can be, you know, there's no budget there
. . . it's an idea . . .*

T G : Everybody who's worked in an office knows about the importance of
the size of your desk, and I love the idea that he's been, what's the word, he's
given a promotion and they actually had to create an office for him, so what
they did is cut the office our friend Harry Lime is in in half. That guy, the
day before, had a complete desk and now he only has half a desk. He's been
reduced to this sorry state. . . . Yeah, it's the ruthlessness of things in the film,
where, to deal with a problem, they're very pragmatic—the people who put
those ducts that frequent most of *Brazil,* if there happens to be a beautiful
tapestry in the way, it goes right through the tapestry. And these are the
things you do. It's very much . . . there's an element in there about the sacri-
fice of aesthetics for the goodies, the things you want, the mod-cons, the
things that make your life a little bit easier. The ducts are there to service
you. And the ducts are also there to keep an eye on you; there's a two-way
relationship with everything, every television you get, you actually see the
world, but the world somehow comes into your life and transforms you. So
that was very much the thinking behind everything. And the technology,
none of it works, basically, in the film. There's a great belief in technology,

but it's like the elevator at the beginning, it doesn't quite come up to the floor, it doesn't do it, it's irritating.

S K :   *Yeah, because this film came out very soon after* Blade Runner, *and there was some superficial comparison made with* Blade Runner *at the time, but I think one fair comparison is,* Brazil *and* Blade Runner *both defined the worn-out future, which has now become a convention.*

T G :   It was that idea that technology . . . I think what we do more in *Brazil* than they did in *Blade Runner* is emphasize the fact that they believe, want to believe, that technology is going to give you goodies, and it never quite delivers what it promises. And that was very much a product of growing up in America, really, in the forties and fifties, when we really believed that technology was going to answer our problems. And it's never done that. It's just complicated our lives.

S K :   *But it was really an economical film, what you talked about, the corridors and everything, and part of the battle that happened over the release of the film in the United States, one thing that everybody had to admit was that this fifteen million dollar film looked like a forty million dollar film . . .*

T G :   We actually made it for thirteen and a half million dollars. We shared out the excess with the crew. (audience laughs)

S K :   *Ah, excellent.*

T G :   We had a fifteen million dollar budget and we brought the thing in a million and a half under budget, which is crazy, since we started out shooting a script that had I shot the whole script, probably would have been ten million over budget, and then it would have been a twenty-five million dollar film. I think it was the twelfth week of the shoot, I suddenly realized, we're not going to make it. We're in real trouble here, this is the twelfth week of a twenty-week shoot, and we stopped for two weeks, and I just started pulling page after page out of the script, because the script was even more ambitious than the film that's up there, the dream sequences were much more elaborate, there were more of them. It was almost as if there were two films going on. And they were almost equally balanced. And I cut huge numbers of the fantasy sequences out so we didn't have to shoot them, so we saved money. The whole thing was very strange, because in the end we ended up doing a lot of the special effects, the flying sequences and all, they all ended up in this warehouse that was Her Majesty's stationery office . . . warehouse. So we actually ended up in the warehouse of all the paperwork of England, which is wonderfully appropriate for *Brazil.*

s k : *It is perfect. I didn't know if we should get into all the disputes about the film. Probably everyone here knows, but* Brazil *was the first and I believe only film ever to be voted best picture of the year by the Los Angeles Film Critics without ever having been released. (TG laughs) A real distinction. But it's a long story. There is a book out—I brought my copy to wave at you—it's by Jack Mathews, who was covering the story for the* Los Angeles Times, *it's called,* The Battle of Brazil: Terry Gilliam versus Universal Pictures, *and it has the screenplay in it, so I didn't want to get into detail unless you wanted to talk more about it . . .*

T G : No, it's a long story, but the end result was that we achieved something you're not supposed to be able to do. You're not supposed to take on the system and win, especially in Hollywood, and we did, and we did it by being silly. This is the kind of weaponry that they don't understand out there. (audience laughs) They understand lawyers, they understand money, they understand all those things, and basically, without going into the whole thing, it turned out Universal was very much the world of *Brazil,* it was the most bureaucratic of all the studios. Literally, you had to wear gray suits, and depending on what level within the organization you were, the tone of gray was determined—dark gray, light gray, medium gray, and it was like that— and because they had basically taken the film away and were refusing to release it, we were in a situation where the producers said, oh, we've got to get lawyers and go to battle, and I said, we can't, we can't win. They don't have to release the film, it doesn't mean much to them, it means everything to us. So I said the only way to do it is to personalize the battle and not let anybody hide behind bureaucratic responsibility or corporate responsibility. And so with Sid Sheinberg, who was the head of the studio, who had fool- ishly got into this battle with me, I decided to personalize it, so I took an ad out in *Variety,* which is—in retrospect when I looked at it, I practically shat myself with how foolish I was to do this. But it was in *Variety,* open the pages and all you're seeing is numbers—ten million in the first two seconds, you know, twenty million in the first hour, you know, it's money, money, money, money—and suddenly you came to a page that was just rimmed in black, like an obituary notice, and there was nothing on the page except in the middle, in smallish type, "Dear Sid Sheinberg, when are you going to release my film *Brazil?* Signed, Terry Gilliam." And this you don't do. (audience laughs) And suddenly, whoa! The journalists, everybody, came to the rescue. Jack Mathews, who was with the *L.A. Times,* basically started a dialogue between me and Sid—by then we weren't speaking—and he would say, "Terry just said this, Sid, what do you say," and Sid would say something, and we kept this thing going, and I was going on talk shows, like Maria Shriver's show and all, Joel Siegel, and Bobby De Niro was very good because he, even though he had a small part in the film, when we needed him he came to our rescue, and they were desperate to have interviews with him, so he and I would go on and she would say, I hear you have a problem with the studio, and I would say, I don't have a problem with the studio, I have a problem with one man, his name is Sid Sheinberg and he looks like this! And I'd pull out an eight-by-ten photograph and say, there, millions of Americans, that's the man! (audience laughs) And he had never been treated like this. This is a man who was very powerful, who sat in his office and the world kowtowed to him, and it drove him crazy. And it was fun. It was painful, because this went on for months, and I thought the film was never going to be released, but in the end L.A. critics . . . I mean, the studio got crazier and crazier, and they even took out an embargo on us showing the film anywhere in America, and we started a series of clandestine screenings . . . a few friends in L.A., and eventually enough of the L.A. critics saw it and realized it was an important film and discovered in their bylaws it didn't say a film actually had to be released to be included in the competition. And this is the year Universal had *Out of Africa,* this was their big thirty-five, thirty-seven million dollar spectacular, and they're all in New York for the premiere, all in their white, you know, their new jackets and all, and the L.A. critics announced the awards, and it's "Best Picture, *Brazil.*" "Best Screenplay: *Brazil.*" "Best Direction: *Brazil.*" And, they died. And the film had to be released, and they released it in L.A. and New York, they didn't have posters, they didn't have anything. They actually had Xeroxed copies of some artwork that they stuck outside the cinemas. And in those two cinemas, we did more business per seat than any film over the Christmas, the holiday season. So it was out. And it was great, and there were a lot of people who were calling—writers who were grateful because they thought we had brought down the system, and I said, no, we haven't brought down the system, we've made a little crack in it that maybe a couple of you can slither through while they're in this state of confusion. (audience laughs) And that was it. A couple of films got made that wouldn't have been made, so we did something useful.

S K : *Well, we're going to go on to other battles now. We're going to show a clip from Terry's next film,* The Adventures of Baron Munchausen, *but before we do that we're going to show another little clip from* Time Bandits. *We're going to start with the clip from* Time Bandits *where Kevin and the Time Bandits go back to the Napoleonic wars, and then we're going to look at something from the very beginning of* The Adventures of Baron Munchausen.

T G : And I'm going to go to the toilet while you're watching it.

S K : *Oh.*

[CLIP]

S K : *So, two versions of the theater of war, separated by what, about ten years in making. But remarkably consistent with each other, and obviously* Munchausen *looks great, it just looks beautiful on the screen, it's a wonderful print they sent; but you had a crane, you had many more people, you had a bigger set . . . you once did a very nice book about the art of animation and I remember, you gave your primary rule for animators, which was, if it looks like it's going to be a lot of trouble, don't do it. (TG laughs).*

T G : I wish I had read that book before I made *Munchausen.* (laughs) *Munchausen* was . . . it was some kind of punishment for hubris. I wanted to make the biggest thing around, and I think . . . I mean, it's a stunningly beautiful film, and . . . it was interesting to have more money, so we could actually wallow in the detail more, because with *Time Bandits* we made the film for five million dollars, and *Munchausen* probably cost forty million dollars, so there's a lot you can do with that extra money. But it's funny, I haven't even thought about the fact that both of them have this, you know, city-under-siege battle, and the theater going on in the middle of it. I think it's me, just making a statement about what is important in life. It's about how the theater and entertainment and art, no matter how dire the world is, have to be kept alive.

S K : *Well, that's certainly the theme of the movie.*

T G : In *Munchausen* I loved the stage set. It was a chance to almost do my animation, because of this huge set, and everything is very close to my original animation, only now it's three-dimensional, it's big, there's real people in there.

s k : *Oh, not only that, but the episode when they go to the moon, you have all these architectural cutouts. But done much more elaborately . . .*
 t g : What's interesting in the moon sequence in *Munchausen* is . . . not having the money to do it properly. . . . The moon sequence, I don't know how many of you've seen it, basically has two people, the king and queen of the moon, and their heads seem to leave their bodies at different points. It's the very symbol of sort of a Cartesian mind-body dualism, is what it ended up. But what was originally in the script, what we set out to do, which was budgeted for, was 2,000 people on the moon, and it was going to be a huge sequence, a Cecil B. DeMille sequence, with Sean Connery playing the king of the moon. And the film reached painfully dire circumstances; it was very much like . . . the beginning of the film and what the film was about were the same thing. Six weeks into the film, we discovered all the money was gone. We were out in Spain and they were going to close down the whole show, they were going to sue me for misrepresentation and fraud, and they were trying to seize all my assets, my house; my wife was pregnant at the time and it was just a nightmare, it was living in wartime. And again we shut down for a couple of weeks, like we did on *Brazil*. I didn't have to convince them, they were closing the movie down. And again, Charles McKeown and I sat down and tore these 2,000 people out of the moon, and ended up with two. And what happened is that we had started building a model of one of the sets, and that was going to be . . . it was this big inverted dome, a cupola like Saint Peter's, and it was going to be this huge dome which was an amphitheater where a big banquet went on. Well, we couldn't, in the end, build it, and what we had was the structure of it, which was a part of this thing, the ribs of it, and so that became our set. Earlier on in the moon sequence, when they arrive, there're all these buildings moving back and forth, and what they were was in fact the drawings of the buildings we were going to make, which we didn't have the money now to do. And so at the end of the shoot we literally took the architectural drawings, blew them up so they were about that high, mounted them on plywood, cut them out, colored them with felt-tip markers—it was back to animation again—put them on runners, and pulled them back and forth. And that was the sequence. Now, what was interesting about it was, the end result was in many ways more magical and

more inventive and more surprising than it would have been had I done
what I intended to do. I think this has happened more times than not making films. I'm curtailed by time or budgets or whatever, and end up having
to make choices that are more original than I would have if I had the time or
money. I'm saved from my own mediocrity by my lack of money, time and
time again.

S K :   *I'd also like to mention the beautiful performance John Neville gives in the*
film, and maybe this can be a little segue for us to talk about the film for which we
won't show any clips, Fisher King, *which was the commercial hit that you made,*
which was recovery for you . . .
T G :   Yeah, because I mean, everything that could have gone wrong on *Mun-*
chausen did, and yet we ended up with a film that I'm really proud of. I think
it's stunningly beautiful and really quite a wonderful film. But it was the
only time I've compromised for political reasons. . . . This happens every few
years: You happen to be at a studio where the person who started the film
with you, who was in charge, is now gone, and this was the case on *Mun-*
chausen—David Puttnam was the head of the studio at the beginning, and
he went the way of most executive flesh and was replaced by somebody else.
So what happens in those instances is that the new regime has no interest at
all in the old regime's films being successful. It's easier to look good if those
previous films have failed. And we got caught in one of those situations, as
did other filmmakers at the same time. We were the one that was more obvious, because we had been in the press a lot for going over budget; it was a
kind of comeuppance for the success of pulling *Brazil* off, you know, okay,
the smart guy gets his comeuppance this time. And the studio said, well, if
you can cut the film down to two hours, we're there. Two hours is always
this magical figure somehow—the film is going to do better—and for the first
time in my life I did cut it down to that time, even though I think the film is
better longer. But they were my cuts and I live by them. But what happened
in the end, having done that, the studio then completely betrayed us and
released the film with only 117 prints, that's all that were ever made in
America. You know, an art film gets four or five hundred prints now. And it
was just a complete betrayal, and despite the fact that the film opened to
reviews and business as good as anything they'd had since *Last Emperor*. And
yet . . . they were in the process at that time of selling, or being sold, or trying
to sell themselves to Sony, and they were balancing the books that year, and

what they discovered is you can balance the books if you don't make films and spend any money on marketing them. So they ended up going in the black for the first time. (laughs) The worst thing you can do is make films, you only lose money when you make films. And so they succeeded in all their things, and *Munchausen* was one of the victims of this successful transfer.

s k : *Nevertheless, we do have the film and we have Neville's performance . . .*
T G : Which is brilliant.

s k : *Which is brilliant, and then in* Fisher King *you had four brilliant performers for the leads, and I wanted to talk with you about that a little bit, because I think it's an overlooked aspect of your work as a director. Everybody talks about your eye, and everybody talks about the production design, but you obviously have a wonderful way with actors, because so many people have given wonderful performances for you.*
T G : It really is, it's one of the most irritating things . . . I remember with *Brazil,* when it came out in England, there was only one review which mentioned Jonathan Pryce's performance, which was an astonishing performance, and it holds the film together. But they were so bowled over by the look of the thing that they spent their time talking about that, and that's not . . . yes, it's part of the film, but it's not the heart of the film, it's not what holds it together. And performances have always been central. John Neville definitely in *Munchausen,* and when it came around to doing *Fisher King,* after the *Munchausen* experience I was really depressed, I really wanted to pack it in, I didn't know what to do, and I didn't want to do a big film, I was actually saying, I want to do a really small film, I'll do a film about a schizophrenic, but only one half of his personality. (audience laughs) This is the way we're gonna work now. And I was banging around, trying to decide what I was going to do, and this script turned up, and it was the first time a script arrived that I read that I hadn't written or been involved in the writing. And there was this wonderful script, by Richard LaGravenese, and it was a script that was good because he wrote it for himself, he didn't write it to get a film made within the system, he wrote a script that came from his heart, and there were these four characters that . . . I understood all of them, I was besotted with them. I thought, I wish I'd been able to write that script, because the ideas in it were things that I felt totally at ease with, and they were saying the same

kinds of things I wanted to say. So here was a chance to go do several things: go into Hollywood, for the first time make a film within the Hollywood studio system, with no special effects, the first time I worked without final cut, as far as a contractual thing, and I just wanted to put my head in the lion's mouth and show I could do it. And it was, in many ways, the most pleasurable film I've made, because it was the easiest. It was four actors, and the trick is to choose the right people and then encourage them to be as good as they're capable of being. For years I was always in awe of the directors who were great with actors, how do they do it, and I still have never learned how to do it except all I know is . . .

SK: *Except you do it.*
TG: (laughs) But by being a good audience, that's all I know how to do. I am intelligent enough to choose good people who are there already, and then you provide them with an audience—you know, when they're tragic you cry, when they're funny you laugh, you encourage them. I mean, my job, it seems to me, is to build this perimeter wall around this playground where we then can go in. They're being paid a lot of money, to get to play, like children; they get to make fools of themselves, they get to fall on their faces, because it doesn't matter, we can fix it later. And that's what happens. I mean, with *Fisher King,* Robin was the beginning of the whole thing. I think that's why I got the job. I think I was offered the job because I'd worked with Robin on *Munchausen* and they were looking for a director who Robin would feel comfortable with. And they went down all the lists of people he'd worked with, and they were all working, obviously, and they got down to this guy who didn't have a job. "Gilliam, okay, that's interesting." And there was a combination of that and [the fact that] the producers, for whatever reason, wanted to be the ones that could tame the beast, the wild beast that I was seen to be in those days. They came, we talked, and then my first job was to convince Robin to do it, which I then did. And then it was about casting the rest of it, and getting that balance right, and getting Jeff Bridges was the key to it because Jeff is like the anchor. He . . . it's his film. People don't seem to recognize that. Robin got nominated for the awards, Mercedes got an award . . . it's Jeff's film, he holds the film together. And he in a sense was the anchor, because I knew Robin and myself, when we get silly, we just float off into the stratosphere somewhere, giggling, and I wanted somebody that would anchor both of us right to the ground, and that was Jeff. He was

solid as a rock. You know, it was wonderful to watch Jeff and Robin work together, learning from each other. Jeff was picking up comic things and Robin was learning to act, as opposed to being funny all the time, and then Mercedes and Amanda just completed the thing. It was a brilliant force.

s k : *Well, it's wonderful to see how you managed somehow to calibrate the performances, because Robin Williams and Amanda Plummer are such high-strung actors and Jeff Bridges and Mercedes Ruehl are so rooted—completely different styles, and yet you made them mesh.*

t g : But it's kind of what you have to do. The job is to choose the team wisely. It's like we're about to ascend Mount Everest, and you've got to make sure the team is the right team, whether it's the actors, whether it's the technicians, all of it, they've got to be able to work together. It was the first time that we had two weeks of rehearsal, so we got to spend time playing and working out things, developing it, and it's interesting with someone like Robin, who's paid a lot of money, he wants to give value for money. He feels guilty that he's paid so much money, and so his weakness is that he tries to be funny all the time. So the trick was to . . . "don't worry about it, you don't have to be funny, just be there." We worked out a way of working after a while: We'd do the takes as scripted, and then you'd feel the pressure building up, and so okay, I'd give him a couple of takes, just play and do something. And sometimes things would come out of that that were good, and then we'd go back to the script. There was this need for this release occasionally, but they were an amazing team, and I just. . . . To me it was so easy, because they were so good, and you'd just . . . "don't do that, do that." That's directing. (laughs) A bit louder.

s k : *Well, from there you went on to do another project where the script already existed, and it's a movie which to me is a miracle, which is* Twelve Monkeys. *Wonderful, wonderful film, and to me one of the most improbable projects ever. Who would have thought that a big budget remake of Chris Marker's* La Jetée *with Bruce Willis and Brad Pitt would be such a wonderful film?*

t g : That was part of the reason for doing it. When the script arrived I said, "You must be joking! This is going through the system? This'll never get through the system." And I said, well, let's do it. I mean there's this awful need . . . I'm constantly trying to show the people out there . . .

s k :   *Let's pause. Shall we look at some of it first?*
T G :   Nah. (audience laughs)

s k :   *No? Come on, let's look at some of it!*
T G :   All right. (laughs)

s k :   *Then we can talk about that. You can talk about how that script links you with Clint Eastwood, too. I mean, you and Clint Eastwood are the two great directors of David Peoples. Let's look at a little bit of* Twelve Monkeys.
[CLIP]
s k :   *I fear we could spend ninety minutes just talking about that one clip.*
T G :   I haven't seen that in so long. It's quite extraordinary sitting that close to it, it's wonderful.

s k :   *Well, what I love about it, it's got all the Terry Gilliam stuff and it's also this David and Janet Peoples script, all merged together.*
T G :   Dave and Jan are just great writers. When *Unforgiven* came out, I thought it was one of the great scripts of all time. Of course it didn't win the Academy Award, but then it was the only one that didn't from *Unforgiven*. But this script turned up and it was just . . . they had a commission from Universal to write this thing, and they're highly paid writers, so the studio had quite a bit of an investment in this thing and didn't know what to do with it. And I, when I first read the script the thing that appealed to me most was the idea of a boy seeing his own death as a man, and not understanding what he had seen. And that just hit a chord that I wanted to deal with. I avoided getting involved in the film for a long time, but then . . . ultimately the idea of taking as intelligent and complex and demanding [a script] as that and pulling it all the way through that system of Hollywood and getting it out using their marketing tools, power, intrigued me. And off we went. Originally, when they asked me, I wanted Jeff Bridges to do the part that Bruce played, and they didn't want to deal with that. We went around for a long time, and the studio didn't like who I was suggesting and I didn't like who they were suggesting, and I walked away from the project. I said, I'm not going to do this unless we can do it intelligently. And then I got a call from my agent saying that Bruce was really interested. Now, I'd met Bruce when we were doing *Fisher King,* because he actually wanted to do the part that Jeff played in that, and we spent an afternoon together, and I really

liked him because there was a side to him you don't always see in films. I'd also been intrigued by the very first *Die Hard*. There's a scene in that where he's in this building, glass everywhere, and he's picking glass out of his feet, he's on the phone with his wife, and he's in tears. And I thought that was really interesting, and he said that was his idea, it wasn't in the script to show that side, this weak side of him, quote. And that really intrigued me. So when he said he was interested, we met in New York, and to me what was important, when you're dealing with some superstar like Bruce . . . it's a very dangerous game you're about to play, because they're very powerful, they get paid a lot of money, and they believe they're right. And so here was an instance of where he wanted to do it, he was at a stage where he wanted to prove he was a good actor, and so I said, okay, but you've got to come to this think naked, totally. You can't bring your entourage, you don't get any of the perks. He actually worked for scale, basic scale of an actor on this thing, and he came with nothing. And that's why it worked, because he wanted to prove something. And I'm very lucky in getting people that, at certain points in their career, wanted to show another side of themselves. And my direction to Bruce was really simple. I said, "You can't do the cute smirk, you can't do the steely-eyed thing you do, and there's that little [thing] you do with your lips when you're nervous, you can't do that." (audience laughs) End of direction. "And if you don't do those things, you'll be great." (laughs) And it was really interesting for him to try—because he's always been such an external kind of actor, it's all out there—to internalize it. And that was a real challenge for him, and I think he's quite extraordinary in the film. The sad thing was he wasn't acknowledged in any way; there was no nominations for anything, and I think, the more I watch the film, the more times I've watched it, the more I appreciate what a great performance there is. Brad, on the other hand, was interesting because Brad wanted to get involved and, strangely enough, he wanted to play the part that Bruce plays. He wanted to play Cole, which makes more sense, because he's the more laconic character, and really, if you're going to cast it, you could have taken a young Bruce Willis and made him into the Brad Pitt character, the smart, fast-talking one, and vice versa. So it was interesting to take two people and cast them opposite type. And Brad took a long time to convince me, because I didn't think he could do it. And yet he was so determined to prove something I couldn't say no. I mean, the studio . . . "You're out of your mind, Terry, why are you hesitating? Brad Pitt wants to be in your movie!" "No, he's going to ruin it, he's gonna destroy it!" (laughs) And so in the end I fell victim to his incredible keenness to do this thing, and I put him together with a guy named Stephen Bridgewater, who trained Jeff Bridges as a DJ in *Fisher King*. He works as a voice coach, and I put him together with Brad, and he said, "Why are you doing this to me, Terry? What have I ever done to you?" (audience laughs) He said, "This kid comes in, the guy smokes, he's got no breath control, he's got a lazy tongue, he can't do the part." And I said, well, can you go to work, and Brad worked for months, he really worked hard at it, and Stephen worked with him. And Brad was supposed to be sending me tapes of his progress, which he relentlessly failed to do, which made me more and more nervous. We're now shooting and I kept calling Stephen, and Stephen said, "Oh, I don't know, it's not going really good," and then one day he called and said, "He can do it. He can do it." And when he turned up, that opening scene in the mental hospital—that was his first day at work on the film—he just exploded. He was wonderful, he was funny and outrageous. And all this stuff he was doing. A lot of people think it's too much. I don't, I think it's wonderful. And I think it's a wonderful combination, the two of them, Bruce and Brad, the way they worked together. It was nice to see Bruce, he's like the old gunfighter, and here's the kid in town, and rather than being frightened by him, he sort of embraced him. And I think that's his way of controlling it, to hold him close. (laughs) It was very interesting. The crew really liked Brad, and Bruce normally didn't come sit around the set a lot, he'd go back to his trailer. Once Brad was there, because Brad just loves sitting on the set, so Bruce was sitting on the set. (laughs) It was one big happy family. It was wonderful to watch the two of them.

s k : *We want to have some time for questions from the audience, and we also have one more clip that we'd like to show to bring us really up to date, with* Fear and Loathing in Las Vegas. *So I'm going to suggest that we show the* Fear and Loathing in Las Vegas *clip, and we've chosen for you the moment when Hunter Thompson and his Samoan lawyer enter Las Vegas (TG laughs), and then after we show the clip maybe we can take some questions from the audience. How does that sound? All right? Let's do it.*
[CLIP]
s k : *To quote Bruce Willis, "They forced me to take drugs."*
T G : I love that line in *Twelve Monkeys*. Why would anybody force you to

take drugs? It all follows on, you see. There's this undercurrent through all
the films.

s k : *Well, we've got a few minutes here for questions, so raise your hands high in
the air, pump them wildly . . . yes, you. . . . The question is, there's a rumor that
Terry Gilliam went to MCAD—Minneapolis College of Art and Design—and was
kicked out. Any truth to this rumor?*
t g : Well, I was probably eleven years old when this happened, so they
probably wouldn't kick me out at that age. No, it's all a lie. I mean, I did go
to the Walker, I think for one weekend, years ago. When I was about ten or
eleven. There was a drawing course.
    [The next question is:]

s k : *Where did the song come from, from* Brazil?
t g : Harry Berrosa wrote it, it's a very famous song, I mean, in the forties
America was all about going south to Rio for romance, for love and all that.
And that song has always been, to me, a wonderful encapsulation of that
sort of innocent, romantic escape. And that's why the film is called *Brazil,*
because the film . . . strangely enough, the film was not originally, the song
was not originally "Brazil," because I was originally using a song that Ry
Cooder had recorded, "Maria Alena." Which is, again, a beautiful Latin song,
and there's a version of "Brazil" which we used in there by Geoff Muldaur,
Maria Muldaur's husband, it's an album called *Cottage Pie.* And it's a very
silly version, which we play when Jonathan is driving to the Buttles' flat in
his tiny little car, and that was the song that sort of got me going again, so
"Brazil" is . . . Harry Berrosa wrote it.

s k : *The next question is: Is there truth to the rumors that Terry Gilliam wants to
direct the comic book series* Watchmen *or* Alice in Wonderland?
t g : After *Baron Munchausen* Joel Silver, who produced *Die Hard, Lethal
Weapon* and all those films, came to me and said he had forty million dollars
and the rights to do *Watchmen.* And Charles McKeown and I sat down and
wrote a script which I wasn't really happy with, because to condense *Watchmen* into a two-hour film is like, you know, you're throwing away half the
material. And by losing the detail you're really losing the point, so I wasn't
totally convinced, and Joel didn't have forty million dollars, in the end.
We're walking around L.A., I'd just made *Munchausen,* which has gone way

over budget and has flopped, he'd just made *Die Hard 2,* which went ten trillion dollars over budget and hadn't done as well as it was supposed to, and we're asking for money for this very dark and complicated comic book. So we didn't get it and it didn't get made and, in a way, I think it would be better to be done as a miniseries for television, because you actually need about five hours to do that thing properly. Alan Moore, when I talked to him about it, he said, basically, that he would rather I fuck it up than he did, I think was the term. And as far as *Alice in Wonderland,* I think I keep making *Alice in Wonderland* in one form or another. And there's a script that has been pouring out of my fax machine for the last several months by some people who I don't know who they are, and every day I get another three pages of *Alice in Wonderland.* Which I then put in the bin. I'm not going to do it that way. (laughs) If I do it, it'll be my script. But at the moment, no plans for it.

S K: *Let's get some questions from this side of the audience. In the blue shirt, there.*
S P E C T A T O R :   *Well, I was just wondering, we've talked a lot about you as a director, but it's the screenwriter part of you that I'd like to talk about. How do you go about writing?*
T G :   I mean . . . there's no simple way. A script I was working on after *Fisher King* is called *The Defective Detective,* where basically I started going through all my notebooks and all the other bits I had left out of films I had done, and put them all out there and said, can I make any sense of this? I like that, I like that, let's see if we can stick them together. And it started that way, and I actually worked out a story based on these disparate elements and sticking them together. I always need to work with somebody else, because my dialogue is not good, and that's why there is always somebody else there who can write better dialogue than I can. At the moment, I'm working on something called *The Man Who Killed Don Quixote.* It was partly because I had been working on *Don Quixote* and found it's such an impossible book to translate, so by shifting it, I could take the bits I like and put them in my story, and use the good bits and rearrange it. So there's no rule. A lot of times there is an image that sits up there, that starts the process. Oftentimes that image is not in the final film, strangely enough. It's a catalyst that starts things going. But I kind of work out a story, I work out a shape of something, that's the first thing, and then I start dealing with more details.

S P E C T A T O R :   *On video, the immense scale of your movies. . . .*
T G :   It's sad in a sense that most people probably end up seeing the films on

video. I just hope you've got a big television set at home. (laughs) Sit really close to it, it's better that way. My wife prefers *Brazil* on video, because she found the image is so terrifying up on the big screen, it actually was an unpleasant experience for her. But suddenly in that box, it's contained, it's okay. I actually do supervise the videos when we master them, because I try to make them as good as we can, because I know there's going to be more people watching them that way. And I love the fact that retrospectives come along occasionally. I mean, as you get older you get retrospectives, so people get to see these things. We were just talking about this guy at Universal who's going to make new prints of things. . . . I use wide-angle lenses partly [to make you feel like you're] *in* the thing. When I'm looking through a camera I can never get into the film enough. I'm trying to get in there and there's this distance between me and it. Unfortunately on video it's safe, it's tame. The beast is tamed.

S K : *Let's see if we can hit one more question, and we'll take one from the back. Yes.*

S P E C TAT O R : *Do you have any idea what your next film will be?*

S K : *Excellent last question.*

T G : No, I don't, actually. I'm working on this script, this *Man Who Killed Don Quixote*. There's a couple of other . . . there's this *Defective Detective* script I wrote several years ago with Richard LaGravenese [that is] becoming possibly disentangled from a particular producer in Hollywood, who was sitting on it. I really don't know. My problem is, until I have finally given total and utter birth to whatever my latest project is, I can't really think that much forward. Like *Fear and Loathing*'s about to open in England, and once it's open next week in England I think I then seriously have to think 'bout getting a job.

S K : *We'll all look forward to that. Thanks to all of you for being here, thanks to Terry Gilliam for tonight and for all the years before. (applause)*

Childhood, Vocation, and First Experiences of a Rebel Dreamer

JORDI COSTA AND SERGI SÁNCHEZ/1998

TERRY GILLIAM IS NOT a clear exponent of the law of Flaubert. He is not, as Martin Amis said while talking of J. G. Ballard, methodical and normal in life, and uncontrollable and original in art. He seems, at first sight, as original and uncontrollable in life as in art. However, to these two journalists that rang the bell of his mansion in Highgate Village a slightly cloudy 31 July, he gave the impression that the many-sided inventiveness of Terry Gilliam could only evolve in that house, which the creator shares with his wife and three children: Amy Rainbow, Holly Dubois, and Harry Thunder. A British house, green, comfortable as a dog panting by the heat of the fireplace. Going up the winding and narrow spiral staircase to his enormous study, behind his wife and right-hand man Maggie Weston, we expect to meet Baron Munchausen, shut away in his comfortable ivory tower, happy to see, from the heights, the sights of a definitely imaginary country, a country where the word "horizon" has no longer meaning.

A back. That was the first thing we saw. A back surrounded by models from his films, illuminated by the neon of *Brazil,* sitting in front of a computer. It was the study (and the back) of an explorer, upholstered in rugs and wooden furniture. It was an oceanic study: large as a sea of sand. The Arabian music that Gilliam's back was listening to impeded him from hearing his wife. The journalists had arrived. It took the back time to understand, but

From Jordi Costa and Sergi Sánchez, *Terry Gilliam: El Soñador Rebelde,* trans. Piasca Arbe and Rosa Sáez (San Sebastián: Euskadiko Filmategia-Filmoteca Vasca, 1998), 301–09. Reprinted by permission of Jordi Costa and Sergi Sánchez.

once it understood, it rose like a spring and it became a face. Barefoot and smiling: that was how his words were going to be, barefoot and smiling. In a room attached to the study, covered in art books and mountains of scripts piled up in the corners, a chat of almost four hours was going to take place during which Gilliam, clutching his knees, like a big child without new shoes, would answer, would laugh, and would burst out in noisy laughter. Robust, energetic, insultingly frank, Gilliam is like his house, and by extension, like his films: pleasant and lively, hospitable and excessive, untidy and uncontrolled.

Q : *In your cinematographic work, the figure of the child and the childish glance have a great importance. Did the small Terry Gilliam resemble any of the child characters that would later appear in your work?*

A : No, I don't think so. I grew up in the countryside. We lived a few blocks away from the lake, so I was like Huckleberry Finn or Tom Sawyer. I almost always played outside. As a child, the most important thing for me was listening to the radio, because my family didn't have a television. We only had a radio. I think that, somehow, the radio developed my visual sense, because I had to imagine everything. There, there were neither faces nor suits. So you had to create all of that. I believe that it is really excellent training for a visual artist. It does not seem to be, but it is. It makes your imagination work.

My father was a carpenter. We both used to build houses in the trees. We used to make igloos in the snow. It was so physical, I was so close to Nature. . . . In fact, I lived in nature, I lived surrounded by it. And that was how that little game of inventing and creating things with all you had around you came about. The ingredient had always been there.

It's funny. We lived in the countryside and later we moved to the city, but I continue [to be] obsessed by the countryside. I have always believed that it is more real. However, in the countryside I have no creative impulse. Only very basic creative impulses, such as to build a stone wall or things like that. It is only when I am in the city that I need to express myself. The society is a disaster, a permanent disaster. It always makes me feel angry and critical. And my films come about from that anger. I think that if I had always lived in the countryside I would never have been able to do any creative work.

I also used to do magic. It was because of my father. He had a little theater to do tricks, but it wasn't for me. That was the great moral of my experiences with magic: the tricks did not work, like what happens in my films (laughs). Or, at least, they never completely worked.

It's strange, as a child I did not have the type of political anxiety as I have had as an adult, although all the children of my films always show political and social attitudes. I think the only thing I share with them is that I also spent all my childhood asking things, asking why, why, why . . . why this has to be like that or why it doesn't. In my films, the children are always angry with the adults. The adults put limits and the children don't know their limits. I was like that as a child, and, in fact, I am still like that. I don't know my limits. It is a way of staying young because you don't know up to what point you can reach. You don't know what your abilities are. It's like a permanent state of childhood, of innocence . . . or of stupidity. I'm not sure (laughs).

Q: *Your childhood was spent in a rural community in western Minneapolis, Medicine Lake. Do you think that that environment had any influence on your later creative work?*
A: I think that, probably, I'm stuck to the idea that having lived in the countryside as a child was like a utopia, something magical, and because of that my films are always trying to go back to that idealized place from an adult place, from the frustration and the anger. It's as easy as that. If I had been born in the city, it's possible that I would try to do that journey in the opposite direction.

Q: *Why is the idea of the city so important in the work of someone who, like you, comes from a rural environment?*
A: After Los Angeles, which is not really a city, I went to New York. When you move from the countryside to New York, you have the sensation of having been dragged there. New York was the great American city. If you have dreams and ambitions, these end up carrying you to the great metropolis. It was a nightmare. For me New York turned out to be completely claustrophobic. But it wasn't only a nightmare; it was also a fascinating place. I remember when I didn't have money; it's a difficult city to live in without money. I think that the only thing that I really liked about New York was that it used to break its own rhythm: "Pum!, pum!, pum!," like a musician playing the drums. But that also made it difficult for me; I had to find my own rhythm within another that made me go on: "Come on!, come on!" You can go

crazy. It was because of that that I had to go. New York left such a mark on me that I think all my films deal with the three years I spent there.

Something that really catches my attention is that in New York nobody looks upwards. In that way nobody sees how extraordinary it is. For example, they don't see the castles. . . . All of that is magical and nobody sees it! In *The Fisher King* I tried to draw a line that went up towards the skyscrapers to show that nobody looks upwards in New York. London, however, is a marvelous city. Los Angeles is too slow. New York is too intense. London has a lot of energy, but you can avoid it. London distinguishes between the place that the individual occupies and the place of society, between the intimate and the collective.

Q: *In 1951, the Gilliam family moved to California. How did that affect your learning years?*
A: I think the fact that we were next to Hollywood was very disturbing. I was there! I went to school with boys whose parents worked in the cinema world. If I had stayed in Minnesota I would not have taken the same path. It's obvious. In California I spent my school years. I suppose I used up the biggest part of my energy at school. Back then I did not plan on being a film director. Progress and technology were really thriving after the war. All of us wanted to be engineers or scientists, because we had gone to the moon. So I was busy with that. I didn't start to break the rules until I went to university.

Q: *You have spoken of those little magic shows that you organized with your father. Sometimes you have declared that this experience was related to your admiration for Georges Méliès. Can you talk about that? When did you see Méliès's work for the first time?*
A: I used to do the type of magic trick that you can buy in a magic shop. The Chinese rings and all of that. . . . I wasn't very good at the tricks but I knew all of them. In a certain way, my films try to be like magic tricks. I want to surprise the people, leave them astounded. Magic leaves you dumbfounded, it makes the impossible possible. That is what I try to do with my films.

Ah, Méliès! I probably saw some of his films before knowing they were his. They always had something so marvelous. They were so funny and silly, a mixture of everything I liked. There was something very special about his sincerity, about the intensity of his cinema, about that capacity to convert everything into a game. I loved the idea of a guy able to dare to use references to the legend of Mephistopheles for his films. He used cinema as a means that has many more resources to take the spectator in than theater. In theater you had to use mirrors, and in films you don't need those kinds of tricks. What I want to say is that what he used to do is more or less what I have been doing since I was at high school. I used to design castles for the dances on some panels that my father used to make, some panels of eight by eight. It was what Méliès did in his studio many years before. I was already doing it at sixteen. At least, that's what I felt when I saw his films: that we did the same. He always tried to trick the eye or the brain, and that forms part of what I do: try to trick the brain, do a trick to make you see the things in another way. He did it literally and I do it—more or less—metaphorically. It all comes down to doing tricks so as to make something that you wouldn't have believed five minutes earlier, happen . . . but, it's possible! And I think that magic achieves that. I hope not to end up selling toys in some train station. Well, it wouldn't be a bad job.

Q: *How did your passion for the cinema arise? What films left a mark on your childhood?*

A: The first I remember are things like *Snow White and the Seven Dwarfs* (1938), *Pinocchio* (1940) . . . *The Thief of Bagdad* (1939) was important for me. I saw it when I was very small. I had nightmares for years. I was always trapped in the cave that appears in the film and when I woke up in the morning, it was as if I was tied up, the sheets were all messed up. And the spiders used to come down. . . . That nightmare repeated itself for many years. In that period the films were always magical. Now they are not as much. That is the sad thing about growing old and making films. You go into that dark room, that temple, that magic space. . . . It's the same sensation that you could have when, at midnight, you used to sit around the bonfire, with the glow of light from the fire, and used to listen to a storyteller.

I have always loved adventure films. As you can see, I'm very unsophisticated (laughs). I think that until my adolescence I didn't begin to get to know other things, international cinema. . . I was a great fan of Jerry Lewis, as now my son is of Jim Carrey. I liked the epic films: *Ben Hur* (1959), *The Silver Chalice* (1954). . . . Those films were extraordinary because they talked of other civilizations and other times. It was a way of travelling in time and being able to live, dress, and eat in another way. Each time there was a Roman or a Viking

I was there, stuck to the television. For an American boy that lived in a country where everything was very similar, very monotonous, all of that proved to be very emotional. And I think that because of that I ended up in Europe, as a result of those films. I think that the first film in which I was conscious of a real social background—the first film in which I realized that cinema could do something else rather than entertain—was *Paths of Glory* (1957), by Stanley Kubrick. I was about fourteen years old. It was Saturday, but I stayed at home watching the film, astonished. Later I went running to tell all my friends about it. Nobody had seen it. But, dear God, that film was something different. It made me realize two things: that you could deal with a social theme and that you could move the camera in such a way nobody had done before. Suddenly I was conscious of what is called cinematographic technique: those travelings were marvelous.

Later, when I started university, I discovered great films by Bergman, Kurosawa, Fellini. . . . I became obsessed by all those foreign directors to such an extent that American films seemed rubbish. Actually, I didn't want to see any more American films. Those films drove me crazy.

You know, I began to learn cinema in a very casual way, not like other directors that already know they want to be one from when they are little. They are like encyclopedias, and I am not an encyclopedia of cinema.

Q : *Often your films have a note of myth or of perverse fairy tale. Does this have anything to do with your childhood reading?*
A : I used to read loads of fairy tales. I loved the tales of Aesop. I also used to read adventure books such as *Treasure Island,* by Stevenson. Stories about dogs delighted me. I don't know why I was obsessed by stories about dogs. I liked a Scottish author a lot, who nobody knows now, who used to write books about Scottish dogs. They were part of my basic reading. In some way it was logical that, later, many of my films had a literary base. Sometimes I think that I make films so that, afterwards, the people will go to buy and read books about the same themes.

I grew up with the Bible. We were a very religious family. As you know, in the Bible there are great stories, fantastic tales. I felt very sensitive about those types of stories. They always seem to have a moral, especially in the Bible, and because of that they are like fairy tales or myths. They don't only tell you something to entertain you, but they try to describe a way of life, a way of seeing the world. That is what I look for in my films. Because of that, when I read a script, I let myself go with my searching spirit, and I love that from that search questions and answers arise.

Q: *The influence of cartoons, especially of directors such as Tex Avery, is also apparent in your work. Were they also a childhood influence or was it a later discovery?*

A: Me and cartoons. I'm always ready to make a cartoon. My interest in drawing was an early discovery. I didn't know who Tex Avery or Chuck Jones was until I was thirty, but I loved cartoons, they were marvelous. I never cared who made them. My son is great: he knows exactly who Tex Avery is, he knows his style. I only knew that it was something entertaining. They make me laugh and that's it. I have always worked in a very instinctive way. I never approach the things I like in an academic way. There are people who have studied and say: "Oh, that's by Chuck Jones!" I haven't . . . however, I know the voices of the cartoons . . . (He pauses. Terry hesitates. He can hardly remember the name of the dubber of the Warner cartoons) . . . it was Mel Blanc!!!!

It is strange, but I knew Mel Blanc's name before Tex Avery's. It's as if the actor who put the voice was more important than the guy who made the cartoon. I thought cartoons simply existed. Even though I was always making cartoons, since I was very small. If I had been asked the name of the cartoonist, I would have said Walt Disney. That's all. I didn't know any cartoonist. And what I liked about Disney was his visual power, his taste for detail. . . . I think that a film like *Pinocchio* is terrific. The Disney universe is complete, complex. Compared to Disney, Chuck Jones was a joke. Disney is far superior. The real art is superior.

Q: *Why did you use the cartoons of Tex Avery in* Twelve Monkeys?

A: Because it was cheaper to use them than any others. It's true! (laughs) What Universal asked us for were cheap cartoons. We saw many others that we liked, but we found ourselves with Tex Avery's work. When I saw it . . . oh! it was perfect: brilliant and cheap. The aim was not to get Tex Avery's cartoons, but to get the cheapest cartoons.

Q: *In 1969, Ward Kimball won an Oscar for the animation short* It's Tough to Be a Bird, *a short that used the technique of cut-out animation and had certain*

Gilliamesque touches. Do you think that it was you who influenced the Disney cartoonists in that period?

A :   Maybe it was. Before Monty Python began using it, very few worked with the cut-out animation technique. I think that using this technique was important, because the people could see a new form of animation that had nothing to do with the perfection of the Disney design. It was all very elemental but it was also entertaining. And that was the interesting thing. I'm thinking that in my next film, the special effects might be very rough. I think the public would love it and that they would find it completely new. It would be a form of recuperating the period in which I had the opportunity to use that technique and I was lucky that millions of people could see it. Now the MTV designers use that technique a lot. The American series *South Park* also uses it. The only thing that annoys me is seeing advertisements done with the cut-out animation technique, sound effects and images in the Python style, in such a way that it looks as if it's Monty Python who is promoting the product.

Q :   *Where does that interest for the medieval mythology, present in many of your works, come from?*

A :   I suppose from the films that I saw when I was small, and from Disney. The medieval mythology is a very archetypal imagery, very simple, fundamentally made up of castles and knights. I remember that one of the first things I did as a child was make a shield for myself. The idea of a medieval world made up of a king, a castle, and its knights always fascinated me. A very simple world (laughs). All fairy tales are essentially based on that. So I must have come from a Disney fairy tale.

I still find it moving. I see it in my son. The power a sword has for a child is extraordinary. It's like an extension of his own power. . . . And dragons. I have always been fascinated by the imagery of the Middle Ages. The demons are marvelous, much better than what Freud invented. Freud's theories can reduce the world to a series of nightmares, simplify the psychosis explaining how the mind works. My visual sense tends to be more literal. For me pain is not an abstract idea, it is something that we really see: a monster with its jaws chewing my head. Recently, medicine has been trying to visualize illness. God, that's what they used to do in the Middle Ages! They simply saw it and now we are trying to repeat it. Freud put it all into an abstract world, and I prefer the literal worlds more than the abstract ones: the real demons, the real angels, and the authentic monsters. There is a book I love about the Holy Grail: *Illustrations and the Margins of Medieval Manuscripts*. . . . Oooh, so many things happen in that book! What I want to say is, that there were less limits during that period. The odd thing about the abstract thought is that it doesn't expand but it limits. Or at least that's what I think.

Q : *In California, you went to Birmingham High School and you became one of the best students of your class. Doesn't that fame of the model student contradict your later reputation of a free spirit, irreverent and uncontrollable?*
A : Yeah, okay, maybe! (laughs) I think I was very diligent and I did what I was supposed to do. I was simply doing my job well and my job then was to be a good student. Maybe it was a fools' school, but the truth is I passed everything with distinction.

On the other hand, high school is very good because there are many people, many activities you can join. I like people a lot, although I also like to be independent. Sometimes I can't find a moment to be alone, there is a point in which I hate people.

Later I liked university. We formed a small community of prepared people. In New York, although I was working with the magazine *Help!*, I felt very alone; we weren't a team. I think that because of that I like to make films: because a community is created. When you are making a film, everything is about a common aim. It's marvelous to see how that complicity arises every time I begin a new film.

As for the model student . . . when I went to university I realized that there were more interesting things to do. It was more amusing to be a joker, to play. Playing was very interesting, because the results of any game are often satisfactory. I decided that academic studies were not what I wanted. I felt that I needed the most varied education possible, that would include learning theater, learning how to do silly things. . . . All of that seemed to form part of my education and I think I was right.

Q : *The influence of the magazine* Mad *and the role of Harvey Kurtzman in your creative formation has often been talked about, but were there other comedians who left a mark on you in those years? When did you start drawing? What influences helped you to define a personal style?*
A : I used to read comics at the same time as I read books. I loved the classic illustrations, but I also enjoyed the comics about superheroes, such as Super-

man or Captain Marvel. . . . At the beginning I only read the books and later I began to copy the drawings. By the time I was ten I used to draw quite well, and I improved my technique thanks to the comics. I took almost everything from them. I remember when I was at university, my art teacher used to go mad. He never stopped giving out to me over doing caricatures. "Look at life! Look at the reality! And draw things as they are," he used to say. But I had been drawing comics for so long that it was difficult for me to stop. And, in fact, it was a question of laziness on my part, because I could have done what I was asked to, but I enjoyed doing my drawings. That way, I didn't concentrate on drawing real life as something "serious." I probably should have done so.

Suddenly, I began to pay attention to the comic strips that are printed in newspapers. Things like *Pogo* by Walt Kelly. Then I came across *Mad*. That magazine took the world I knew and made it really enjoyable. When I was at university I began to get to know great cartoonists, such as Jack Davis, Willy Elder. . . . I really liked the drawings of Willy Elder. There was one gag after the other. The drawings were so complex, so full of amusing things . . . like what my films have become. He made you adopt various points of view to be able to grasp all the richness of the drawing.

I was at university when Harvey Kurtzman and other cartoonists founded the magazine *Help!* It was a great magazine, very amusing. It was the only national humor magazine. All the cartoonists of "underground comix" came together in *Help!* because it was the only way they could express themselves with complete freedom. When I finished university, as I had nothing better to do, I went to New York. I had been sending copies of my magazine (*Fang*) to Harvey. Luckily, a guy who worked as an assistant in the magazine *Help!* had left and they were looking for someone; so they gave me the job. It was really extraordinary. After graduating from university, I had got many diplomas in a summer camp. I was reading the autobiography of Moss Hart, who wrote very successful comedies with George Kaufman. It told how much he had admired George Kaufman when he was a boy, and that one fine day he went to New York in search of his maestro and he ended up becoming his partner. It's exactly what happened to me with Harvey. I don't know if it was a coincidence, but that was how it happened.

Working on the illustrated novels that we used to publish in *Help!* was, basically, like making a film: There were actors, costumes, locations. . . . The only difference between both artistic expressions was that, in this case, noth-

ing moved. In some ways, it was my first opportunity to do something similar to a film. It was like drawing a storyboard.

Q : *How do you remember the hectic sociopolitical panorama of the United States*
during the sixties? When, in your youth, was that political standing born?
A : When I was in New York it was a surprising period. The fight for civil
rights was at one of its most explosive moments. The first cartoon I published
was about that subject. I used to make many cartoons about the fight for
civil rights in the magazine *Help!* America was changing very quickly. My
father was from the south, from a very charming and very civilized and
polite place as long as everyone was where he was supposed to be. America
started to change and it became a really ugly, horrible place. That was when
the Vietnam War began. I used to do loads of political caricatures. The good
thing was that all these changes took place within a frame of complete freedom of expression. In the sixties, it seemed as if we could fix America, but
then *Fear and Loathing in Las Vegas* appeared, to show us that it was a country
far from improvement (laughs). Many people I loved had a bad time. I
remember I was in the National Guard, in a regular training session, when I
started to read the *New York Times* articles about David Halverston: it was the
first time I read something credible about the war.

In 1964 I came to Europe. I was very critical about America but I found
that the English, the French, the Spanish . . . used to say horrible things
about my country and I used to answer: "Hey! What are you saying?" Suddenly I surprised myself defending a nation that did things that I didn't agree
with at all (laughs). I thought that I could criticize it, but that those strangers
did not have any right to do so. It was strange to discover that feeling in me.
I am still American, although I don't agree with many things that happen
there.

In Europe you get the feeling of belonging to a very, very long history. In
America you are taught to believe that the world began when you were born.
That creates a very energetic society but, at the same time, it is a society that
behaves like a big child. I think Europe is much more balanced. I'm happy
here. I can keep going back to the past. This house, for example, was built in
1691. In Italy I have another one from the eleventh and twelfth century.

Q : *In all of your films there is an important influence from great artists such as*
Goya, Bosch, or Bruegel. Where does your interest in painting come from? What
are your main influences?

A : I only started off with the paintings of famous artists because everybody knew them and understood them; and then I turned them into something stupid. That always proves to be surprisingly amusing. It's very youthful, very childish. But later I began to draw using works of art that I really admired, such as Bruegel's and Bosch's. I find those artists incredible because of the worlds they are capable of creating in their paintings. I think they could have been film directors if they lived nowadays, because they tell great stories and they love people, the personages from their paintings and what "happens" in their paintings. The strange thing is that I have never thought of any Goya for my drawings. The credit titles of *Cry of the Banshee* (1970), by Gordon Hessler, were inspired from Gustave Doré's illustrations. All of these artists share a powerful imagination and a great sense of reality. They love humanity, although they show it through tortured and painful scenes. They are talking about human experience.

And then there is the surrealism. I love . . . Dali, De Chirico . . . All that world of great painters! They are there, I simply listen to them and . . . wow! The fact that I find some more interesting than others depends on their temperament. Realistic painting has always attracted my attention more. I don't like abstract art a lot. Jackson Pollock or Mark Rothko . . . they are not bad, but I don't connect with them. I thought Matisse was a decorative painter and later I liked his paintings at an exhibition I saw in New York. I don't know, I can say that some painters are more useful to me than others in my work: I admire some, I laugh at others (laughs). Any type of religious paintings, great classic paintings, academic paintings . . . I have enjoyed myself with all of them. I love Daumier: ingenious, satirical. I saw one of his exhibitions in New York. It took my breath away. Paintings really leave a mark on me. Is that what they call the "syndrome of Stendhal"? Well, it happened to me in Brussels. I was looking at a great triptych by Bosch and I got shocked. With art, I can become like Pavlov's dog (he imitates a dog). I would have liked to have been a painter and I'm not. I can't. When I am very old and no longer able to make films I would like to become a great painter. We will see what happens (laughs).

Q : *Max Ernst influenced your animations for Monty Python . . .*
A : It's strange, because I didn't even know Max Ernst until I read a criticism about Monty Python. There are always gaps that you fill in as time goes by. It's entertaining.

Q: *Before you mentioned your favourite directors. Could you tell us what most interests you about each one of them?*

A: I liked the worlds that Bergman created a lot. The first one that I noticed was for sure *The Seventh Seal* (1956). It begins with a medieval story but, suddenly, it takes a very different path. It takes you to a place where there are knights fighting on horseback, but the battle is very different; it seems terribly believable and real. The characters are so fascinating that your interest goes from the action to the character. Visually it was incredible. The great image creators have always impressed me, and in that Bergman and Sven Nykvist (his director of photography) were phenomenal. The images, the faces . . . I felt I was there, with them. And his dream world . . . I love it as well. Moreover, when I started to watch Bergman's films I realized that his actors resembled real people, their faces were believable. On the contrary, in American films the actors look like actors.

When I discovered Fellini I felt I was watching ballet. It was so beautiful: how the camera moved, the people singing, letting their voices flow. For me it was a case of changing from cinema as a form of entertainment to cinema as an art. I adored the sense of grotesqueness of Fellini.

And Kurosawa . . . I was beginning to get so fed up with American cinema that everything that was not American seemed good. He was the king of action. I had never seen action performances like the ones in his films, especially *Seven Samurai* (1954). I remember an action scene through the woods . . . wow! I felt the same as the first time I saw *Paths of Glory.* Spectacular! I was fascinated by his capacity to combine different visual elements. They were sensual films. Despite being intellectual, or whatever, they were sensual, while the sensuality in American films was banal, superficial.

I loved Pasolini. Again, he made me feel I was there in those places. I could hear them, feel them. They were alive.

I prefer Truffaut to Godard. In the beginning Godard interested me, but he has always seemed too intellectual, too academic. I liked Truffaut, because he was very human; the actors used to nearly jump out of the screen.

The only American material that surprised me was the rediscovery of Buster Keaton. He was absolutely great. In a film such as *Sherlock Jr.* (1924) he uses the camera in a surprisingly original way.

On the other hand, I find it magical to watch and listen to something in another language. The sensation was very special, because I had to read and watch the film at the same time. Sometimes it was like reading a book and

watching a film at the same time. It had the good side of both things. And
the sounds and voices were marvelous.

Q: *However, in the period of Monty Python, many of these creators were the subject matter of your jokes, weren't they?*
A: Yes, the Pythons taught me that you could amuse yourself with everything you take seriously, with everything you really love. It's like a way of
testing it. The things that interested us, what we had read and seen, was what
we later played with in our films . . . and in that way they were funny. I
suppose that because of that it annoys me so much to see a film surrounded
by pretentious specialists. They are pretentious in a very boring way.

In my opinion a good artist makes you enjoy yourself, as with Pasolini or
certain medieval stories. They are so good that they are invulnerable to criticism. If a determined public doesn't like them, much better! I hate those
long faces saying: "Oh . . . mm . . . yeah, yeah." I remember once when I
went to a cinema in the east of New York where there were loads of very
serious film fans and neighbourhood kids who had gone to see the film. I
think it was shit and the kids were shouting, talking, and the formal people
reproached them: "Sssh, silence!" It was marvelous to see that film with the
conflict that broke out among the public (he shouts). I like to take things
seriously, but only with myself. We could say that I don't like to share my
seriousness.

Fear and Loathing in America: Gilliam on the Artist's Fight or Flight Instinct

GREGORY SOLMAN/1998

G S : *What are you working on now?*
T G : Actually nothing. I'm still actually promoting *Fear and Loathing [in Las Vegas]*, which hasn't opened yet here in England. It's opening in November.

G S : *So you're still in the mood to talk about it, then?*
T G : No, I hate talking about it! I hate the movie at this stage—I've been talking about it, non-stop, for six months now.

G S : *Do you have a DVD player?*
T G : No, I don't. I have a laserdisc player, but not a DVD. How are the sales of these now?

G S : *Very good, from what I understand.*
T G : Our laserdiscs are history, now, aren't they? They're just vinyl $33^1/_3$, aren't they?

G S : *I'm not worried about my collection, since they already have machines which play both laserdiscs and DVDs, so that folks like us won't have to replace our collection after the amount we've already spent on laserdiscs.*
T G : They already have the multi-use players?

G S : *Yes, they do. They are pricey now, and I expect they'll come down like everything else does. So, that overrules some of my questions, because I wondered*

---

whether you'd done something specifically for DVD releases, or will the DVDs of
your movies be essentially what has been released on laserdisc?
T G : Yes, that's the thing. I don't think one should waste time trying to make
two formats when one does the job very nicely. I've been surprised at how
good the quality of DVD is, though. That is disturbing, as good as it is.

G S : *Have you seen it in component? Because it is impressive in component out . . .*
T G : What is component?

G S : *Well, there is a spigot that allows it to come out in RGB, a non-coaxial cable,*
not even the S-VHS YUV that we are used to.
T G : I'm going to have to learn about DVDs, seriously. I've seen demonstration versions of DVD that impressed me, but that's about all.

G S : *I haven't been impressed on the whole. The amount of compression being*
used right now is distracting.
T G : Well, I thought that's what it must do, but the demonstration must
have been a special, souped-up version demonstration, because it looked
pretty good to me.

G S : *You mean the flower floating gently in the breeze? The demonstrations are*
careful to avoid stuff that shows up badly on DVD, I'm afraid. But you were well
ahead of the curve when it comes to the director's cut, and I think much to your
chagrin, in many cases . . .
T G : Yes, I can't usually rerelease a film as the director's cut, because that's
what it is the first time out.

G S : *You're back with Universal on this project, but originally Universal had cut,*
what, seventeen minutes out of Brazil?
T G : Yeah, something like that. And it wasn't just cutting out. They reor-
dered, they made a different film. If you look at the *Brazil* laserdisc that Crite-
rion did, they actually include the Universal version, and it is just a different
film.

G S : *Was it one of those discs that allowed you to watch either version if you*
wished?
T G : The *Brazil* disc is maybe one of the best laserdiscs ever made, because

it's got my version of *Brazil;* it's got interviews with all the people in all the different stages; it's got a documentary on the making of the film; and there is a battle of *Brazil,* with all the participants being interviewed, again, ten years after, or whatever it was. And then they put out Sid Sheinberg's Universal cut. That's all on the disc. It's amazing. It's wonderful.

G S :   *I like that you call it Sid Sheinberg's cut!*
T G :   Well, I have to give credit where credit's due!

G S :   *He's an* auteur *and he didn't even know it. What are you preparing for the* Fear and Loathing *disc?*
T G :   I haven't actually done a voiceover yet on that. We actually put in some additional material, scenes that were cut out. This is, again, one of the nice things about DVD and laser, that you can include that. So I think there are three or four scenes that we ultimately cut out of the movie that are there for us to look at. It gives people a chance to see some more of the internal workings of the thing, and then decide whether I made an intelligent choice, or a really stupid choice, by cutting something out.

G S :   *Give us a sneak preview of what will be put back into the film?*
T G :   I don't want to put it back into the film: That is the whole point. It is stuff cut out of the film for very definite reasons, because the film played better without them. And, in certain places, it is just like anything, you edit, you tell a story, and certain scenes that you shoot which seem in script form to be essential, and you realize, ah, you don't need those, or the pace is slowing down, or the story itself has gone a slightly different direction in the course of the shooting. When you are making a film you are sort of discovering the film as you are making it. I don't believe in this idea that you write a script, that's it, then you put it on film. The whole thing is a continuing process, right through to the final cut.

G S :   *So you are of the mind to include the additional material, but not interweave it back into the theatrical version?*
T G :   Yes, it is supplement at the end, it is the bits. It is the scraps from the table.

G S :   *In an article I wrote for* Film Comment *years ago, I considered that sort of presentation the best of both worlds . . .*

T G : Yes, I think it is a great thing because you can see these scenes that on their own are really good, but in the context of the film they didn't work as well as they should have, or they didn't work to the overall benefit of the film. So, that is what happens. Things get lost. And so I like that fact that you can say, you know, there's the dustbin, you look in it and see what's there.

G S : *I was more philosophical about the whole point. I know that you are a fan of* La Jetée, *so you will appreciate that it has to do with memory for me: The memory of how I saw something at a theater is very important to me, almost sacred. I am disturbed by director's cuts that radically alter my memory of the way a film was.*

T G : I agree totally. My attitude about director's cuts is, why didn't the director fight hard enough at the time to make sure his cut was the cut that he put his name on? He put his name on the film, and so it seems to me that he is responsible for it. Either you fight, or you don't fight, and a lot of people clearly don't fight, and then they in some cases have the opportunity to rerelease a film as they intended. And I would rather fight at the time and make sure it is the way I wanted it. But I don't mind letting people see bits and pieces that I cut out, and they can decide for themselves.

G S : *Yes, I admire that. Because with directors whom I admire, such as you, there's a kind of intact quality to scenes that is just fun to watch on its own. You are used to working in a short format, particularly, so I imagine some scenes that might have involved digital special effects or hallucinogenic recreations of drug experience, those scenes might be fun to see . . .*

T G : It is very interesting, the cuts that we've put back in. There is a scene at the race, the Mint 400, that takes place at the bar inside the tent after the racers have taken off. It is a very funny scene, and it is a great performance from Tim Thomerson, but it slowed the pace down at that point. We're not interested in his story at that point, we want to get on with something else. There is a big cut, which is at the end of the film, because I actually had another ending on the film, an extra scene that I really liked. But it turned out the only people who really liked it were Lesley Walker, the editor, and myself. We're the only ones who seemed to have got the scene as it was intended. Everyone else found it confusing, or just too . . . they'd had enough, it was time to go, and we were making one more point. And, in the end, after trying it with enough audiences, I said okay, great, we lose it, and it is gone. This way I get to stick it back in and say, all right, this is one more point we were making. And maybe you get it and maybe you don't get it. But there it is for your consideration, ladies and gentlemen.

G S : *Do you feel you are more disciplined as a filmmaker now, Terry?*
T G : Nope. I've always been disciplined as a filmmaker. That's what I think is so bizarre about what people think I'm doing out there. I'm a very disciplined filmmaker. I make films for a fraction of the cost most other people do, and it is *only* because I am organized and disciplined. It doesn't mean that I'm not always discovering what the film is, because that is just the reality of it. That's just the way I work. But it is discipline. You do something like *Time Bandits* for five million dollars, because we're disciplined, or something like *Twelve Monkeys* for twenty-nine and a half million dollars, it's because we're disciplined. We couldn't make those movies unless we're disciplined. So it is very funny, my reputation for being a madman, which I'm very happy to allow to continue, because it is just more fun. But oddly I'm pretty pragmatic in the way I make films.

G S : *Would you rather be known as the madman or Merchant-Ivory? You have your choice.*
T G : Exactly, if you are going to be thrown into one lot or another, I know which one I would choose. I'm happy to be "the lunatic."

G S : *It is interesting, though. I've always thought you were a disciplined artist as well, and people confuse your narrative interests with* modus operandi . . .
T G : Yes. Sometimes it is the film that confuses people. I think that what people get lost in is that I don't always think that narrative is the most important part of the film in some cases. And it isn't that there isn't a narrative, that there isn't a structure there, it is just not necessarily your normal structure. You can tell the story in different ways, rather than narrative being the primary way of doing it. I also find that people just don't seem to be visually literate, so when I am throwing all this imagery out at them they get overwhelmed, they get confused. They can't "read" the tale, just because they are not used to seeing juxtaposed images, or images that make you think, I suppose, is what I'm trying to say.

G S : *Or images that are evocative in some respect . . .*
T G : They get lost. Some people, because the images are so complex, seem to

get confused in the complexity of the image and lose the story. *Brazil* was always criticized for that; I remember when the reviews came out on that, they barely talked about either the story or the character, they were so busy talking about the visuals, and I thought, this is ridiculous. Don't they look at paintings?

G S : *The answer is "No," by the way!*
T G : That's what I'm discovering!

G S : *We're in a visually illiterate culture.*
T G : You know what's wonderful, we don't even have a word for visual illiteracy. Illiterate means one thing, it has to do with literacy! So we need a word like a-visual.

G S : *Let's invent one right now . . .*
T G : Blind, I think.

G S : *You see, there* is *a word for that.*
T G : Blind . . . but that's *technical.*

G S : *Really, I don't know what the word is.*
T G : I guess a-visual . . .

G S : *But, nobody really uses it like that. You're right. I used tone deaf a lot as a critic, which, again, is borrowing . . .*
T G : You can be tone deaf, you can be illiterate, a-visual is not really ever used as a word.

G S : *It's an interesting conundrum. I'm going to get back to you with my top ten suggestions. I know there must be an animator lurking within you. How does that animator manifest itself? I don't think once you are an animator that ever really goes away in some respect. It is too much a part of your artistic personality.*
T G : It is, partly. What is frustrating is that I can't do what you can do in animation in live action very cheaply, and that is the problem. A lot of the ideas that I have . . . there is one particular project that I keep trying to get off the ground called *Defective Detective,* and it is very much imagery that an animator or a comic-book artist would be playing with, but to try to get it on

film is incredibly expensive. It's not that you can't do it. But trying to get those images on film, within a story that is not simple and mainstream, that becomes the problem. The costs don't match. So that's why I play down in the lower half of the budget range of films and get away with murder. And that's what I continue to do, because beyond a certain price, everybody gets nervous and says, "Well, you can't do that, you can't do that, you can't do that." So I'm stuck.

G S :   *I am curious to know how you approach the digital world and if you have enjoyed computer-generated imagery, because I know there is some of that in* Fear and Loathing . . .
T G :   Yes. And there is computer-generated stuff in *Twelve Monkeys* as well. And it is just a tool; that's my approach to it. I mean, I like it. I like the fact that I can get on a computer and fiddle and make things, so in many ways the technology has made it very easy for me to do what I would have done with an animator.

G S :   *I'm guessing that you are either the most difficult director to do CGI for or the most gratifying.*
T G :   Well, the thing is, I actually have my own company. It is a company called Peerless Camera Company, which I set up with my partner Kent Houston after [*Monty Python and the*] *Holy Grail,* because I made some money on that and I bought a camera and an optical printer. All of my films have gone through the company. All the effects I've done have always been there. We sort of learn together as we go, so I can usually go in and fiddle on the machinery myself.

G S :   *Terrific. Peerless is your baby in some respect?*
T G :   Yes, it is sort of my attempt at being a British ILM, but much smaller, where we've always kept it down to about a dozen people working there. So it has allowed me to play a lot more, and also allowed us to survive the ups and downs of the effects world.

G S :   *Having admired your vivid imagination and your animation technique for so many years, I've always thought, "What would Terry Gilliam do with the ability to infinitely layer and invisibly composite, and what would he do with CGI's particular characteristics?"*

TG: So far I've used it when I've needed to use it. I never sat down to actually design something based on CG work, except solving the problem that the story demanded.

GS: *So in this case, the director, or filmmaker, or the storyteller has taken over . . .*
TG: Yes. That's what's interesting about the story *The Defective Detective*. It is designed more from an animator's point of view. So with the technology that exists, I can do it, but it would probably cost $60 million, and so far I've not been able to get it off the ground because it is doing what I do in all my films: mixing genres, mixing experiences. They say, "Well, who is it for? Is it for kids, for adults?" I tell them, "For everybody. Don't you remember I made *Time Bandits,* once upon a time?" Again, they said, "Who's it for?" and I said, "It's for everybody. It works on all levels." But, at the moment it is not happening.

GS: *I would say that* Fear and Loathing *is pretty specific in its audience, wouldn't you?*
TG: It's an odd one. I didn't actually know who the audience was, to be quite honest. I wasn't even approaching it that way. My approach was, "Can I interpret that book and get it up on the screen intact," or what I felt would be true to the book? We'll find out afterward two things: We'll find out whether it is a film after I've got it up there; and, second, we'll find out who the audience is. And to me it has been very interesting. I've begun to think there are two groups of people, the main groups, those who were there the first time around, who get a chance to relive some extraordinary times, and the other, it turned out to be, high school kids . . .

GS: *I'm sure. The new drug generation.*
TG: What's interesting there is, again, people said, "Ah, well, it is the drugs and the rock 'n' roll that they are impressed with." But when I started talking with these kids, that's not what it's about. It is interesting. I get this comment again and again: *That what they like about it is that it is honest.*

GS: *Or that it represents a certain anomie or disconnection from society?*
TG: I think it is that. I think it is that it doesn't apologize, that it doesn't pretend to be anything other than what it is. And most kids are living in a world, or we're all living in a world, that seems to me to be one Big Lie. Very

few people are actually dealing with the truth. They are running from it in ten million different ways. And whatever the film does is, I think, truthful, and that's what the kids seem to be responding to.

G S : *Let me suggest something that I did not think was truthful about it, and hear your response to it. The subject of whether Hunter Thompson is effortlessly talented, as the film kind of suggests, or whether what he did really represented hard work that was constructing what I would call an* ad hoc *persona, where he is inventing a character that is himself in some respect. I think the film is not showing the hours of labor Hunter Thompson may have spent making his pieces readable. As a writer, I was particularly sensitive to that.*

T G : I didn't think that's the story. That's not what the book does. I was trying to do the book. The book doesn't spend time talking [about] the hours he spent honing it down. "And then I spent months honing this thing"— that's not what it is about. And that is the point. We don't have to sit here and see what a serious journalist he was, oh, my god, he worked and worked and worked. We see him typing twice in the film, and both times he is very serious in the doing of it.

G S : *That's a fair response . . .*

T G : That's what it is about. I'm not telling the life story of a journalist. I'm recreating, hopefully, that book. The fact is that Hunter *does* write surprisingly effortlessly at times. I think he was a child prodigy, frankly. It flows out of him very fast. It is very interesting the way he writes. Because he does constantly make lots of corrections, but not as many as you'd think.

G S : *Your point is that the only part of Hunter Thompson's life you are interested in telling, really, is the portion which he himself wants to reveal in his book.*

T G : What is actually very interesting about this is that, yeah, he created that character, Raoul Duke, and Raoul behaves and does what he does. But at the beginning of the project I actually talked to Hunter and he said, "You gotta understand, that book is *not* the most important book I've ever done. I mean, it was just something I did in a frenzy." And, "Really, I'm a very serious journalist; Oscar Zeta Acosta [Dr. Gonzo] was very serious." "Yes, I know, Hunter, but when I first read that book I didn't know that, and what I responded to was the book that you wrote"—and that was the end of it. I said, "Hunter, I'm not making a memorial to your life here. I'm trying to get the book you wrote up on the screen, as honestly as I can." And he accepted that, and that's how we approached it.

GS: *Terry, was this era part of your American experience, or were you already in Britain by then?*

TG: I left in '67, but I left for most of the reasons he wrote the book. I had become very disillusioned with America. I mean, into the '60s were magical, and well through most of the '60s were quite wondrous, because we were making great progress with the civil rights movement. The early free-speech movement was quite extraordinary. And it really kind of felt like we could change the world, change it for the better, and in a very short time. But then it started going bad. And it wasn't so neat, and it was uglier. And we were then all fairly young, and I think our expectations were that we could do it overnight, and of course it takes much longer than that.

GS: *Did you go through Occidental [College], was that the last part of your American citizenship?*

TG: No, I actually graduated Occidental in '62, that was in the early days, that's when things were great. The Peace Corps was starting up, people were going off. That was really exciting. I went to New York. I worked in magazines, the civil rights movement. A lot of kids out of college were going down to the south, going straight in. It was like . . . those of us who had the privilege of being educated well really felt we had a responsibility. And that was all happening: It was quite fantastic.

GS: *Have you seen the documentary,* Berkeley in the Sixties?

TG: Yeah.

GS: *I think that really expresses what you just said.*

TG: We used some of that footage in the film, during the Wave speech. That's actually footage that was part of that documentary. And I hadn't seen that documentary until we were in the middle of working on the film. And it brought everything back to me. It was painful how extraordinary it was, how hopeful it was, and how bold and totally committed everybody was.

GS: *The level of articulation of those students was astounding.*

TG: Brilliant. Brilliant!

GS: *I thought to myself, what happened to college education?*

TG: Education became the first step on your career, not about education. It became a careerist move, it seems to me.

G S : *But also the personal commitment of those kids . . .*

T G : Yeah, the effort. So that was the time I was around, and I finally left in '67 because I was involved . . . with, ah, I was involved in . . .

G S : *It was the paternity suit—go ahead, you can admit it!*

T G : [Laughs] No, actually I was involved in the first police riot in Los Angeles, when Johnson came to Century City. And it was the Century Plaza Hotel, which was basically a huge empty lot except for the hotel at that point.

G S : *There was nothing around it at that point?*

T G : No, there was nothing there. There was nothing but open land. And Johnson came, and there was a police riot that went absolutely out of control and just was violent and brutal. That just shocked me. Again, the interesting thing about the times was that the *L.A. Free Press* came out immediately on the street with interviews with all the people because the *L.A. Times* was basically selling it as "hippie, Communist, drug-addled people rioting." In fact, it was probably mainly middle-class people, college professors, doctors, lawyers, all kinds of people involved. And the *Free Press* came out on the street and said, "No, no, that's not how it happened, and here's interviews." And they were just handing it out to commuters, people in their cars, wherever they passed a street corner. And, interestingly enough, by the end of the week, the *L.A. Times* reporters actually stood up and demanded that the editorial staff admit to the truth of the whole thing, and that following Sunday the *L.A. Times* recanted on the whole story. And that was extraordinary. But, little by little, I was getting more and more angry, to the point that I felt I'm going to have to start throwing bombs soon. I think it was better that I keep drawing cartoons and get out of the country.

G S : *So, was it a slippery slope of disillusionment, or could you pin it on a critical moment when you decided this is just not a country you could live in?*

T G : It was continuing things. The fact is, about a year and half earlier. . . .

G S : *You know, George Wallace died yesterday . . .*

T G : Really? Wallace was just one more demagogue. He wasn't the worst person in the world, but he certainly knew how to play the mob.

G S : *At least he repented his positions, and, even more important, he repented his positions at a time when it was not to any particular advantage, which means it was probably an honest repentance.*

T G : Although sitting in a wheelchair slows you down a little bit.

G S : *It even slowed Larry Flynt down. I guess we shouldn't be giving it that much credit.*

T G : Time to think. Time to reconsider a few things! I had actually gone to Europe in '64 and '65, hitchhiked around for around six months. And I really fell in love with Europe, and it certainly opened my eyes to the rest of the world and to the way the rest of the world perceived America. The fact that there were so many different cultures waiting outside the country, that all put a certain sophistication or a certain awareness of history and our place in it. So, I was sorely tempted to stay in Europe, but I came back to the States, and it was just this continuing ugliness that started developing, and I thought, "Okay, I've got to leave. I've really got to leave."

G S : *How did you feel about England, in contradistinction? Did you really feel that, as a culture, it was better, or was it rather that you didn't have to be as tortured by its own problems?*

T G : A little bit of both, to be honest. Yeah, I wasn't responsible for the mess of Britain. As an American, I felt if I was in the country I had to accept my responsibility and do something about it. And, also, I felt that England was a country that cherished and nurtured eccentrics, whereas in America, peer pressure is so great. And it's worse now than it was then. It is very hard for true individuals to exist. America begins as a great nation of individualists, and I just think that's not true.

G S : *It's odd to hear you speak that way, considering that Monty Python, to which you were an important contributor, was about the only show my peers watched when we were in college. It was about the only thing that spoke to my college generation.*

T G : It was interesting. I was trying to do comedy work in the States with friends. In fact, there was this trio of us who were working closely together. One of the trio was me, and one of the others was Harry Shearer. Harry and I were doing this together. And the third one was Joel Siegel, from *Good Morning America*, the film critic. The three of us were doing stuff.

G S : *You know what Harry goes by now, don't you?*

T G : No, what's that?

G S : *The artist* currently *known as Prince.*

T G : [Laughs] I actually saw him a couple of weeks ago. It is nice that Harry's really becoming well known, because for a long time he just wasn't, and he was really stuck in there, and I think he's really unique.

G S : *You can hear his radio show over the Internet now. In fact, Alternate Scenario Theatre, one of his regular skits, is some of the best radio writing around.*

T G : That's what's very interesting. We were all getting very frustrated and I popped over to England, and within a year, a year and a half, Monty Python started up and suddenly, ah! In some cases we were doing things that we were trying to do in the States, but now there was an audience for it, in England, and ultimately in America—and seemingly throughout most of the world, these days.

G S : *Was animation something you insisted upon, or did you fall into it?*

T G : It's definitely something I fell into, because I always really wanted to make live-action films. But I was on a program as a cartoonist, and they had a thing, and I animated it, and overnight I became an animator.

G S : *You mentioned the frustration of live action. Other animators who work in live action describe it as liberating, that it would take them all day to make a character smile in animation, but in live action the character simply smiles.*

T G : Well, and I more and more enjoy working with wonderful actors. It is really great fun, and it is easier doing the other stuff. It is just that I've proba-bly got certain images in my head that I have to get on film and I have different ways of approaching this stuff. But I'm getting to the point where I might start doing some very strange sideways stepping up to get what I want. I don't know what the answer is. I was just thinking that I've always worked with . . . if I keep banging my head against brick walls, I'm being stupid. So let's just find a way of getting around the wall by not going through it. I don't know what that means yet. But it's reaching the point where I'm going to come out with solutions. And I'm beginning to think that because of the way effects are becoming slick now, and so seamless, and so incredible, maybe the best thing to do is make films where everything looks really phony, like it is cardboard cutouts, like my animation, but instead it is live action.

G S :   *Do you remember Resnais's film,* Providence? *He experimented with intentionally giving away illusions. That could be an interesting area for you to explore, because photographic reality is dead.*

T G :   I think that's the sad thing about the way CGI is being used. It is only being used to recreate naturalistic things as opposed to really inventive creative things.

G S :   *Or it is the digital mucking with photography to the point that photographic realism is meaningless. And that is a sad day for cinema in some respect. When I see a shot that I admire, I'm not sure whether it has been dragged through a computer or not.*

T G :   That doesn't bother me because all of cinema is artifice. It's all artifice. And it doesn't matter to me how one achieves it as long as it achieves the effect you are after and the audience . . . well, it is kind of like magic. I don't think I want to tell you how the magic tricks are done.

G S :   *I agree with you on the artifice point. But I would say when you let a magician entertain you there is a sort of contract between him and the audience. There is a bit of calculation in trying to make the image perfect.*

T G :   What bothers me is, *that's* why my films are *not* naturalistic. They are hyperrealistic or stylized. Because, in a sense, I'm trying to say, "This is artifice." I'm not going to make a documentary; I'm not going to cheat by pretending that this is a documentary.

G S :   *That's what's admirable about your artistic style, I think. You're very honest as an artist.*

T G :   *Saving Private Ryan,* for instance. I think the Normandy landing is *phenomenal!* And now, having now convinced me that this is real, this is the real stuff, we start sliding into Spielberg land. And I found it a very strange film because it just kept shifting from something that convinced me of its total and utter verisimilitude, to things that I knew were just wishful thinking on the part of someone who's lived his whole life in Hollywood. That's what disturbed me about the film. Because I think. Ultimately, it was less truthful than it would have liked to have been, and yet it was conning me with naturalism. It is kind of like, I remember years ago there was this Ken Loach movie, I can't remember the name, it might have been called *Family Life* [a.k.a. *Wednesday's Child*, 1972], that I loved, and it was wonderful, and it was done in this semi-documentary style, it was so Kitchen Sink-y. It seemed to be real. Then I found out that what was told me was not accurate; it was not truthful, and yet because it seemed [truthful], well, it must have been truthful. It was a documentary, and that's why I stay away from that kind of filmmaking, because it is too deceptive, it is too easy to cheat.

GS: *You like the artifice as part of the readily understandable surface of the film that is in some way an honest part of filmmaking.*

TG: That's the only thing I can do. At least I'm not relying on any Pavlovian documentary tricks.

GS: *Of course, when you are a filmmaker such as Spielberg—not that you have to argue* Private Ryan *here, since it is more about you—but when you have the sound being drawn away when Miller is shell-shocked on the beach at Normandy, et cetera, there are all kinds of cues and interesting suggestions that the artifice is not realistic. I agree it was a harrowing sequence, but to me the interesting thing about what Spielberg did in the Normandy sequence is that it more had the emotional or psychological impact of being realistic . . .*

TG: Yeah, I think you are right. I agree with you on that. I think that it was actually a brilliant sequence.

GS: *And I do too, and because of that, I forgive the intermixture or artifice in a way that you've always intermixed artifice.*

TG: Well, I just found I couldn't believe a lot of what he was telling me there. I just found it a very strange film in that I couldn't feel my way through it, even though he had me completely by the throat for the first half hour, and then he kept losing me. It was like, "Okay, you're cheating now." And it is kind of like *Schindler's List*. I think the first part, through the ghetto massacre, I thought it was astonishing again. And then I think he started sliding into what I think are cheap tricks. And by the end I'm getting angry, because he doesn't favor a basic trust in the material.

GS: *I think this is what Spielberg is about, take him or leave him.*

TG: I know, and there is no question that it works for a huge number of people and that it is very effective. But I think they disturb me, those films . . .

G S : *It is interesting because you are animated in your personal life by a certain political gestalt and maybe that affects the way you see films . . .*

T G : I think so, yes.

G S : *. . . as maybe more or less propagandistic. I'm sure that you thought to your-self when you made* Fear and Loathing *. . . that you probably have your greatest-fear scenario and your greatest-hope scenario.*

T G : And it is all mixed in there.

G S : *Exactly. I suppose the greatest fear would be that young people would like the film for the wrong reasons.*

T G : I think the one thing that people have said is that when you walk out, there is no way you can say that it is a pro-drug film. This is not a film that is going to encourage people to rush out and start taking drugs. I don't think. I'm pretty certain of that.

G S : *But would you admit there is the possibility that it is a pro-narcissism film?*

T G : [Laughs] It is pro-indulgence. It is pro-excess. Pro "push things to the limit" . . . those things, so what does that make it?

G S : *What was this rumor that you'd worked with Alex Cox [Repo Man] on the film?*

T G : No, not at all. There is a long story about the Writer's Guild, why those credits are out there. That is absolute bullshit. That's why I resigned from the Writer's Guild.

G S : *What was it all about?*

T G : That's because of the way the Writer's Guild worked. It will take a few minutes. The small print when you are part of the WG, you definitely won't read. You only discover it when you've made a film that has been on previous writers involved with previous scripts, one you worked on with previous scripts. And it turns out that was it in this instance. What the studio submit-ted to the Writer's Guild were Tony Grisoni's script and my script and Alex Cox and Tod Davies' script. As a director, *and* a member of the Writer's Guild, any script that I am involved in goes into arbitration automatically. Auto-matically.

G S :   *Wow. Somebody's making money on that agreement.*

T G :   That's an interesting one, yeah. So, we're going to arbitrate between Tony and me because they want to make sure that I did my fair share of the writing. So Tony and I both write our letters in, saying, yes, we wrote this side by side, holding hands, blah blah, and each of us did exactly 50 percent of the work. And then we discover, no, it's not about that, it is about that Alex and Tod are contesting. Oh? This is getting interesting. Then the rules get interesting. As the director, and someone who works with me, we have to produce substantially more than 60 percent of the script to get a credit— not to share a credit, but to get *any* credit. Any other writer or writers only has to produce 31 percent of the script, something like that, to get a credit. Not me and my cowriter. We are second-class citizens. We have to do twice the work to get credits, because I am the director, and the WG refers to directors as "production executives."

G S :   *What is the thinking behind that?*

T G :   I never spent much time thinking about it. It is a fact.

G S :   *Is it because as a director you get things your way, anyway?*

T G :   Yes, that's the idea. The actors will push their way around, and the writers like to do it the director's way, blah blah blah. The directors will take credit. The reality is, in practice, that certain directors who I won't name, who are well known for this, actually pay their cowriters to fuck off, basically, and they end up getting the credit. So it is very corruptible, this whole thing. But anyway, the rules are this and now that it goes into arbitration it gets even more interesting. Because if the previous script, i.e., the Alex Cox script, uses X number of scenes and we use some of those scenes, they get credit for choosing those scenes first. If we use the same scenes, we don't get credit because they chose them first. Now, the fact is, you've got the book and there are X number of scenes that are the building blocks of the book, and if you don't use them you are clearly not doing the book. So we don't get points for choosing those scenes, they do, and we don't. So at the end of the process . . .

G S :   *So what happens if the first scriptwriters have cherry-picked all the good scenes?*

T G :   Yes, of course, any good writer is going to do that!

G S :   *You're left with, "I want the scene where Hunter is in his room staring at the wall."*

T G :   Right, that's it. So here's what happens: Then you've got to write a document putting your case forward why. So Tony and I write a very long letter. Basically, before Alex's script there were probably twenty previous scripts; [the book] has been going around for a long time. It's been made into a stage play; it has been made into a CD; all these things exist and all of them use the same basic scenes. So we explained what we've done and how it is different and why ours is the script that we made the film from and why it is totally different. And, anyway, three arbiters read the book, the two scripts, and the letters, then they arbitrate. And there is no appeal from the arbitration. We are not allowed to know who they are or to see their report and why they arbitrated as they did. We're not allowed to see anything. And there is no appealing their decision, and their decision was that the screenplay of the film that we made was written by Alex Cox and Tod Davies, and we didn't have a credit. So that's what's happened. Then we got into a very long, protracted and ugly set of events. And, basically, here's what we were able to do: We couldn't appeal, but we were able to open, reopen, the situation because we were able to prove that one of the writers involved in the project had been involved in previous scripts before Alex Cox. So it was reopened with the submissions of these other scripts, and it went in this time. Tony and I spent longer writing our, ah . . . our ah . . .

G S :   *Exegesis, your defense of the realm . . .*

T G :   . . . exegesis, than we spent on writing the fucking script! At the end of all of this (and we said, "We've written 95 percent of the entire script, there is a couple of points that Alex and Tod made that we used, and that's it. Everything else is ours"), they re-arbitrated. And at least this time they gave us credit. But apparently this had never happened before, that writers and/ or a writer who were *not* given credit the first time were not only given credit but given first-position credit. So it ended up with us in first position. But the whole thing was ridiculous and I said, "Why am I paying my dues to be a member of the WGA, one-point-something percent of my earnings, and I get this kind of treatment, that I have to do twice as much work, that I am a second-class citizen?" The irony is that Alex and Tod aren't even members of the WGA! Fucked by our own Guild!

GS: *Knowing Alex a little bit, I'm sure that would be* his *attitude about joining it.*
TG: What's interesting about this is that some of the reviews I've read say, "Well, the script's a mess, but that's obviously the product of too many cooks with four writers." When, clearly, it's a mess because *two* of us fucked up!

GS: *The scene I might have guessed was Alex's, simply because he made* Highway Patrolman, *is the scene when the highway patrolman stops Hunter on the way out of Las Vegas.*
TG: That scene in Alex's script took place at the end of the film. And it was a fraction of that length, and it didn't have the end line about, "Can I have a kiss?" That was something I added.

GS: *That was my favorite scene. It took me to a different narrative space. What's interesting is that, for me, that was more hallucinogenic than the actual hallucino-genic scenes.*
TG: It's a very great scene because the pace is totally different. It slows, it comes screeching to a halt, and you're wondering, what is the point of this scene? It is going on and on and he's caught out there with this guy, and it is just a different rhythm than anything else.

GS: *You had me on that one . . . the different rhythm, the different narrative space, and it takes place on the desert, so it seems almost existential, this meeting . . .*
TG: I agree. Oh, I liked that a lot. That's one of the things: In playing around with the film we're shifting the pace and throwing the audience constantly. And it is clear that a lot of people just don't want that treatment; they don't go to the movies for that kind of treatment.

GS: *Did you draw out, as a cartoonist and animator, some of the hallucinogenic fantasies?*
TG: Nope. I didn't draw anything. The only time I drew on it was during the shot of the cop chase—the car, the shots of the cars and all that. I gave that over to the second unit, so I did a little drawing on that, a little storyboard for them, as a guide. But, no, I didn't storyboard anything else. I didn't draw anything.

GS: *Not even conceptual work?*
TG: Well, that's true—I do little sketches, little things like that.

GS: *That must be fun.*

TG: Yeah. I can do a little scribble and then some really talented people can make it look wonderful.

GS: *That's what* [The Simpsons' *creator*] *Matt Groening says. He told me that it was a surreal experience seeing twenty-five people, all of whom could draw better than him, doing his characters.*

TG: That's what's nice about doing live-action films. I can do little cartoon sketches and then somebody can translate that and make it really good and I get to be the supervisor, add a little bit more of this or that. But they're doing it better than I could if I had to do it all on my own.

GS: *Must be fun being in this supervisory capacity, because I know you were a one-man show when it came to Python.*

TG: Yeah. Sometimes it is frustrating when you've got somebody who, no matter how good they are, they can't quite get what you are after, and you don't have time to do it yourself. Those are frustrating moments.

GS: *But it's your company, so you can fire them . . .*

TG: No, I'm not actually talking about special effects at that end, but stuff when you are in production.

GS: *I was just kidding. I can't see you walking in and saying, "Well, that's not working. So goodbye."*

TG: Nobody gets lucky enough to get fired off my films!

GS: *What else does Peerless do for you, then? The compositing?*

TG: They do all the optical work, all the CGI work, the compositing, every-thing. They've literally been doing everything, from *Brazil, Time Bandits* to *Munchausen* . . . everything has gone through there. Ridley Scott has a lot of his stuff going through there as well.

GS: *So are you near Wardor Street?*

TG: No, in Covent Garden. We have about four CGI workstations, and motion control and animation stands.

GS: *It's funny to see commercials rediscover a kind of Gilliamesque animation style. They are probably doing it different ways than you did, but cutout and collage has come back.*

TG: You can do it at home on a computer a lot easier than I could have done it. You could sit there at home on a Mac and use a couple of regular software programs and make the stuff look just like my old animation. The only difference is it would probably be hard to make it look as jerky as I used to be able to do it.

GS: *Those nights at four in the morning when you said, "I think I'm going to animate on 4s or 8s or 16s now." Let's go on: Are there particular films that you would have DVD collectors see in order to understand your work? For instance, folks should see* La Jetée *before seeing* Twelve Monkeys. *Are there films you would attach to the films you've worked on?*

GS: *I think that everyone ought to look at* The Earrings of Madame D.
TG: Oh, Ophuls. It's wonderful.

GS: *And a lot of people don't know that film. And I only discovered it about five years ago when somebody said you ought to see this. I am incredibly oddly educated when it comes to films. I didn't go to film school and what I know about films is what I'd seen by going to the movies.*

GS: *And you'd deprived yourself of the American experience of having films everywhere. I don't know that it is that big in England, is it?*
TG: No, it is harder to get to see things. Like *La Jetée,* I didn't see it until the Paris premiere of *Twelve Monkeys,* and we had *La Jetée* on as the short. Have you seen Marker's latest one, *Level 5?*

GS: *No, I have not.*
TG: It was at the London Film Festival last year . . . and it is quite interesting. He is trying to tell two stories, a love affair between a man and a woman, when the communication is via a computer. They never see each other. He works at night on the computer and she works during the day on the computer. So there's that story. It is primarily—well, the best part is—about Okinawa and the battle of Okinawa and everything that went up to it, the brutality. It is horrifying.

GS: *It sounds like the Marker mode I like best.*
TG: I finally met him in June, near the Summer Solstice. There is a festival

in Finland called the Midnight Sun Festival that the Kaurismäki [Aki and Mika] brothers do. And I went up there and Chris Marker turned up incognito . . .

G S: *As if so many people would recognize him!*
T G: . . . that's what I was about to say! He's behaving as if at any moment he's going to be spotted.

G S: *He could deliver my mail today and I wouldn't know him.*
T G: He looks like he should have been in the French Foreign Legion: trim, tough, sort of tight-skinned. I think he works at being enigmatic full time.

G S: *It's a full-time job, not for hobbyists. So, what else,* La Jetée, *and what else?*
T G: All the Buster Keaton films.

G S: *He's great, isn't he? I must say that* Seven Chances *is the underrated Buster Keaton film.*
T G: *Seven Chances* is fantastic.

G S: *People have always extolled the virtues of* The General *and others . . .*
T G: *Seven Chances* and *Sherlock Jr.* are my favorites. *Seven Chances* is all about rhythm. He is extraordinary. And I keep trying to get people to see *One-Eyed Jacks.* An amazing film, and, again, it was just vilified at the time.

G S: *You like that surreal quality, don't you?*
T G: Yeah. I remember coming to New York and seeing it on 42nd Street and seeing it at one of the flop-house cinemas. And it was on a double bill, and I just sat there, and I think I watched it three times that day, having to sit through this other movie which I can't remember. I was just transfixed by that film.

G S: *I love Brando's performance in* The Missouri Breaks, *too.*
T G: I got to ask him about that, because I always thought when I saw that, "This is outrageous!" I know what's going on, because Jack Nicholson is so earnest, working so hard, because he was working with the Great Brando. And every day, I was convinced, Brando walked into the costume department and said, "I think today I'll wear this thing . . ."

G S : *Today I'll be an Irish rogue methinks . . .*

T G : So I asked him about it and it's true! That's exactly what he was doing. He was just fucking with everybody and trying to drive Nicholson.

G S : *Well, it got the best performance out of Nicholson.*

T G : And, again, watching Brando, you just didn't know what he was going to do next, and when he finally ends up as the woman in the dress, you go, "Wow!" It's great stuff.

G S : *It's a Gilliam-like moment, you must admit.*

T G : You sort of hunt for those moments in life!

G S : *You'd only expect it to be Terry Jones in that dress. Let's keep going.*

T G : Well, you ought to throw some Buñuel in there. I think *Exterminating Angel,* and for me it has always been *Seven Samurai, Seventh Seal, Seven Chances . . .*

G S : All *the Seven films . . .*

T G : Except for *Seven. Seven* is not one of my favorites. It has to be "Seven" with another word involved. "Seven" on its own doesn't work.

G S : *Seven must* only *be a modifier . . .*

T G : Yes. I'm trying to work out who nobody talks about anymore. That's what intrigues me more.

G S : *I love* The Fisher King. *You were not even in the country anymore [1991] and yet you captured the political zeitgeist of the insanity and homelessness.*

T G : Thank you. Stanley Donen films, like the Gene Kelly musicals. It isn't sentimental: It's just clean.

G S : *Were you influenced by Orson Welles films?*

T G : Well, that sort of goes without saying. *Citizen Kane, Touch of Evil.*

G S : *I was thinking* The Trial . . .

T G : Yes, and *Lady from Shanghai . . .*

G S : *And* Mr. Arkadin *maybe?*

T G : *Mr. Arkadin,* you know, I finally saw it after we made *Fisher King,* in fact. Somebody sent me a tape. And I thought it's got some of the worst acting in the world in that film. Oh, Jesus! Visually I thought it is extraordinary, but the acting is so appalling!

G S : *I love the acting . . . maybe because it is so appalling.*

T G : It drove me crazy! I hate that lead actor, I can't remember who it was, the Block of Wood [probably Robert Arden]. I thought what a terrible bit of casting. Orson! Of the last few years, my favorite films are *Toto le héros* and *Unforgiven.* Those are my films.

G S : *Will you come stateside soon?*

T G : I think I will make my next film in Europe. I don't ever want to come back to America at the moment. I am fed up in Hollywood.

G S : *Was it a bad experience making* Fear and Loathing?

T G : No, I had a good experience. But somehow Hollywood is really starting to get to me. It's almost as if I finished another trilogy. I did *Time Bandits, Brazil,* and *Munchausen,* which is kind of a trilogy. *Fisher King, Twelve Monkeys,* and *Fear and Loathing* is sort of an American trilogy. Now it is time to go back and do a period film in Europe, somehow. That's what I want to do. That's what I feel like. The kind of films that have no audience these days, but why not?

G S : *One more strange question: You call your company Poo-Poo Pictures. Is that after the poo-poo platter?*

T G : What's a poo-poo platter?

G S : *Some sort of Americanized Polynesian or Hawaiian sampler, I think.*

T G : No, it is designed to embarrass serious, suited lawyers who sit around at a conference table talking about Poo-Poo Pictures. It is baby talk for ca-ca.

Lost in La Mancha: The Making, Unmaking, and Remaking of Terry Gilliam

DAVID STERRITT AND MIKITA BROTTMAN/2002

WE CONDUCTED THIS INTERVIEW at the Toronto International Film Festival in September 2002, a few days after the premiere of *Lost in La Mancha: The Un-Making of Don Quixote,* a documentary about the rise and fall of *The Man Who Killed Don Quixote,* a pet project Gilliam had been trying to complete for more than a decade. *Lost in La Mancha* was directed by Keith Fulton and Louis Pepe, who had been invited by Gilliam to chronicle the *Quixote* project in a "making of" documentary. (With producer Lucy Darwin, who also worked on *La Mancha,* they had documented the making of *Twelve Monkeys* in their 1995 film *The Hamster Effect and Other Tales of* Twelve Monkeys.)

Gilliam's attendance at the festival was uncertain in the days leading up to it—not surprisingly, since *Lost in La Mancha* is the record of a failed project that he presided over at every stage of development, from preproduction planning to principle photography in Spain, which was abandoned after a series of disasters including the illness of star Jean Rochefort, a torrential rainstorm that washed away scenery and equipment, and the discovery that military aircraft conducted training flights over a key location with alarming frequency. In the end he decided not only to attend the festival, but also to discuss *Lost in La Mancha* with the press and make a surprise onstage appearance at the end of the first public screening. This interview is published here for the first time.

Reprinted by permission.

DAVID STERRITT: *Were you much involved in making* Lost in La Mancha?
TERRY GILLIAM: I saw it when [Keith Fulton and Louis Pepe] were cutting
it, and gave them a couple of notes on it. But once they finally got it finished
. . . when I watch it, it takes at least a week to recover from it. It sends me
into a spin every time. So I just talk about it now—I don't look at it.

DS: *This is a movie of which you're the star, and it's about a movie of your own
that didn't happen. So here's a silly question: How does it feel to have this film
around?*
TG: As long as it's out there and I don't have to sit and watch the fuckin'
thing, it's fine. But when I do watch it, it brings back all the nightmare and
anxiety. It's that weird thing of thinking I'd got over it, but then realizing I
hadn't got over it. It keeps knocking on.

But looking at the positive side, it's probably the best sales tool that a guy
could ever hope for, to get [*The Man Who Killed Don Quixote*] up and running
again. That's fantastic. I do think it's a really good film. The reason people
get so excited or moved by it is that it's maybe the first time you're seeing
something truthful about filmmaking. It isn't all about how wonderful
everything is and how happy we all are. For better or for worse, it's a true
tale. I think the dangerous thing is if people begin to think, "Well, it's a
unique experience." No, most filmmakers have been through something like
that. They may have ended up with a film at the end, but they've gone
through those kinds of nightmares.

MIKITA BROTTMAN: *It shows how much waiting around there is when you're
making a film, how much depends on the weather, how much paperwork there is,
how much legal stuff there is, how much of it is just phone calls and
organization. . . .*
TG: That's what's so good about it, because most people think filmmaking
is something other than that. What you see here—that *is* filmmaking.

MB: *It isn't glamorous!*
TG: Never! (laughs) What's also interesting is that I have a reputation as this
guy out of control, a dreamer, blah blah blah. My agent keeps saying this
[*Lost in La Mancha*] is really good for me, because you can see I'm responsible,

I'm in touch with all the details, and all that. These things are the good side of it.

D S :   *Looking at things from your perspective today, how do you feel you acquired this reputation?* The Adventures of Baron Munchausen *had various problems, but one movie couldn't have done it.*

T G :   It was a combination of *Munchausen* and *Brazil*. With *Brazil* I took on the system and won, so I must get my comeuppance. Orson Welles knew about this—it's in *The Magnificent Ambersons*. And then *Munchausen* fulfilled a lot of those expectations: This guy's out of control, he's a troublemaker. But there's only one film [of mine] that went over budget and didn't work out financially. And while they talk about financial disaster, they never talk about the fact that only 117 prints were made of *Munchausen*!

Anyway, *The Fisher King* was a reason to go out to Hollywood and show I'm not who [they] think I am, irresponsible and all that. And it was cheap and a big success. So I think it's done, my reputation is back. But no. So then I go and do *Twelve Monkeys*. What was interesting there is that we were half financed by Hollywood and half by other sources, and I had to go see a completion company. I said *Fisher King* came in on budget, and they said no—it's a studio film, so we don't know if it did or not. So I had to start again!

After that I thought we'd cleared our way with the studios and we'd cleared our way with the completion companies, so it was all nice, and *Twelve Monkeys* was a big success. Then *Fear and Loathing* came along. We did it very cheaply in Hollywood and Vegas for $19 million, but it didn't do very well, so it was back to the "old Gilliam." You make one slip. . . !

It's partly because I'm so stupidly outspoken. I say how much I despise these people, and that is not so intelligent on my part.

D S :   *I've been reading interviews you've done over the years, and yes, you've done a lot of that.*

T G :   There's a payback for all of that. I got a new agent this last year. They were so excited, and then they went out and tried to push a couple of projects of mine, and they were getting all this feedback: Gilliam's out of control, he's dangerous, you don't know what he's going to do. They didn't expect this. They were shocked by it, and they actually suggested I go to Hollywood and spend a few weeks out there doing a charm offensive, to let everybody know what a nice guy I am. Wait a minute! This is what you do at the beginning of your career! I'm over sixty, and they're wanting me to go back and start again! So it just goes on.

But I think I've just got to maintain my anger about Hollywood, despite the fact that films I've done in Hollywood were the easiest and smoothest I've done. There's just something clearly out of sync with me, in my own head.

M B : *One of the good things about* Lost in La Mancha *is that the film makes it very clear that you're very much in control. There was just an awful series of unforeseeable catastrophes that happened one after another, but had nothing to do with you or any other human factor.*

T G : Yes. But to be quite honest, there were a lot of production problems that were going to rear their ugly heads in a month or two. At one point I said to Jean Rochefort, "Thank you for getting ill, because you got the blame for it, not me." (laughs) Things were going to come apart. Jean's illness and that storm were the killers. But we had no fat on that budget, no fat at all. Things were right at a knife edge on every point. So even if we'd gotten through those [crises], I think some problems were going to hit us. The production was a mess. What you have to understand about [*Lost in La Mancha*] is that everybody [who appears in it] signed off on it, everybody had to give releases. So some people are let off the hook, because they wouldn't let things go into [the film] that were damning of their lack of skills.

M B : *Vanessa Paradis, who was playing Dulcinea, isn't in it at all. Was material filmed with her?*

T G : There's just a screen test, the day after the insurance company came to the set. She was there, but we never got around to filming her. There's a shot of her double riding away on a horse, but that's the closest we got to Vanessa, because the plug was pulled.

When Jean got that ill [with an apparent prostate condition], the crew and everybody said, "We'll wait, however long it takes. If it takes two months, three months before he's well, we'll wait." Johnny [Depp, cast as a modern-day character in *Quixote*] said, "We'll wait." People said, "We won't charge anybody anything. We'll all reconvene when Jean is ready to go." But the insurance company said, "No, you'd better recast and reschedule." I wasn't in the mood to recast, because we had spent so long getting Jean, and I didn't really know who could fill the bill that quickly. And I didn't know how to reschedule the film, because there was no latitude. We were [scheduled to film] in cathedrals, castles. It was very tight. So if you suddenly started pulling things apart, I think the jigsaw was going to come undone. Phil Patterson, the AD [assistant director], was convinced of that. And I think I knew it in my heart, even though I was pretending we could just keep marching.

D S : *So even if Rochefort hadn't gotten sick, you were going to run into needs you couldn't fill and problems you couldn't solve?*
T G : That was my fear. But I was so exhausted by the time we started shooting, because the run-up to it had been so long and problematic, that I was not in a great mental state. On the first day of shooting I was not filled with joy. I was filled with fear. Which is a terrible way to start a film. I'd been on it two years solid, and already had it collapse once on me during that time. And Phil was going crazy because he was trying to do the job of both first AD and production [manager], trying to hold the stuff together. You get glimpses [in *Lost in La Mancha*] of the horse problem. The horses were gonna kill us, because there'd been this terrible internecine battle in the family that was handling the horses—between the father and the son—and we were the victims of it. There was a lot of stuff that I was worried about. But it may have been my own fear, which you always have when you're going into something. You're worried about everything. And I'm always thinking months in advance. "We need this now, because if we don't do it now, it'll take time to do it later, and it won't be ready." I'm aware of all those things, and I was not in good shape.

D S : *If you didn't have horses, you could have used coconuts! [This is a reference to* Monty Python and the Holy Grail, *where the knights run on the ground and make clip-clopping noises with coconuts in their hands—a comedy idea dreamed up by the filmmakers when the budget wouldn't allow for horses.]*
T G : I was smart in those days! I keep wanting to go back to that [fantasy kind of] world where you're not tied down to a natural world, basically. But too late. We're down another road.

D S : *Will* The Man Who Killed Don Quixote *ever get made? Would you still like to put it into production?*
T G : I'm planning to start shooting September 25 next year. That's how stu-

pid I am. We're negotiating with the insurance company right now to buy it back. We're talking numbers now.

M B : *Is Rochefort back in it?*
T G : Yes. That's why I'm curious about the film he's in here. [This was *L'Homme du train*, a film by Patrice Leconte being shown in the 2002 Toronto festival where this interview was conducted.] I was talking earlier to somebody who has seen it, and he said [Rochefort] spends the whole time sitting down. [Rochefort] has done some [film and television] work [since *Quixote* went out of production], but I don't know if he's fit. And I don't know if he can be insured again. We had a thing called essential insurance, for the essential elements: Johnny, me, and Jean. So [the insurance company] ended up paying [for costs of the terminated production], not the completion guarantor. And now I don't know if we can get essential insurance. The insurance companies are pretty ruthless, and we would need essential insurance. So I don't know. I guess it's just one step at a time. Until I actually have a script in my hand, and we own it, I'm not really thinking about it. Except to everybody around me I'm saying, "This is when we start. Move your ass. Get the stuff under way." Johnny won't be available until then—he's signed up for other things—so that's why I'm saying that [September 2003] date. We'll see.

D S : *Will it be a whole new production? Will you still shoot it in Spain?*
T G : Yeah. The advantage is that we have done the work—we know the locations and all that. I assume they're still standing. I don't know what to do about the F-16s! I had been at that location four times [before principle photography started], and in those times there were maybe fifteen minutes when a plane came through, once a day. I had a feeling [when the planes became a major nuisance] that a lot of it was because Johnny Depp was there. They would actually fly low over our base camp and tip their wings. There's a movie star! Hey, Johnny!

D S : *On another topic, are you still in touch with the Python people?*
T G : Oh yes.

D S : *Might you do more work with them?*
T G : I don't see how it could happen. We keep talking about it. Eric Idle wrote a musical version of *Holy Grail* called *Spamelot*, which was supposed to

be going on Broadway, because of the success of *The Producers,* but the producers dropped out recently. So that was a semi-Python thing. But other than that, no. We're now dolls. There are *Holy Grail* dolls you can buy . . . and they're doing a new set. These are collectibles, and they're very lovely. (laughs)

D S :   *Back to* The Man Who Killed Don Quixote, *you talk in* Lost in La Mancha *about having the whole movie in your head. Given the problems you've had with some of your movie productions, and especially with this latest round of trouble, what is it that keeps driving you to want to make movies? There are other things you could do with those things in your head—books, television, animation—or a different kind of smaller movie.*

T G :   I'm a pinhead. I'm stupid. But in a sense, I did what you're saying. The first time we [went into production] with *Quixote* . . . our budget was . . . about $38 million. Then when we picked it up again with the French money, we took it down to $31 million, because that's all we could get. We probably should have had about $34 or $35 million. That makes a difference, because I still wasn't changing my quote vision unquote of what the movie was. We just tried doing it a different way—we brought a much smaller crew down to Spain, we picked up more local people . . . doing everything to keep the costs down. But I think it was still too ambitious. You need a little bit of fat [in the budget] to deal with disasters.

After that [shut down], I got to work on another project: a book called *Good Omens,* which we adapted. That was an expensive movie, but I thought it was going to work, because all the right people were involved. And it didn't. The backup one, a $15 million movie based on another book, we couldn't get backers for because of the subject matter. It's a book called *Tideland,* written by a guy named Mitch Cullin, who lives in Arizona. He sent it to me, and it was one of those books that sits around until one day you open it and [find that] it's just fantastic. I describe it as *Alice in Wonderland* meets *Psycho* through the eyes of *Amélie.* It's magic. It's about a little girl who's in a very dark, disturbing world. It's about her ability to deal with this. And somehow Hollywood can't deal with that. It's very interesting: You bring children into a thing, and. . . . We couldn't get an American distributor. I was shocked. I've met women who've read [the book] and they really get it. Men, who usually have control of the purse strings in Hollywood, just freak out. I think it unearths all sorts of strange things in males' heads. It's [about] a girl and her reinventing the world around her with four Barbie-doll heads on her fingers, all different characters who talk to her. So you get a five-way dialogue going, and it's all this little girl. Now there's a German former pediatrician who's a financier of films and really wants to do it, so I think I've found the right backing. But I should be doing it *now*, and I'm not. . . .

M B :   *Can you tell us more about* Good Omens?
T G :   It's [a] hugely popular [book]. It sells in the millions, and Hollywood doesn't seem to understand that. There's websites about it. It's by Neil Gaiman, who is huge in graphic novels, and Terry Pratchett . . . in England he sells more books than J. K. Rowling does. He's written more books, that's why, but he's hugely popular and it's a great book.

Effectively, it's the story of two characters. One was the serpent in the Garden of Eden and the other was the angel with the flaming sword. They've been on Earth ever since then, as Hell and Heaven's representatives, and over the years they've worked out an accommodation between the two of them. They like the Earth, and the Antichrist is headed here—depending on which prophecy you believe, it's in ten or twelve years—so it's [going to be] Armageddon, Apocalypse. So they decide to team up and raise the Antichrist, or surround his raising, to balance out his nature with a bit of nurturing. At the end of the [allotted] time, when it's his birthday, there's a hellhound that will accompany him in his anti-Christian behavior. It's supposed to arrive but it doesn't, and they realize there was a mistake at the birth, and they've raised the wrong kid. So somewhere in England is the Antichrist, and they've got to try to find him and stop the Apocalypse. (laughs) It's brilliant. And it ends with the Apocalypse, and Beelzebub, and angels—it's all there, spectacular! And it's a happy ending!

But we came to Hollywood at the beginning of last November—I guess apocalyptic things weren't very popular after September 11—and they just didn't get it. Typical Hollywood. There's a bit in the last act . . . when it gets very dark, leading up to the Apocalypse. I said, "It ends up happily, everybody comes back to life, the world is fine." But they [Hollywood] don't want that moment when the audience might be getting disturbed: "What the fuck is going on? We thought this was a comedy, and suddenly it's descended into something dark." I said, "That's what's so wonderful about it. You're taking them down, down, and then you bring them back up beaming, the sun is shining, and everyone is happy!" But no.

M B :   *Is it actually September 11 that caused the negative reaction in Hollywood, or was that just an excuse for the usual Hollywood mindset?*

T G :   It's another excuse for Hollywood to play it safe. I really do believe that. And there's a combination of things. Hollywood played it safe during the potential actors' and writers' strike. That was a big panic: "We can't do this, we can't do that, we have to rush into production with a lot of crap, just so we get it out of the way." Then after September 11 there was panic, and now as the economy disintegrates, that's even more reason not to do anything. It just depresses me.

But also, this script was not like other films. It wasn't *Men in Black 2* or any of that. It's more complex, there are more characters than you normally would put in a movie, more stories are interwoven. But that's the joy of it. There are probably a million reasons why they wouldn't do it, and it was expensive. It was taking something that's more complex and more original, and saying you need $70 million. They're not comfortable with that. The person I was talking with said, "How can you make this for less than $100 million?" I said, "That's not your problem. I can make it for $70 million. There'll be a completion guarantor." We only wanted $15 million out of Hollywood, and I would go for Robin Williams. We couldn't get $15 million, and I thought, this is crazy.

D S :   *Dare I ask about* The Defective Detective? *[This is another pet project that Gilliam has been trying to launch.]*

T G :   I've sent it out to a couple of people in Hollywood, and one of them really likes it. I don't know where it'll go, but I don't see it [happening] immediately. I want to get this other stuff out of the way

D S :   *You've been working on that for years.*

T G :   Yes, but I set it aside. It sits there. That many versions of it [makes gesture indicating large pile of pages]. It's like *Quixote.* I haven't looked at the [*Quixote*] script since we crashed. I just can't bear to, because I know it's really good! I still have this problem that I haven't found the producing partner that I really need to get things going. Ron Howard has Brian Grazer, everybody's got a team. But I've never had that. Chuck [Charles] Roven was closest, with *Twelve Monkeys,* but he's making *Scooby-Doo* and things like that now. And the terrible thing is that those kinds of successes don't make you more confident in your intellectual tastes.

D S : *Is there any prospect of doing some contract work for the studios, to get back in the Hollywood mainstream?*

T G : That's what I'll probably do. I'm on the verge of signing a deal—it looks like DreamWorks—for a small film. Post-*Munchausen* I did *Fisher King*, a small project, and that's what this is, as well. Without a horse, without a knight, so it's even easier! (laughs) I was attracted to it because it's a really good script, really good characters, good dialogue, good cast. And it's fast and easy. I'm not going to talk about it yet, because it isn't signed. . . .

And hopefully I can get *Quixote* going after that. What's so bizarre is that this last year after *Quixote*, I thought I had a perfect plan. I had *Good Omens*, and as a backup I had the little $15 million one, and then I had the problem that I might be working even harder, because we wrote *Time Bandits II* for Hallmark, for television. We thought that was a shoo-in; I wasn't going to direct it, but I was going to be executive producer, whatever. And they've all collapsed—three in a row, this year alone, all for different reasons, not neces-sarily connected with me. . . .

I don't know what to do anymore. I was talking with Maggie, my wife, and I said, "I've stopped imagining. I can't afford to imagine anymore. Because every time I have a good idea I get excited, and it's not gonna happen!"

So let's assume that this [prospective] project comes off, I'm actually terri-fied of it, because I don't know how to do it anymore. I just have to dive in and get through all this blockage that's going on in [my mind]. It frustrates me because it's a good piece, but it doesn't require *me* necessarily—it only uses a fraction of the things I'm good at. But I know I've got to shoot. It's like a writer's block that's taken over. I've got to get through it.

D S : *Is there a part of you that wishes you'd started out making "normal" movies and gone on making "normal" movies, and maybe in your spare time you'd write crazy books or something? As of now, looking at the number of films you've man-aged to make, do you feel you've done the right thing in your career?*

T G : I can't do the other. I can't get excited by doing the normal stuff. I don't want "jobs." That's my problem. I'd rather go to my place in Italy and build stone walls. And that's exactly what I do—just build stone walls, because that's good, solid, basic work.

I mean, I hate the waste of my life. The years are going by and so few films are being made. That pisses me off. But I can only work on things that thrill me, that excite me. They actually give meaning to existence. And if you don't do that, what's the point? I'm not interested in making movies, per se. I'm interested in doing things that blow people's minds, that change the view of the world.

D S :   *You do commercial things from time to time.*
T G :   Yes. I did a commercial last December for Nike, for the World Cup. I do a commercial about every five years, when I get really depressed. And it was a bizarre experience. Ultimately I had no control—it was a big World Cup commercial that had all the leading players. And directing traffic is what it is. As simple as that. You come in, the camera's there, and there was no thrill. It was a way of spending time and playing around with the equipment, but nothing more than that.

And then it turned out to be a huge hit. I didn't edit it at all. We shot sixteen and a half hours of film for what was basically supposed to be a sixty-second commercial. They also did a three-minute version. It made Elvis [Presley] Number 1 again in the world. It's the song that was in *Ocean's Eleven,* about "less conversation, more action." It went to Number 1 in England—up until then the Beatles and Elvis were tied at seventeen Number 1's, and this knocked the Beatles down when he went to eighteen. It's a remix of an Elvis song, and it's in this commercial, and it's the MTV video in Australia for this song. And I had nothing to do with it! I shot this commercial, and saw a rough cut of about four minutes, and said, "Just trim it down," and somebody at the agency came up with the idea of putting the Elvis song on it, and it's a huge hit, and I'm getting all the credit for it, and I didn't do it! It's just absurd!

D S :   *There's a lot of absurdity in this business. Have you thought of making a movie about moviemaking?*
T G :   Keith [Fulton] and Lou [Pepe] just did! I actually had the galleys of *The Player* when it was in book form, and I thought it was great, but I didn't want to do it. There's a kind of incestuousness about moviemaking, but everybody wants to see it—*The Player, Day for Night, Safe Passage,* [which is] the new [Bertrand] Tavernier film [2002]. That's about moviemaking in occupied France under the Vichy government and German film production. I think it's a wonderful film, but probably just for people like us who love movies. It

didn't do well in France, but I think it's a great film. It's three hours long and I was never bored, I was engrossed.

D S : *Returning to* Lost in La Mancha, *if I were you I think I'd be tempted to say it's very nice they made this movie, and I think it'll do good things for rehabilitating my image with people who might have the impression the* Quixote *fiasco was my fault. But you could lay low and let the movie just be out there, and here you are visiting Toronto and talking about it!*
T G : I think Lou and Keith are very talented. I wasn't planning to come here, but there was a lot of pressure on me, and I decided to do whatever would help them, because they're really good. It would be nice to see them have a real film career, because they're now moving into proper filmmaking, not documentaries.

M B : *However difficult you find it to face the thought of* Don Quixote, *you have the comfort of knowing that a wonderful film came out of it.*
T G : That's right. I "participated" in somebody else's very good film. And I feel I have to support it.

INDEX

CONVERSATIONS WITH FILMMAKERS SERIES
PETER BRUNETTE, GENERAL EDITOR

The collected interviews with notable modern directors, including

Robert Aldrick • Pedro Almodóvar • Robert Altman • Theo Angelopolous • Bernardo Bertolucci • Jane Campion • Frank Capra • George Cukor • Brian De Palma • Clint Eastwood • John Ford • Jean-Luc Godard • Peter Greenaway • Alfred Hitchcock • John Huston • Jim Jarmusch • Elia Kazan • Stanley Kubrick • Fritz Lang • Spike Lee • Mike Leigh • George Lucas • Michael Powell • Martin Ritt • Carlos Saura • John Sayles • Martin Scorsese • Steven Soderbergh • Steven Spielberg • George Stevens • Oliver Stone • Quentin Tarantino • Lars von Trier • Orson Welles • Billy Wilder • Zhang Yimou